City of the Ram-Man

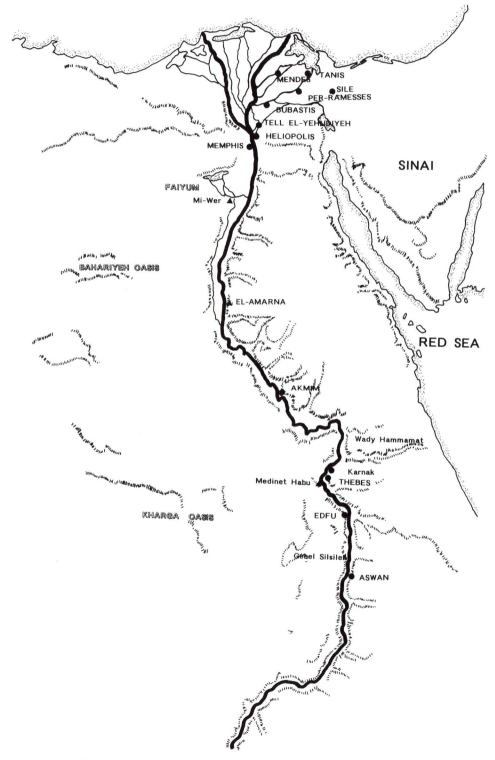

Figure 0.1. Map of Egypt.

City of the Ram-Man

THE STORY OF ANCIENT MENDES

....

Donald B. Redford

Princeton University Press
Princeton and Oxford

Library of Congress Cataloging-in-Publication Data

Redford, Donald B.

City of the Ram-man : the story of ancient Mendes / Donald B. Redford.

p. cm.

Includes bibliographical references and index.

ISBN 978-0-691-14226-5 (hardcover : alk. paper)

1. Mendes (Extinct city)—History. 2. Mendes (Extinct city)—Religious life and customs. 3. Rams—Symbolic aspects—Egypt—Mendes (Extinct city) 4. Mythology, Egyptian—Egypt—Mendes (Extinct city) 5. Mendes (Extinct city)—Antiquities. 6. Excavations (Archaeology)—Egypt—Mendes (Extinct city) 7. Egypt—History—To 332 B.C. I. Title.

DT73.M54R43 2010

932—dc22   2009021605

British Library Cataloging-in-Publication Data is available

This book has been composed in Pro Minion

Printed on acid-free paper. ∞

press.princeton.edu

Printed in the United States of America

10 9 8 7 6 5 4 3 2 1

Contents

List of Illustrations   vii

List of Sidebars   xiii

Preface   xv

Introduction   xvii

List of Abbreviations   xxi

Chapter One   The Beginnings   1

Chapter Two   The Advent of Horus   8

Chapter Three   In the Time of the Residence   18

Chapter Four   The Collapse   42

Chapter Five   The Mysterious Centuries: The Middle Kingdom   58

Chapter Six   Mendes under the Empire Pharaohs   67

Chapter Seven   The Great Chiefs of the Meshwesh   95

Chapter Eight   Egypt in the Time of Troubles   111

Chapter Nine   The Ram, Lord of Djedet   124

Chapter Ten   The Saite Revival   138

Chapter Eleven   Mendes, the Capital of Egypt   144

Chapter Twelve   The Great Disaster   179

Chapter Thirteen   Dusk and Darkness: The End of Mendes   188

Notes and Further Readings   211

Index   231

Illustrations

0.1. Map of Egypt.   ii
0.2. The outer (eastern) harbor looking east at dawn.   xviii
1.1. Putative distribution of the Predynastic levees of the Mendesian branch
      of the Nile.   2
1.2. Excavating at Buto, 1968, illustrating the major problem that arises if
      the water table is high at a site.   3
1.3. The lush environs of *Anepat*, which arguably occasioned the name.   3
1.4. Lower Egypt, the "Land of the Flood," as it was in Greco-Roman times.   5
1.5. *S(h)erakhu*, "lordly, uplifted (building)."   7

2.1. Map of the central and northeast Delta.   9
2.2. Map of the Near East in the late Naqada II–III (Gerzean) period.   9
2.3. Decoration on a Naqada II pot.   11
2.4. Heraldic devices conveying symbols of power.   12
2.5. Standards of the Mendesian township.   14
2.6. Tableau depicting King Den's "outstanding deed of smiting the east."   16

3.1. Section through Excavation Unit AJ-A Extension, facing south.   19
3.2. "Silos" beginning to emerge.   20
3.3. "Silos" of Phase V (AJ-A Extension).   20
3.4. "Silos" and rectilinear buildings of Phase VI (AJ-A Extension).   20
3.5. Sealings from AJ-A Extension.   21
3.6a–3.6k. Old Kingdom pottery from Unit AJ-A.   22
3.7a–3.7d. Shrines of the Archaic Period.   23
3.8a–3.8b. A semicircular "silo" of late Old Kingdom date. The same "silo"
      under excavation (AJ-A Extension, locus 100).   24–25
3.9. Ceramic contents of the "silo."   25
3.10. Plan of the "silo."   26
3.11. Structure at the southwest corner of the Old Kingdom temple enclosure.   27
3.12. "Holding" area for containers of foodstuffs.   27

3.13. The Old Kingdom temple and adjacent mastabas. 29

3.14. Limestone mastaba of Ishtef-Tety. 29

3.15. False door of Nefer-shu-ba, 6th Dynasty. 30–31

3.16. *Anzata*, the "shepherd," of Busiris. 34

3.17. Osiris. 34

3.18. Plan of the Old Kingdom city in the late third millennium B.C. 37

3.19. Plan of Unit AJ-A, due west of the Old Kingdom temple podium. 37

3.20–3.21. The initial sondage, undertaken in 1996, to uncover the pre-Ramesside levels. 38

3.22. The mud-brick podium on which sat the temple of the Old Kingdom. 39

3.23. The northern façade of the podium. 39

4.1. Sealing of an official (name lost) of Pepy II. 44

4.2. View looking south of the bastion. 45

4.3. Section through the bastion, facing south. 46

4.4. Bricks, fired in the conflagration. 47

4.5–4.6. Multipurpose mixing vats. 47

4.7. Body of an old woman. 48

4.8. Two men under a collapsed wall. 48

4.9. Fallen sub-adult, sprawled in front of the bastion. 48

4.10. Bodies of man and pig. 49

4.11. Clusters of bodies in the depression along the central axis. 49

4.12. Plan of Unit AJ-E/F, showing the larger of two mud-brick mastabas. 52

4.13. Unit AJ-E/F under excavation. 52

4.14. Vaulted tomb with part of the plaster removed. 53

4.15. Unit AJ-E; vaulted tomb with superstructure removed. 53

4.16. Unit AJ-F. Bronze mirror found over the face of a woman in an intrusive burial (early First Intermediate Period). 53

4.17. Unit T-A, facing south (First Intermediate Period). 54

4.18. Secondary use of T-A vaults. 54

4.19–4.21. Pottery from the T-A vaults. 55–56

4.22. Cleaning a multiple burial under a single mat, Unit AJ-E. 57

5.1. Surviving wall of the Middle Kingdom temple. 63

5.2. Chambers (perhaps magazines) along the south side of the Middle Kingdom temple. 63

5.3. First Intermediate Period bread-pot, with whitewashed exterior. 64

5.4a–5.4c. Pottery from the chambers on the south side of the temple. 64

5.5.   Map of Egypt, illustrating the Second Intermediate Period and
         Middle Kingdom.   65

6.1.   Ethnic groups of the Egyptian empire.   69
6.2.   Map illustrating Egypt's African empire in the New Kingdom.   70
6.3.   Western balk of excavation Unit AJ-A Extension.   72
6.4.   The Temple of the Ram-god at its greatest extent.   72
6.5.   East reveal of the easternmost aperture through the Thutmosid façade. 73
6.6.   Reconstruction of east reveal.   73
6.7.   Conjectural restoration of the temple of Ba-neb-djed.   74
6.8.   Section through the foundation trench of the first pylon.   79
6.9.   Pylon block with part of the name of Merenptah.   79
6.10.   Foundation trench of the eastern lateral wall of the first court. 81
6.11a–6.11b. Gate of the Second Pylon under excavation.   81
6.12.   Jamb of the postern gate.   82
6.13.   Part of the reveal of the gate of the Second Pylon.   82
6.14.   Foundation deposit of Merenptah.   82
6.15.   Vessels from the foundation deposit.   83
6.16.   Stone "brick" from the foundation deposit.   83
6.17.   Haunch of beef as a sacrifice under the deposit, in situ.   83
6.18a–6.18b. Bricks of Thutmose III, laid ceremoniously across the
         foundation trench.   84–85
6.19a–6.19b. Sections through Excavation Unit AL-I, trenches I and II.   87
6.20.   Section through Unit AL-I, trench III facing south.   88
6.21.   New Kingdom temenos wall, cut away by the Nektanebo
         foundation trench.   88
6.22.   Votive vessels in situ.   90
6.23.   20th Dynasty wine-jars.   90
6.24a–6.24b. Fish-stelae.   91
6.25.   Fragment of hieratic stela of Neb-ma'a-re.   93
6.26.   Late Helladic IIIc strainer spout beer-jar, with Cypriot overtones. 94

7.1.   Sardonians ("Shardana") from the west coast of Asia Minor.   96
7.2.   Libyan tribesmen, as depicted in the tomb of Ramesses III.   97
7.3a–7.3d. The ruins of Tanis.   101
7.4.   Sheshonq I from a relief on the Bubastite portal, Karnak.   104
7.5.   Map showing the position of Mendes, Thmuis, and Hermopolis Parva. 107
7.6.   A Great Chief of the Me(shwesh) "offers the field."   107
7.7.   Excavation Unit HF, south of the temple.   107

7.8.	Excavation of the "Libyan Palace" (mound AK-E).	109
7.9.	Doorjamb from the palace, showing the head of a Great Chief of the Me(shwesh).	109
7.10.	Rendering of the "Libyan Palace" and the temple.	109
8.1.	Amun crowns his Divine Worshiper.	113
8.2a.	The Divine Worshiper Shepenwepet II.	113
8.2b.	The Divine Worshiper Amenirdis I.	113
8.3.	A Kushite king libates to Amun.	114
8.4.	Nine Egyptian potentates do obeisance to Piankhy.	116
8.5.	Taharqa, shown in typical "Nubian" cap with double uraeus.	120
8.6.	The eastern Nile Delta, showing the disposition of border forts.	121
9.1a–9.1e.	The roofs of three of the four naoi unearthed in the central temple.	125
9.2.	Hathor capital with abacus from a pier in the *mammisi* at Mendes.	127
9.3.	A prophet of the Ram and lector priest, Smendes, "burns incense to his lord."	129
9.4.	Three priestesses (from the Hieroglyphic Papyrus from Tanis).	130
9.5.	Bronze figurine of Osiris; surface find at Tel er-Rub'a.	132
9.6.	Figure of Harpokrates, "Horus-the-Child"; surface find, Tel er-Rub'a.	132
9.7.	Faïence aegis of the feline goddess, probably Bast.	132
9.8.	Figure of "Ba-neb-djed, the fornicating ram who mounts the beauties."	133
9.9.	"Arsaphes-re Ba-neb-djed," after a figure in the Book of the Fayum.	135
9.10.	Amun-re identified as "Khnum-re, Lord of the Cataract," after a figure in the Book of the Fayum.	135
9.11.	"Amun-re, Lord of the Lagoon," after a figure in the Book of the Fayum.	135
10.1.	East gate of the fortress of Pelusium (late Byzantine period).	142
11.1.	Shawabti fragments of the deputy high priest of the Ram, Ny-su-ba-neb-djed.	145
11.2.	Head of royal statuette, probably a likeness of Neferites I, from his tomb at Mendes.	146
11.3.	Fragment of a stela found in the debris of Neferites' tomb, showing a kneeling king worshiping the Ram.	148
11.4.	Plan of the city of Mendes at its greatest extent (fourth century B.C.).	149
11.5.	Phoenician "torpedo" jars from the northwestern harbor.	150
11.6.	Eastern face of the Nektanebo temenos wall in the vicinity of Neferites' tomb.	152

11.7a–11.7b.   Views of the Nektanebo wall at the point of an inset.   152
11.8.   Figurine of the god Shu with arms raised to hold up the sky.   153
11.9.   Pottery drain at the bottom of the foundation sand in the court of
          the temple; Saite period.   154
11.10.   Fine sand as foundations for the renovated temple of the Saite period.   154
11.11a–11.11b.   Section through the Saite foundation sand, showing the "slots."   155
11.12.   Limestone fragment from the upper part of a wall in the inner part of the
          central temple.   156
11.13a–11.13b.   Quartzite dado of alternating nomen-cum-prenomen
          of King Akoris.   156
11.14a–11.14b.   Views of the single surviving naos of an original four that stood
          in the southernmost court of the Saite temple.   158
11.15a–11.15b.   View of the south side of the cut where the southeastern postern
          gate of the naos-court once stood.   159
11.16.   The earlier (Old or Middle Kingdom) wall of small bricks through which
          the Saite engineers cut.   160
11.17.   Mud-brick foundation of the southern gate of the naos-court.   160
11.18.   Excavation plan of the Mansion of the Rams.   161
11.19.   The columned(?) hall at the start of excavations.   162
11.20.   Mud-brick vaults of two preserved cubicles beginning to appear
          in excavation.   162
11.21.   Reconstruction of the Mansion of the Rams, facing east.   163
11.22.   Alternate reconstruction of the western approach.   163
11.23.   Foundations of the northwest corner of the installation.   164
11.24.   A sarcophagus still resting in its cubicle.   164
11.25.   The variety of shapes and types of stone assumed by the sarcophagi.   164–165
11.26.   Miniature Lower Egyptian type of shrine.   166
11.27.   Miniature column capital, of a type known in the 30th Dynasty.   166
11.28.   Plan of the hall in Field T where, possibly, the diorite sarcophagi
          were housed.   167
11.29.   Reused New Kingdom sarcophagus.   168
11.30.   Plan of Neferites I's tomb.   169
11.31.   The sarcophagus of Neferites I before excavation.   169
11.32.   The burial chamber of Neferites I, viewed from the east.   169
11.33.   Fragment of limestone relief showing the horn of the avatar of the Ram
          known as "the living soul of Re."   170
11.34.   "The Ram, the Lord of Djedet."   170
11.35.   Plumes and sun-disc surmounting the vertical, alternating cartouches
          of Neferites I.   170

11.36. Vulture goddess, with *khu*-fan in her claw, extending her wings above the king. 170

11.37. The night-barque of the sun, with names of part of the crew. 170

11.38. Head of a priest. 171

11.39. Architrave with the epithet "Beloved of the Gods," one of the appellatives of Neferites I. 171

11.40. Pilaster(?) fragment with the epithet "Founder of the Two Lands," one of the appellatives of Neferites I. 171

11.41. So-called Sacred Lake, southeast of the main temple. 171

11.42. Samian amphora, c. 575 B.C. 172

11.43. East Greek ware, fifth to fourth century B.C., from the great harbor. 174

11.44. Basket-handle jars from the great harbor. 175

12.1. Nektanebo I in red crown of Lower Egypt. 180

12.2a–12.2b. Six "falls" of fragments from the destruction of Neferites I's tomb. 186

12.3. Section drawing through the destruction debris of Neferites' tomb. 186

13.1. Section through the burial chamber of Neferites I, facing north. 189

13.2. Statue of Philip Arrhidaeus as it appeared in excavation. 191

13.3a–13.3c. Views of the kneeling statue. 192

13.4. Facsimile of the inscription of the back-pillar. 192

13.5. Inner, western face of the Ptolemaic temenos wall. 198

13.6. Vessels from the foundation trench of the present temenos wall. 198

13.7. Outer glacis of the Ptolemaic temenos (T1), facing south. 198

13.8a–13.8b. Early Ptolemaic coinage from the harbor. 200

13.9a–13.9c. Demotic ostraca from the harbor. 200

13.10. Terra cotta figurines from the inner harbor. 203

13.11. Corner of "Roman" building constructed of field brick. 203

13.12. Cache of Roman pottery. 204

13.13. Amphorae in the *depinto* style, of sixth to seventh century date. 205

13.14. Fragments of a limestone sarcophagus used to block up the entry in Christian times. 208

Sidebars

1.1	The Chief Brings Verdure	6
2.1	The Uruk Phenomenon	10
2.2	"Yellow Face," King of the Baboons	12
3.1	Domestic Arrangements to the Cemetery	32
3.2	False Door of the Priest Nefer-shu-ba	33
3.3	Mendes in the Pyramid Texts	34
3.4	Osiris and the Deceased in Mendes	36
3.5	Osiris and Life	41
4.1	A Royal Decree of Exemption	43
4.2	Occupation at Mendes at the Close of the Old Kingdom	44
4.3	From the "Instruction for King Merikare" (c. 2070 B.C.)	50
5.1	Prophecy of the Coming of Amenemhet I	61
6.1	Statue Inscription of Ibaba	76
6.2	Sety, as Vizier, Visits Seth, Lord of Avaris	78
7.1	The Libyan Menace	98
7.2	"Hit-Men" and Anarchy: Pharaoh Derided	102
7.3	The Tribulations of One Caught in the Civil War	102
7.4	Favors to a Mendesian in Royal Service	103
7.5	Land Donation	108
8.1	Tefnakhte	114
8.2	Revere Amun!	115
8.3	Pharaoh Piankhy on the Uncouth Libyans, c. 720 B.C.	115
8.4	Shabaka Conquers His Enemies	117
8.5	The "Kings" of Egypt	119
8.6	The Prowess of the Kushite Troops	120
9.1	Provisions for Sacred Animal Burials (Djed-Hor)	128
9.2	To the Ram Deceased	129
9.3	The Mysterious Link: Osiris and the Fornicating Ram	134
11.1	An Egyptian General Still Functioning under Darius I (519 B.C.)	145
11.2	Shawabti of King Neferites (from His Tomb at Mendes)	147

11.3	Nektanebo's Self-Laudation	149
11.4	Mendesian Perfume	176
11.5	Ny-su-ba-neb-djed	177
11.6	A Saite Worthy Honors the Ram	178
13.1	The Gods Return!	193
13.2	Ptolemy II, Son of the Ram	195
13.3	The Cult "Gazetteer" of Mendes	197
13.4	A Greek Banker and the Perfume of Mendes	201
13.5	An Egyptian Boy Makes Good under the Ptolemies	201
13.6	The Mendesian Branch	209

Preface

The present work is an attempt to set on record in readable form the interpreted results of a century and a half of investigation of the site of Tel er-Rub'a/Mendes. Until the early 1960s these investigations involved the desultory visits and/or treasure-hunting of individuals whose names would best be forgotten. Only beginning in 1963 was formal excavation undertaken, first by New York University (1963–80) and then by a consortium made up of a team from the University of Washington, the University of Illinois, and the Pennsylvania State University (1990 to the present). The work is by no means finished and, judging from the results so far, it is altogether likely that discoveries, some of a sensational nature, will be made in the future. What has already been found, however, has cast such a flood of light on the history of Egypt and the eastern Mediterranean that it is high time to set it forth for the predilection of layman, student, and scholar.

Many people placed me in their debt in the writing and production of this book. Of these the late Bernard Bothmer and Professor Herman de Meulenaere must be mentioned first. They both encouraged me from the first expression of interest I divulged in the site. Equal encouragement and offers of help came from two close friends, Christine Liliquist and Richard Fazzini, both of whom had accompanied the New York University expedition under Donald Hansen in the 1960s. With colleagues Robert Wenke and Douglas Brewer we enjoyed close collaboration in the early seasons, and one hopes their work is not completed. Without the Supreme Council of Antiquities of Egypt the expedition could have neither started nor sustained itself, and thanks are due the chairman, Dr. Zahi Hawass, Mansura director Naguib Nour, and Chief Inspector Salim el-Boghdadi. Over the years we have been privileged to play host to a number of distinguished visitors, including Ambassador Michael Bell of Canada, Manfred Bietak of the Austrian mission to Tell ed'Dab'a, Gregory Mumford and his team to Tell Tebilla, and Terry Waltz of the American Research Center in Egypt, to name but a few. All were generous with comments and useful advice. Last but not least, the indefatigable field staff is to be acknowledged as perhaps the key element in turning the Mendes expedition into an unqualified success.

The following contributed directly to the present volume: Keith Meikle, Susan Redford (plans), Tracy Butler, Patrick Carstens, Sandy Nesbitt, David George (photographs), Rupert Nesbitt, Troy Sagrillo, Heather Evans, and Stephanie Palumbo (artwork). Isometric renderings were done by the author, and Kyle Long edited the manuscript. Unless otherwise stated, the translations of Egyptian texts are those of the author.

The notes and suggested readings gathered at the end of the book are not intended to be exhaustive but to provide a sort of *Einleitung* for the interested reader. Colleagues may well detect gaps they think ought to have been filled. The author tenders his regrets.

Introduction

···

Anyone who has not visited Mendes cannot appreciate the wonder of approaching from the south or west and seeing the vast, low mound arise on the horizon out of the flat Delta landscape. Before 1900 a visit often took on an eerie aspect in that, because of the proximity of the flat Daqahlieh plain, the approach was often of necessity by boat. Even today, when the fields are flooded for the rice planting, Mendes again becomes an island, and it takes little imagination to visualize the marshes of old.

Yet, for those visiting the site in July or August, another unexpected experience awaits. Arising at dawn the traveler finds him- or herself engulfed in thick fog. Heavy moisture drips like rain from indistinct tree shapes, mere silhouettes in the mist. Donkeys and humans go haltingly, unsure of the terrain, swallowed up as they perceive themselves to be in a mantle of grey darkness. All things, even those which are normally comfortingly familiar, are completely hidden from the gaze of animal or man. And the fog is everywhere; it never ends, it is infinite. Worst of all, perhaps, one cannot help but go astray, for sense of direction is stifled: the fog is "directionless." And always there is the croaking of frogs! Only when the sun mounts high in the sky does this mantle of unknowing begin to draw back: gradually the mists retreat before the heat, and the ordered world begins to appear. Such is the daily act of creation during the summer at Mendes.

Modern times have come to Tel er-Rub'a and its environs, but the site and its satellite villages still lie off the beaten track. Reflections of an agricultural past are seen from time to time. Fishermen abound on the banks of local canals, and the *schilby*-fish, misrepresented as a dolphin, lives in garden statuary. On our first visit to Mendes our progress on the last kilometer was impeded because of a strange procession in the dust of an August afternoon: a seemingly endless flock of well-fed sheep, led by an enormous ram, was shuffling slowly westward along the road.

The city whose ruins one sees today owes its size and general configuration to the activity of a relatively late period, from approximately 540 to 350 B.C., and would have differed markedly from the New or Old Kingdom settlement. Although excavation has not yet tapped prehistoric levels of the fourth millennium B.C., it is highly likely that the shape of the first habitation differed yet again, and in many respects, from what was to follow in the 1st Dynasty. Coring has suggested that the earliest occupation was a modest

Figures 0.2. The outer (eastern) harbor looking east at dawn on a foggy day in July.

affair, established on levees left by the meandering Mendesian branch of the Nile. The evidence of toponymy makes it tempting to identify a substantial segment of the earliest population with a West Semitic–speaking element, with demographic ties northeastward along the Levantine coast. It is one of these groups that the first chapter imagines trekking into the Nile Delta in the late fourth millennium B.C. and settling on the site that was to become Mendes. To enhance verisimilitude and depict a culture on the threshold of its historic evolution, the conceit of translating familiar place-names rather than transliterating them has been adopted in the early chapters.

While Mendes does not mirror, nor even broadly illustrate, the conventional history of Egypt, the longevity of occupation on the site, spanning as it does over four thousand years, provides a useful gauge against which any period of Egypt's long past may be measured. To the extent that the prosperity of the city appears directly linked to the strength of discharge of the Mendesian branch, one might view that gauge as a sure indicator of the ecology of northeast Africa at any given time. Unexpectedly, through archaeological investigation, certain periods in the city's history have turned Mendes into a virtual type site for interests sometimes broader than those of Egyptology. One might mention the prosperity of the site during the third millennium, which has left four meters of stratified deposition; the destruction and massacre at the close of the 6th Dynasty; the evidence of international trade with the eastern Mediterranean; the violence which attended the Persian occupation of 343 B.C.; and the papyrological evidence for town layout and distribution of economy during the Roman period.

What makes Mendes an important source for evidence on ancient Egyptian history and society is not the city's strategic, cultic, or political importance but the fact that over 80 percent of the original settlement has physically survived. Whereas neighboring cities of comparable size, such as Busiris and Sebennytos, are now either under a modern city (the latter) or have become farmland (the former), Mendes has remained largely intact and inviolate. Drawing from both archaeological and textual evidence, and with the advantages just adumbrated, I shall now attempt to tell Mendes' story.

Abbreviations

AJA	*American Journal of Archaeology*
ANET	J. B. Pritchard, ed. *Ancient Near Eastern Texts Relating to the Old Testament*, 2nd ed. (Princeton, 1976)
ASAE	Annales du Service des Antiquités de l' Égypte
ATPN	*Akhenaten Temple Project Newsletter*
BA	*Beiträge zur Assyriologie*
BASOR	*Bulletin of the American Schools of Oriental Research*
BES	*Bulletin of the Egyptological Seminar*
BIFAO	*Bulletin de l'institut français d'archéologie orientale*
BN	*Biblische Notizen*
BSFE	*Bulletin de la société française d'Égyptologie*
CAH	John Boardman, ed. *Cambridge Ancient History* (Cambridge, 1982–)
CdE	*Chronique d'Égypte*
CRAIBL	*Comptes rendus des séances de l'Académie des inscriptions et belles-lettres*
CT	Coffin Texts
GM	Göttinger Miszellen
IEJ	*Israel Exploration Journal*
JAOS	*Journal of the American Oriental Society*
JARCE	*Journal of the American Research Center in Egypt*
JEA	*Journal of Egyptian Archaeology*
JEOL	*Jaarbericht van het Vooraziatisch-egyptisch genootschap "Ex Oriente Lux"*
JESHO	*Journal of the Economic and Social History of the Orient*
JSSEA	*Journal of the Society for the Study of Egyptian Antiquities*
JWH	*Journal of World History*
KRI	K. A. Kitchen, *Ramesside Inscriptions* (Oxford, 1968–)
LD	R. Lepsius, *Denkmaeler aus Aegypten und Aethiopien* (Berlin, 1846)

LdÄ	*Lexikon der Ägyptologie*
MDAIK	*Mitteilungen des deutschen archaeologischen Instituts zu Kairo*
OLZ	*Orientalistische Literaturzeitung*
P-M	B. Porter and R. Moss, *Topographical Bibliography of Ancient Egyptian Hieroglyphic Texts, Reliefs and Paintings* (Oxford, 1923–)
PT	Pyramid Texts
RdE	*Revue d'Égyptologie*
RT	*Recueil de travaux*
SAK	*Studien zur altägyptische Kultur*
UF	*Ugaritische Forschungen*
Urk.	G. Steindorff, ed., *Urkunden des ägyptischen Altertums* (Leipzig)
ZÄS	*Zeitschrift für ägyptische Sprache und Altertumskunde*

City of the Ram-Man

Chapter One

The Beginnings

Just when it seemed the taste of death had entered their mouths, they were across. A dark band of vegetation in the distance rose before them, and a slight cooling of the air signaled the presence of water. Though strength had all but failed, hearts now revived and the pace quickened: there was life by the river.

Although this was their first passage, others had described the route for them. And no one had underestimated the rigors of the crossing. Nine days of waterless desert, the undulating dunes, the stony path, the adders and scorpions—the facts had been known to them before they set out. But still they came as others of their community had done before. Some had sickened, a few had died; the flocks had thinned, thieves had robbed them. And now the god had proven faithful and their salvation drew nigh. All knew that they would never be in want again.

By sunset they had come to a river. The current was sluggish and the banks thinly lined with herbage. The flocks drank greedily; the men waded and washed. Tents were pitched and a frugal repast enjoyed. When the sun went down the star-filled desert sky showed that the course of the river was leading southwest. No human beings presented themselves at the encampment, and the wild animals stayed far away from the fires. The families could sleep at their ease.

Beyond the river the clansmen found themselves in a new world. Papyrus marshes closed in around them, restricting the paths and concealing the firm ground. Flatness and wateriness replaced the dry undulations of the desert, confusing their depth perception and their ability to detect motion from afar. More upsetting and disconcerting, simply because it was unexpected, was the mist. Each morning thick, milky walls of fog arose everywhere, drenching the skin and disorienting the vision. The fog made it hard to breathe, and even animal life seemed to stop for a while. It was as though the landscape was each morning thrust backward in time to that remote primordial moment, before shape, before limit, before motion, when all that was was part of all that was not. Gradually, as the sun rose, the mists burned off. First the tops of the reeds and papyri would appear out of the gloom, then muddy protuberances; and finally living things would begin to move. The newcomers called the marsh *Laḥaḥta*, the "Watery Place." Fish and fowl abounded everywhere in it, and fishhook and throw-stick made it easy to live.

But the clansmen did not stay in the Watery Place: preferable terrain offered a domicile beyond the marsh. On the south side another river, flowing from the south, debouched into the bog; and a mere two days' trek to the west an even greater waterway ran north directly into the sea. The tract of land watered by these two rivers exceeded anything the weary travelers had ever seen for its verdure. Green pastures and meadows stretched to the west and south, while groves of sycamores and palms everywhere broke the monotony of the flat land. At the point where the eastern river entered and then crossed the marsh a series of close-packed sand levees protruded from the earth, like the vertebrae of some partly buried animal giant. On these, safe from the marsh and the annual flood, the visitors established their camp of reed huts. 'Anepat, "Place of Greenness," they called the place in their own dialect; they called a watery branch of the river penetrating between the levees 'Agen, "the Anchorage."

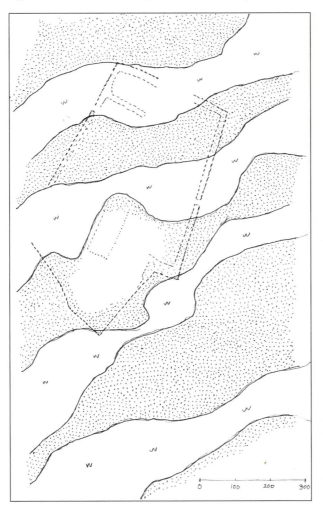

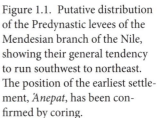

Figure 1.1. Putative distribution of the Predynastic levees of the Mendesian branch of the Nile, showing their general tendency to run southwest to northeast. The position of the earliest settlement, 'Anepat, has been confirmed by coring.

Figure 1.2. Excavating at Buto, 1968, illustrating the major problem that arises if the water table is high at a site. Here, within the temple of Edjo the cobra goddess, the water table closes in just beneath the floor of the temple, at a date contemporary with Pharaoh Amasis, sixth century B.C. Fortunately at Mendes the water table is very low, permitting excavation of both Archaic and Prehistoric levels.

a

Figure 1.3a and b (right). The lush environs of ʾAnepat, which arguably occasioned the name.

b

It was easy to live here. In spite of the fact that the ever-present hippopotamus posed a threat, the river and the pools teemed with fish. In particular, a small fish with a spine on its back abounded to such an extent that the people called it "the Foremost of the Inundation." Fava beans were plentiful in the region. The flocks of sheep and goats began slowly to increase, and pigs grew numerous in the environs of the settlement. Villages appeared south and southwest of ʾAnepat: ʿUmmah, "Clan-Town," and ʾAneze, "the Pasturage." Emblems proclaimed growing self-awareness and identity, and signaled the numina rising in the consciousness of the community out of the fertile landscape to attain the status of gods: the Ram, the Fish, the Shepherd ʾAnzeta, the Child, the Calf.

ʾAnepat was located not far south of the shore of what was later called the "Great Green" or the "Great Syrian Sea." Ships hugging the Levantine coast southbound from the mouth of the Orontes could gain easy access to the interior of the Land of the Flood through the mouth of the river that ran by ʾAnepat. Contact continued overland, over the desert across which the migrants had long ago trekked. Whether by ship or by donkey, goods from Asia came into the possession of the settlers: lithic implements, oil, resin, perfumes. Pottery containers might be secured by rope when they arrived, an expedient eventually inspiring locals to copy a rope design in clay on pots of their own manufacture.

We know little of the mechanics of this importation, whether the Asiatics were private entrepreneurs or chiefs' agents, whether the commerce they engaged in was trade or gift exchange. But one thing is certain: the sailors from the north had tapped a potential source of great riches. For the Land of the Flood boasted resources that other localities could only covet: plentiful food-stocks, aromatic and medicinal herbs, papyrus, and, in the adjacent deserts, natron, copper, and turquoise. Perhaps more important, through the intermediary of such towns as ʾAnepat, ʿUmmah, and ʾAneze, the Asiatics could gain access to the valley of the "River" further south and the Eastern and Western Deserts. Here was gold, carnelian, amethyst, hematite, malachite, and the tropical products of Africa. The result was to turn the Land of the Flood into a middle ground in the exchange of goods, and its cantons into entrepôts where Asia mingled with Africa. Though little remains archaeologically from this early period of settlement development 5,100 years ago, glyptic art and several discrete excavations enable the mind's eye to conjure up a scene of proven accuracy.

The settlements expanded. The river flooded faithfully each summer and food-stocks continued abundant. Perched on its levee ʾAnepat offered safety from the Inundation, a central location for fishing and fowling, and proximity to the shore of the Great Green. The occupations of fisherman, fowler, shepherd, and trader shaped the community at an early date into a rich and prosperous town. While the origins of the workings of the community are buried in the oblivion of preliterate times, careful extrapolation from political structures of historic times makes possible a reconstruction. We may pre-

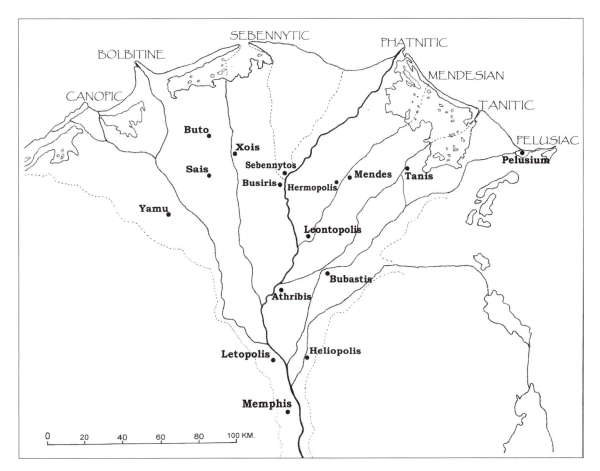

Figure 1.4. Lower Egypt, the Land of the Flood, as it was in Greco-Roman times.

sume the will and consensus of the community at large was expressed and articulated through a "council" (later called *djadje*) probably composed of elders, but from an early stage the need for executive action would have thrown up a "Big Man" (Egyptian *wer*, "great [one]" or "magnate"). Presumably the community, through its council, approved of and selected the Big Man, but the selection mechanism is unknown. Far from being a sinecure, the function of communal leader was one of grave responsibility. The Big Man protected the settlement from the violence of untamed animal life: the hippopotamus, the crocodile, the wild pig had to yield to his harpoon or spear. He guaranteed law and order in the community and judged the townsmen according to local custom. He represented the community in an ineffable sense and embodied its very essence: he was the supreme cultivator, herdsman, shepherd, and fisherman.

But the Big Man was conceivable only in isolation: he had no precursor, no succes-

1.1 The Chief Brings Verdure

(The king) has come today on the crest of the flooding waters! The king is Sobek (the crocodile) with green scales, alert face and raised forefront—the glistering one that emerged from the shank of the "Great Tailed One Who Is in the Sunshine." The king has come to his lagoons which are in the riparian land of the great flooding waters, to the place of offerings, with green fields, which is in the horizon land. The king makes green the herbage which is upon the two banks of horizon land, in order that he might bring greenness. [PT no. 317]

sor. His death was traumatic for the community. It deprived them of one who had seemed to promote and guarantee, nay to incorporate in his very being, the fertility of the landscape and the prosperity of the town. His passing was in fact wholly debilitating to humankind; it was as bad as a murder! In the colorful language of the time, drawn from the natural world surrounding the town, the community attempted to instill into the event a deep and universal meaning that would deny the psychological pain of the existential. The fledgling sat in the nest among the marshes of the Delta, the father dead, the mother in panic. The wild pig stalked the nest; the mother fled with the fledgling into the inner swamps. But salvation was at hand. The friendly cow in the thicket, the cobra twined on its reed, the heron and the ibis—a menagerie of the denizens of the Land of the Flood took the widow and the fledgling unto themselves and protected them during the childhood of the chick. And at last his time had come. As a robust youth with his friends in his train, the fledgling appears out of the marshes to defeat the forces of evil embodied in the wild pig.

Religious texts of the historic period are shot through with such "mythological" imagery. Two things are clear: it is of great age and in origin derives from a Delta setting. While its original form constituted the story of "how we got our Big Man and what he means to us," shortly it was to become "how our Big Man championed his deceased (murdered) father." And with this added twist to the narrative, an *hereditary* principle was introduced: the fledgling became Big Man not because he was approved by a council but because of his ancestry. He was Big Man son of Big Man.

The typical settlement in the Land of the Flood must already have assumed an imposing aspect. A new kind of architecture employing small, rectilinear blocks of mud dried in the sun made possible structures of durability and height. In imitation of up-to-date architecture in Asia, the visitors from the Orontes Valley and the Asian hinterland taught the locals to stagger the mud-bricks in plan to produce wall surfaces with vertical niches. Sometimes, again in imitation of Asiatic prototypes, walls were decorated with geometrical patterns made of colored clay "nails" embedded in the mud. Skillful use of

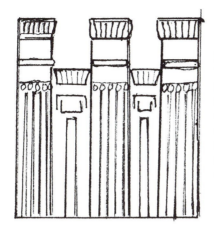

Figure 1.5. *S(h)erakhu*, "lordly, uplifted (building)," a mock-up used from a very early period to represent the dwelling of the Big Man and later to inscribe his "Horus-name"; from the stela of Hor-edjo of the 1st Dynasty.

reeds, wooden beams, logs, and lotus-plants produced corner posts, cornices, and roofs of organic material integrated into the brick. Apertures were provided with wood or reed "drums" at the top, wrapped around with long mats which could be let down as a cover in inclement weather. While the lower classes of the population probably clung to the old wattle hut as their preferred type of domicile—could they afford more?—the *wer* (Big Man, chief) dwelt in an imposing building of brick whose niched (crenellated) walls and towers rose above the surrounding hovels. The people called it, in their own language their ancestors had brought across the desert, *s(h)erakhu*, "the elevated, glorious (building)." Occasionally mud-brick might also be employed to construct a large wall, equipped at intervals with towers, all around the settlement. This served not only to provide protection against marauders and wild animals but also to concentrate the inhabitants in a cluster where the complexity of industrial and commercial interrelationships could best serve the interests of the community.

Routines of life within the town increasingly centered on formalized public acts. The processional, the act of "Coming-Forth," held prominence of place. Here was the Chief in regalia drawn from materials of the landscape—feathers, flowers, garlands, horns—borne by his henchmen, followed by his women carried aloft in carrying chairs covered with curved roofs of matting, and escorted by standard-bearers holding emblems aloft. Then there was the "Rowing-on-the-River." Each local "numen," while housed and honored within a bower and hut made of reeds, mud, and wood, would be seen to best advantage by the populace when his or her fetish or image was rowed in a sacred barque upon the local waterway. The chief struck the first brick for a new building, opened a new canal, sacrificed to the Ram, or Fish, or Cobra, or whatever the supernatural patron may have been. The chief himself took to the water and was rowed along the river, and as he came cresting the flood, both banks burst forth in verdure.

Chapter Two

The Advent of Horus

···

'Anepat was not the only, nor the most dominant, major center in the lower system of rivers. In the period of rapid development which was in full swing 5,200 years ago in the Land of the Flood (the Nile Delta), there were numerous communities dotting the broad tracts bordering the many river branches. Each was self-contained, self-supporting, and to a large extent functionally redundant. Each was presumably governed by a *wer* (magnate, chief) with hereditary rights, his ancestors having graduated beyond the status of a simple Big Man. To what extent conflict characterized relations between these settlements is unknown; but political unification, by force or otherwise, seems not to have come about in prehistoric times.

To judge by later textual allusions to its remote past, the settlement called Pe, later Buto, may have exercised a loose influence over its Delta sister communities, but it is doubtful whether its chief was considered anything more than a *primus inter pares*. Like 'Anepat, Buto was situated on a secondary branch of the Nile, not far from the shore of the Great Green. Lakes, lagoons, and marshes abounded in the vicinity, as the names of local satellite hamlets indicate: "City-of-the-Lakes," "Lake of the Apiculturists," "Basin-Lagoon," "Mansion of the Marshland of Pe." Buto and its numina display the classic form of "chieftain" mythology: the falcon Horus was born in Khemmis, a reputedly floating island lying off Buto, and it was from this mysterious lair that he at last emerged to champion his dead father. The cobra reared up on his head, spitting venom at his enemies, and as Edjo, the "Green One," she took up residence in Buto as tutelary goddess.

While prehistoric Buto left no evidence of any expansionist designs, she enjoyed extensive foreign contacts. Forty miles to the west, beyond the great western river, the desert began stretching many days' journey toward the sunset and the western support of heaven. Here lived the Tjehenu, who dressed like wildmen and spoke a barbarous tongue. Cattle and asses they possessed in some numbers, and the oil they produced was coveted in all of northeast Africa. But apart from the irritant of an occasional sortie, they excited little interest in the Delta, and no one would or could permanently subdue them. From the north came ships with more valuable merchandise: the products of Syria, Lebanon, the Orontes basin, and the western Euphrates, all within the penumbra of the Uruk/Jemdet Nasr culture of Mesopotamia. Goods of northern manufacture pre-

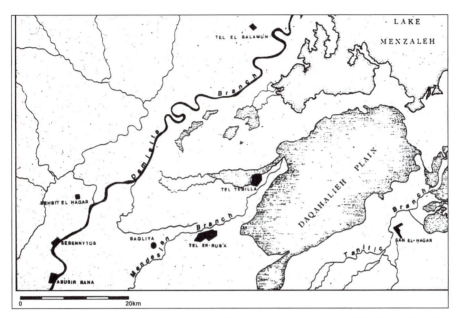

Figure 2.1. Map of the central and northeast Delta. The site of Mendes is marked by the modern Tel er-Rub'a, Hermopolis Parva by Baqliya, and Busiris by Abusir Bana. The Daqahlieh plain (the ancient "*Laḥaḥta*-water") was frequently flooded in antiquity.

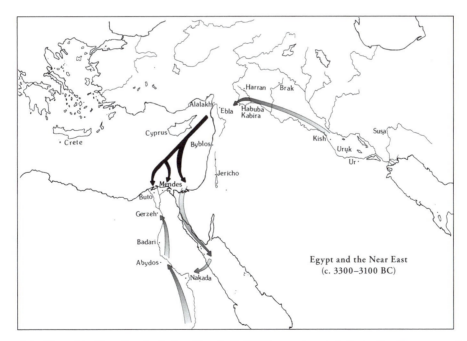

Figure 2.2. Map of the Near East in the late Naqada II–III (Gerzean) period, illustrating the commercial expansion of the "Uruk Phenomenon."

2.1 The Uruk Phenomenon

By the second quarter of the fourth millennium B.C., Lower Mesopotamia had begun to develop a truly urban culture, centered on a number of large cities of about forty thousand inhabitants, each with a relatively small territorium. These settlements, displaying sophisticated elites and complex social stratification, survived through long-distance acquisition of foodstuffs, commodities, and minerals. A network of trade routes led Sumerian prospectors and merchants to the northern plains for grain, northwest into Syria for timber, into the uplands of Iran for minerals, and to Anatolia for copper and silver. These traders eventually, by sea around the Arabian peninsula and the Red Sea, and across the Mediterranean from Syria, penetrated Egypt in search of gold, copper, foodstuffs, and sub-Saharan products. Their insatiable demand increased competition among Egyptian headmen for control of the products the foreigners were seeking and constituted a catalyst in the accelerated evolution of sociopolitical forms that eventually produced the monarchy.

sumably filtered in also from the east where the overland routes from the Levant made landfall in Africa. Copperware, pottery, asphalt, and basalt were beginning to find their way from the land called Lotianu (the Levantine coast and Syria) into the Delta.

But it was from the south that the greatest impact would be made on the inhabitants of the Delta, one that would change their lives forever. In the remote south, hundreds of *itrw* beyond the point at which the great river split, three major settlements were beginning to expand and to dominate the Nile Valley. Each stood at a point where a land corridor met the Nile and thus controlled the movement of goods and people over vast distances: Nekhen and Abydos at the head of desert routes from the west, and Ombos ("Gold-Town") opposite the mouth of a wady running to the "Great Black" (the Red Sea). The chiefdom resident at Nekhen thrived at the expense of the other two centers, but both Ombos and Abydos contributed to the nascent political power of the region. Ombos and its god 'Ash became part of the embryonic royal mythology, and Abydos provided the site for the burying ground for the chiefs of Nekhen.

These were halcyon days for the Valley. Population expanded and settlements spread to the apex of the Delta, many marked by the sophisticated brick architecture described above. "Industrial" techniques were in the throes of a great leap forward, evidenced by beautiful ripple-flaked stone tools, cast copper implements, decorated pottery, jewelry of gold and gems, and decorated palettes for the grinding of eye paint. The population was growing beyond the aggregate of the small "neolithic" communities of the preceding age; and now the range of architecture and tomb size, as well as the availability of luxury items, all bespeak the growth of an elite in an hierarchical society.

The Valley, the "Land of the *Shma*-plant," was giving birth to a vibrant and expansive society. Everywhere, over a stretch of river three weeks' journey in length, the great river yielded unexpected advantage to human settlement. Besides being an inexhaustible source of fertile soil, fish, fowl, and game, it offered itself to humankind as an easily negotiated transit corridor. Why, if subsistence and manufacture dominated human needs, locate a large settlement at any specific point on the river? If food and resources were more plentiful in another sector of the Valley, the ships could sail a one- or two-day journey to fetch them! The entire Valley, from the apex of the Land of the Flood to the First Cataract, was within surprisingly easy reach of anyone with a sturdy craft. Advantage in location became a factor in choice only when movement of goods and personnel could be more easily tapped by settling and controlling a particular node at the junction of transit corridors. And so ships and movement and conflict became the hallmarks of the evolving society of the Land of the *Shma*-plant, and all of these soon appeared in the symbolic discourse of the time.

Figure 2.3. Decoration on a Naqada II pot. The Nile craft is identified by a standard on the forward cabin and carries a dancing(?), steatopagous woman and two males. It is a moot point whether this triad is a grouping of divinities or whether the males are humans worshiping a goddess.

The inhabitants of *Anepat* knew what was happening upriver. A new culture from the Land of the *Shma*-plant was breaking in upon them. It could not be resisted: its new ideas were superior, its power overwhelming.

Out of the south came beautiful ships, descending each river-branch in the Delta. Their profiles defined graceful sickle-shapes, trimmed with colorful fringes of cloth. Amidships they bore simple cabins of wood and plaited reeds with curved roofs. Sometimes a window in the cabin allowed the mysterious occupant to peer out. Almost all bore a standard which raised aloft the insignia of the owner(?). Apart from any merchandise they may have carried, many showed forth markings that betrayed divine ownership. The figure of a woman with broad hips and bared breasts danced with arms uplifted upon the decks. Beside her often stood two males with throw-sticks in hand and feathers on their heads: the Great Mother accompanied by consort and son.

Other symbols defining this "son" were soon displayed to the inhabitants of the north. The Delta folk became aware of a power residing far to the south, personified in a Big Man who could make his will effective wherever he chose. Heraldic devices on ships, pottery, palettes, and even the living rock made him an ever-present lord whose might rivaled that of the local municipal numina. Here he was, as "Bull-of-His-Mother," tram-

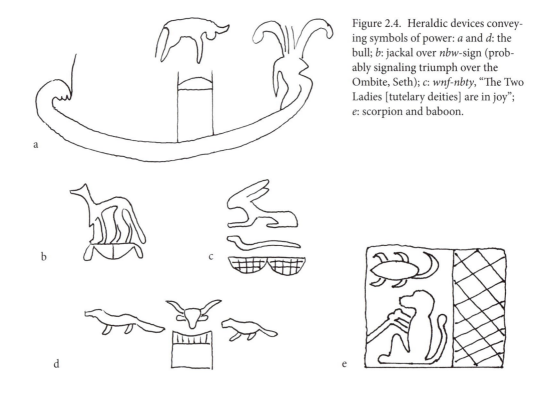

Figure 2.4. Heraldic devices conveying symbols of power: *a* and *d*: the bull; *b*: jackal over *nbw*-sign (probably signaling triumph over the Ombite, Seth); *c*: *wnf-nbty*, "The Two Ladies [tutelary deities] are in joy"; *e*: scorpion and baboon.

2.2 "Yellow Face," King of the Baboons

Here is the king, O baboon, O ape, O pȝtt-monkey! The king's bum is on his back, and the king's "revered state" is in his hand. Let the king make jubilation and chatter, and may he sit among you! [PT 315]

The king has cleared the night sky, and has sent forth the stars, the "Powers" have made an appearance in order that they might confer the dignity of "Baby" (the monkey-god) on the king. The king is the son of the Insouciant One: she bore the king to "Yellow-Face," Lord of the Twilight Skies. [PT 320]

pling enemies or goring his way into a fortress; here a lion tearing at his prey; here a crocodile or a scorpion; here the King of Baboons, the great "Yellow Face"; here the jackal, the "Trail-Blazer" cunning and wise; here the speedy hare. Primarily, though, he was the falcon "Horus," the "Lord of Heaven." In whatever avatar he appeared the great man exuded an aura of power and triumph. He was demanding of goods and services and was apt to construe reluctance or tardiness as opposition. Then he became implacable and vengeful, and began to talk of people "not being on his water," that is, disloyal. Punishment soon followed in the form of "quelling," "curbing," or "smiting" the recalcitrant.

The Land of the Flood rapidly came to know what such punishment meant. The sight of burned settlements, demolished walls, and decapitated townsmen provided macabre inspiration for the artist and decorator. Wherever the themes were displayed their chastening message could not be mistaken: this is how the falcon Horus punishes recalcitrants and malefactors. So be loyal, do what he says, hand over what he wants, do not entertain thoughts counter to his will.

Then the time came when it was heard tell that Horus, Lord of Heaven, and his followers had alighted to take up abode much closer to the Land of the Flood. Half a day's sail south of the point at which the river divided they had founded a new abode, the "White Fort," and there Horus and his men now resided. Although its every aspect spoke of warlike things, it was far from being a menacing place. It was well stocked with a certain supply of food, for Horus was the champion of the fertile Black Land against the sterile desert. A support staff ministered to his needs and those of his men, and if he went to war it was not over competition for resources. Everyone in the Valley succumbed to the attraction of White Fort: if you were in Horus' employ, you lived well.

Acceptance of Horus was mixed north of White Fort. Horus had "united the Two Lands" and every second year rather pompously made "the circuit of the walls" of White Fort, an act symbolic of taking possession; but these phrases at first expressed a pious hope rather than a statement of fact. From time to time a settlement in the Delta refused to cooperate and thus removed itself from "the water of Horus." Out would come the host and march to the walls of the rebel town. The rebels could not resist this overwhelming force and after their inevitable defeat would witness the hacking up of their walls with hoes.

But whether under coercion or of their own volition, the northerners yielded much of their goods, property, and intellectual capital. Gradually isolated parcels of land, bodies of water, and some towns passed into the possession of Horus, and his men began to occupy the entrepôts on the route through the Delta and across the desert to the east. Tracts of land were leased or ceded to pasture Horus' cattle, and vineyards were planted, especially in the west, to provide him and his men with beverage. The "Fields of East and West" began to attract the attention of Horus' agents, and the prospect dawned on some of them of tapping into agricultural riches as well. For ease of control of these riches the country was subdivided into townships, or "nomes," twenty-two in the Valley and (originally) eleven in the Land of the Flood. While the identifying standards of the nomes often drew their symbolism from the avatars of the incipient monarchy—bull and falcon are prominent—the township of *Anepat* retained the image of its favorite denizen, the *schilby*-fish, Ḥat-meḥyet.

Figure 2.5. Standards of the Mendesian township.

Apart from these concrete acquisitions accruing to Horus and his coterie at White Fort, elements of ideology were beginning to slip into the legacy which the Land of the Flood was bequeathing to the "Union of the Two Lands." The mythology of the fledgling in the nest, the future ruler of the earthly community, became grafted onto the rationalization of kingship, the royal myth about the dynamic duo Horus and his deceased father. The cobra Edjo of Buto was translated into the patron goddess of the Land of the Flood and, in concert with her counterpart the vulture Nekhbit of Upper Egypt, shed her protection over the Horus-king. Her shrine, the "House-of-the-Flame," became symbolic of all northern shrines and lent its form to the northern "type" of shrine at all conclaves of the gods. The principal festival at which such a conclave was required was the *sed*-festival or jubilee. This encompassed a reenactment of the coronation and the approbation of all the gods of Egypt in favor of the present Horus.

The exact relationship of towns in the "Periphery" such as Mendes to the central authority of White Fort, the "Residence," remains to be defined at this early stage (if it ever can be), but the general configuration is clear. The Residence sought to establish its authority over outlying districts through a combination of ideological presumption and outright intimidation. The sealings (see fig. 3.5) on the documents arriving at Mendes from White Fort on the morrow of the extension of federal power, the reign of Hor-aha, have been recovered in part on the floors of 1st Dynasty buildings at the site. For all their primitiveness, the designs hammer home certain raw truths: Horus was the "Seizer," who had seized his inheritance and authority; he could not be got at, since he enjoyed maximum security; a higher authority, identified by Upper Egyptian symbols of power and sacred space, ensured his absolute authority.

But one contribution of the Land of the Flood to the new phenomenon of the "state" that Horus was in the process of creating at White Fort lay in the sphere of what might be called "visible language." The small, self-contained community of fishers, fowlers, and agriculturalists possesses a collective memory sufficient to provide an adequate continuum in the life of the inhabitants. Mutual trust, communal awareness, and oral transmission ensured the smooth working of interpersonal exchanges at any of the few and basic levels at which its members interacted. A town in regular contact with strangers, however, or one grown too large for ease of personal acquaintance, suffers a disadvantage if it continues to rely on orality. Record of action and actor cannot be allowed to pass "from mouth to mouth" or to abide in the remembered "sayings of the ancestors." One needs a tangible and visible talisman of the stranger who did business yesterday and will return a year hence; one needs to leave one's own mark on that route of transit triumphantly negotiated; one's own moniker must abide, for the purely practical advantage of one's progeny, in some permanent form other than on the lips of the next generation. For oral tradition decrees functional obsolescence for the action and actor in the third or fourth generation. As the life of the community broadens and becomes increasingly impersonal, the individual experiences a territorial imperative in time and space: he must make a mark, literally; he must assure strangers of his presence; his name must survive.

Identity finds a complement in visible enumeration. The appearance of an "authority" distinct from ancestry brings in its wake property, dependents, and long-range contact. The complexity of the nascent socioeconomic system once again constitutes a disincentive to continued reliance on orality. The decorative arts, once guided solely by available surface and aesthetic considerations, now must produce noninterpretive images and a number system simply to keep the proliferating accounts straight. While eventually the need to keep accounts will be felt most strongly by the elite of a community administration, there is good evidence that in origin pictograph and number-sign were surprisingly the preserve of the small farmer, and possibly his invention.

The same cannot be said, however, of the commemorative tableaux. Here and there, on the slate surfaces of cosmetic palettes, on rock walls in wadys running out from the Nile, on ivory veneers on furniture, and occasionally on plaster surfaces and pottery, someone who was clearly a member of the power-group has authorized and seen to completion a graphic record of an event. The latter is not necessarily, nor even primarily, the registering of a timeless cultic or mythic act. The "scorpion," the "falcon," the "bull," and so forth were once here, and they punished and triumphed over the "dirty brigands" on that occasion. Although the present record has reference to a specific occasion, the punishment may have to be repeated. On that reading the tableau carries with

Figure 2.6. Tableau depicting King Den's "outstanding deed of smiting the east." The standard of Wep-wawet, "opener of the ways," goes before, and the king is identified by his Horus-name over his head.

it apotropaic overtones: it is also intended to awaken chastening thoughts in the brigands' minds.

The social dislocation of the Nilotic communities and crystallization of individual needs called forth a new phenomenon, which we would call a "script." Many communities in the Valley (and presumably the Delta) experimented with this newfangled aidemémoire in the late prehistoric run-up to state formation; but it was only with the appearance of Horus and the Union of the Two Lands that these needs became those of the incipient administration. The need to keep accounts on a large scale perfected number- and picture-sign; commemorative art, with its ideological agenda, provided the hegemonic discourse of symbol. But when the sense-sound to be rendered graphically neither was concrete nor suggested an homonym which was concrete, a one-to-one correspondence between picture and word proved impossible. The problem was first encountered in the attempt to render identifying markers (i.e., names and, to a lesser extent, epithets) into visible record; its solution paved the way for a true breakthrough, ultimately issuing in the invention of a true alphabet. Personal names derived from concrete objects or living things—mountain, earth, star, dog, falcon, rabbit, cobra—could easily be conveyed by a picture of the object itself. A squatting figure, male or female as the gender demanded, might be added to pinpoint to whom the term applied. But when the name was derived from a quality, a color, or an abstraction, no obvious graphic prototype would suggest itself as an unambiguous equivalent. How do you "write" the name "Shorty" without introducing the possible confusion which would produce the misinterpretation "midget," "dwarf," "stunted," or even "baby," "coward," and the like? Will the drawing of a large human figure to represent the name "Champ" misleadingly introduce the notions "hefty," "stretch," "fatty," and so forth? And however can we render such complex names as "My-Life-Force-Is-My-Lord," "He-Is-Mine!" or "The-Foreign-Lands-Are-the-King's"? Even prior agreement among the "literate" would require volumes of arbitrary equations to make the new invention user-friendly. The only solution comes with the realization that sense-sounds can be phonetically resolved into individual oral articulations and, with application of the rebus principle, "rendered" graphically. The resultant list of two dozen "signs" is enough to convey all the articulated consonants and provide a skeletal alphabet for the new script.

The phonetic value of a sign, however, will derive solely from the language of the people who invented it. It is a curious fact that the values of many of the most basic signs in the Egyptian hieroglyphic *script* do not derive from the Egyptian *language*. They make sense only as inventions of a community speaking a West Semitic dialect (with some awareness of Sumerian). In a Nilotic context this clearly points to the northeast quadrant of the Delta, the Land of the Flood, with its settlements 'Anepat, 'Ummah, and 'Aneze.

For all its power, glory, and celebrity, the regime of the Horus-falcon was not universally deemed a blessing. Individual communities in the Land of the Flood continued to rebel; even at the Residence there were signs of stasis from time to time. And then a king arose whose very name presaged the solution: Khasekhemwy, "The-Power-Has-Appeared." Short texts, all the more shocking for their brevity, proclaim "the year of smiting the inhabitants of the Land of the Flood"; a crude scratching on the king's statue records laconically, "slain northerners 47,209." An epithet of the king declared "The Two Lords (i.e., Horus and Seth) are at peace in him," but it was for many the peace of the grave.

Chapter Three

In the Time of the Residence

···

Anepat grew and flourished in spite of the catastrophe which had engulfed the Delta. In the centuries following Khasekhemwy, the halcyon days of the "Time of the Residence," when the unity Horus had brought to the Two Lands was celebrated by ever grander pyramids, the settlement found its own niche within the new state structure of the Two Lands. The kingdom centered upon the city at White Fort and the Memphite residence, as well as the individual pyramid-cities or work-camps erected to service each new royal burial. Here was headquartered the ever-growing civil service with its newfangled mechanisms of script, assessment, revenue collection, celebration, and propaganda. But while the Memphite "Center" milked the Great Cow, Egypt, of its cream, the Periphery at least was given the skimmed milk. And *Anepat* together with other Delta settlements benefited greatly.

The archaeological unearthing of settlements and cemeteries in the Delta within the time frame of the late Predynastic to early Dynastic is yet in its infancy. Nevertheless, several burying grounds have emerged recently in the central and eastern Delta, and the excavations of the temple and town site at Tell Ibrahim Awad promise to contribute greatly to our knowledge. Certainly during the Time of the Residence the settlement of *Anepat* prospered as the center of a number of satellite communities. The sheer depth of occupational debris datable to this period attests to the vibrancy of urban life. The city was divided roughly into two quarters, a northern mound occupying two-thirds of the space of the later northwest enclosure and a southern expanse of unknown extent. Between them ran a watercourse, and into both there penetrated watery inlets from the marshes to the west.

Deep corings on the mound of the temple demonstrate that the depth of the deposition from human occupation above basal sand amounts to over eight meters prior to 2000 B.C. Half of this depth (see fig. 3.1) represents occupation during the third millennium B.C. Our deepest sounding abutted the later temple on its west side, just north of the later entry into the naos-court. (Presumably a precursor to the later temple was standing on the same spot at the turn of the fourth millennium, although at present we have no archaeological proof of this.) Six building phases are in evidence in the excavations to date, the lowest two dating from the Archaic Period (c. 3050–2650 B.C.). Here

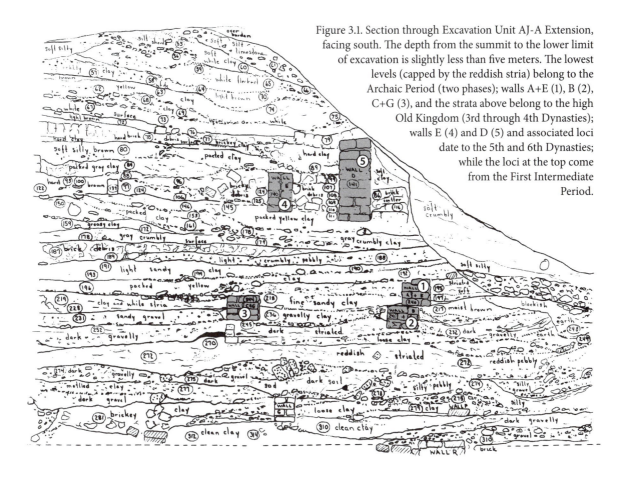

Figure 3.1. Section through Excavation Unit AJ-A Extension, facing south. The depth from the summit to the lower limit of excavation is slightly less than five meters. The lowest levels (capped by the reddish stria) belong to the Archaic Period (two phases); walls A+E (1), B (2), C+G (3), and the strata above belong to the high Old Kingdom (3rd through 4th Dynasties); walls E (4) and D (5) and associated loci date to the 5th and 6th Dynasties; while the loci at the top come from the First Intermediate Period.

were uncovered semicircular "silos," the walls of a thickness of a single brick, with pottery bread-pots, water-jugs, and bowls with vertical burnishing. Fragments of clay sealings with archaic epigraphy, sealing rolled-up missives dispatched from the Residence, were also recovered, with traces of names and titles. Several fragments came from a large clay sealing of Hor-aha, second king of the 1st Dynasty, with his epithet *Atjotji, "the Seizer" (i.e., of his birthright, his inheritance), a title which, three millennia later, Manetho remembered as *Athothis*. There was also a sealing of "the seal-bearer Seka," a powerful official of King Den, fifth king of the dynasty. All these sealings had been impressed in a lump of mud laid across the tied string binding a papyrus document. The latter, no longer in evidence, could have belonged to several different types of administrative text from the central government: a rescript (*mdꜣt*), a work-order (*wpt*), a conscription order (*srw*), or an assessment (*mdd*) are equally likely. In any case the city was clearly already within the administrative web of Horus and the Residence.

Figure 3.2. "Silos" beginning to emerge (Unit AJ-A Extension, Phase V), c. 2nd Dynasty.

Figure 3.3. "Silos" of Phase V (AJ-A Extension) built over "silos" of Phase VI (1st Dynasty).

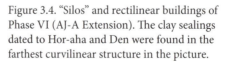

Figure 3.4. "Silos" and rectilinear buildings of Phase VI (AJ-A Extension). The clay sealings dated to Hor-aha and Den were found in the farthest curvilinear structure in the picture.

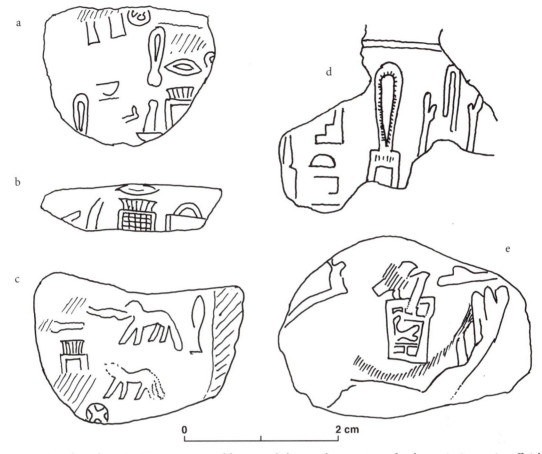

Figure 3.5. Sealings from AJ-A Extension: *a* and *b* seem to belong to the same type of seal, mentioning a mitr-official (unknown function) in association with the shrine types of the tutelary goddesses of Upper and Lower Egypt and the white crown (it is doubtful whether *Djedet* occurs above); *c* may contain a reference to a town near Mendes named *Shetj.wy*, literally "Mongoose-ville"; *d* is an impression of the personal seal of the "Seal-Bearer Se[t]-ka," an important functionary of the reign of King Den (fifth king of the 1st Dynasty); *e* contains the Horus-name of King Hor-aha (second king of the 1st Dynasty).

The uppermost (Phase V) of these early strata had suffered a demolition that left a thick layer of tumbled mud-brick and some ash. On top of this destruction new structures had arisen, and this building phase (Phase IV) proved the longest-lived of the six, with upward of five superimposed floor levels. The well-built walls and fine Old Kingdom pottery point to a period of stability and prosperity, undoubtedly coeval with the 3rd and 4th Dynasties.

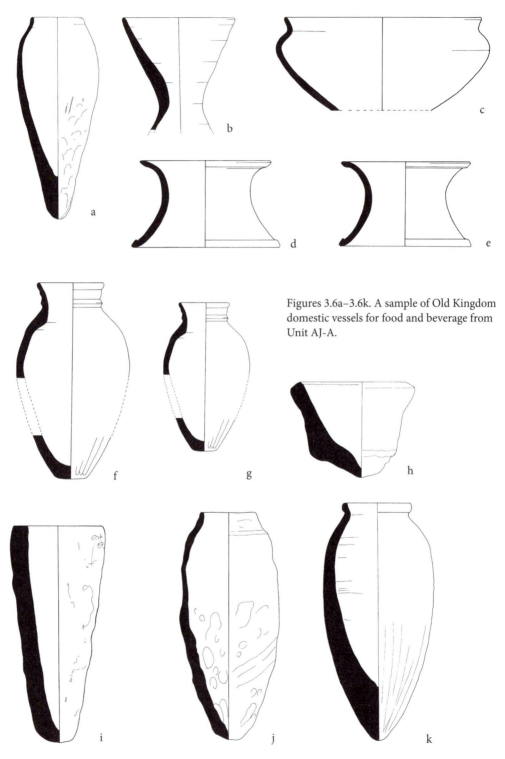

Figures 3.6a–3.6k. A sample of Old Kingdom domestic vessels for food and beverage from Unit AJ-A.

The "House of the Ram" at *'Anepat* occupied a point at the northern end of the site. At any Delta location such a northern exposure constituted a privileged choice, as it took advantage of the cool breezes of the prevailing north wind. We presume that some time early in the third millennium B.C., prior to the building of the large podium, a shrine of brick and reeds had been constructed here (see figs. 3.7a–3.7d). Although this shrine was swept away by later construction, we can visualize it as a modest affair, very similar to the unsubstantial sacred buildings shown in contemporary art. A mystery as yet unsolved relates to the means and direction of access: in the area thus far excavated no staircase or ramp is in evidence to provide the necessary approach, and we have provisionally concluded that the entry lay perhaps on the south side. This would have been swept away in the renovations of Amasis fifteen centuries later.

a

b

c

d

Figures 3.7a–3.7d. Shrines of the Archaic Period: modern renderings with the ancient depictions. The upper two (*a* and *b*) represent a type of shrine, in origin at home in the south, inspired by the shape of an elephant; the lower two (*c* and *d*) are the shrine of Neith, goddess of Sais in the Delta.

a

Figures 3.8a–3.8b. A semicircular "silo" (a) from the late Old Kingdom, abutting the western wall of the temple area (AJ-A Extension, locus 93). The same "silo" (b, opposite) under excavation (AJ-A Extension, locus 100).

The shrine of the Ram was the center of this growing city, now served by the strong "Mendesian" branch of the Nile. For 250 meters north, east, and west of the temple the city stretched out to the edges of the prehistoric levees. Houses were relatively small—three or four rooms sufficed the needs of the occupants—and were constructed of small mud-bricks. Rooms show all the signs of domestic occupancy: built-in basins for grinding flour, hearths, and refuse pits. Certain areas were reserved for storage, not on a house-by-house basis but apparently communally. These areas display recurrent series of curvilinear "bins" or "silos," built of small mud-bricks, the walls never more than one brick thick and only two or three high. None exceeded 1.50 meters in diameter, and many took the form of semicircles abutting other bins. Unlike the function of modern silos, it was not grain that was stored here but jars and pots. A curious feature of life at Mendes was the mortuary arrangements of the middle and lower classes. From time to time in Old Kingdom strata the dead were interred in close proximity to the domestic and storage areas, sometimes even under the floors or walls.

Until the early 6th Dynasty the terrain immediately west of the temple, to an extent of perhaps twenty-five meters, was reserved for the temple's food preparation and storage. Here stood the *pr-šnꜥ*, literally the "House of the Plough," where bread was

Figure 3.8b

Figure 3.9. Ceramic contents of the "silo."

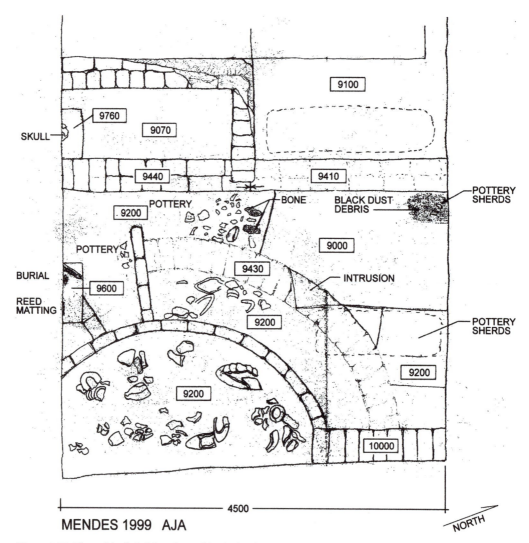

Figure 3.10. Plan of the "silo" (see fig. 3.8b). The broken oval lines are burials.

baked and beer brewed. The ovens here have yielded considerable quantities of ash, and palaeobotanical investigation has produced evidence of sizable quantities of emmer wheat and barley. In terms of the faunal makeup of the environs of Mendes in the Archaic Period, pigs abounded and even hippopotamoi are in evidence; but from Phase IV (3rd to 4th Dynasties) bovoids predominate. This is not fortuitous. With the evolution of a technology adept at quarrying, transporting, and constructing in heavy units of the hardest stone, oxen had become of paramount importance at pyramid construction

Figure 3.11. Structure at the southwest corner of the Old Kingdom temple enclosure, tentatively identified as a *pr-sn´*, a food production unit. At least five ovens are in evidence. Flotation yielded substantial quantities of emmer wheat and barley.

Figure 3.12. "Holding" area for containers of foodstuffs, located immediately west of the structure pictured in fig. 3.11. The wall on the left belongs to the administrative building for the complex.

sites. Pyramids demanded concentrations of manpower and draught animals not seen heretofore, and with their presence a support infrastructure had to keep pace. Work gangs required increased capacities of food production, specifically bread and beer, and larger containers for both commodities appear in the ceramic record from Phase IV onward. The increased concentration of oxen and cows at construction sites had a similar impact on the pottery repertoire. The heightened production of milk and cream—both for workers' consumption and, in the case of cream, for the lubrication of slipways—required the invention of a new and larger type of milk bowl. Thus appeared the so-called Meidum bowl, which became increasingly common throughout the realm and today provides the archaeologist with a good dating marker.

Sometime during the early 6th Dynasty (mid-twenty-fourth century B.C.) the domestic nature of the environs of the temple changed. The food production facilities described above were drastically reduced in size while around and in front of the shrine there grew up a cemetery called "the Abiding Place" or *Djedet*. Here under the aegis of the Ram and in the shadow of his temple, "those that abide," the ancestors "who were aforetime," were laid away in their tombs of mud-brick. Excavation has yielded limestone stelae, false doors, and offering tables inscribed with the names and titles of the tomb-owners, enabling us dimly to discern a profile of the local community. Service of the "Ram, Lord of the Abiding Place," dominated employment in the community. Such titles as "Priest of the Ram," "Overseer of Priests," "Privy to the Mysteries," "Chief Lector-Priest," "Priestess of Hathor" indicate the overriding importance of the town-god in the life of *Anepat*. But civil offices appear as well. Several worthies bear the title "king's agent," a royal appointee who handled state business (sometimes of a paramilitary nature) in the townships. Plantation managers, irrigation engineers, and overseers of messengers were dispatched to Mendes from the Residence and were clearly "Residence men," that is, natives of the environs of the capital city. Three (probably four) large mastabas, built with considerable amounts of stone, stood to the northwest of the temple. A most impressive mastaba, dating from the late twenty-fourth century B.C., belonged to the "Seal-Bearer of the King of Lower Egypt, Unique Friend (i.e., of the king) and General of the Army Ishtef-Tety." His titles remind us of the fact that the city lay fairly close to the eastern frontier of the Land of the Flood. Next to Ishtef-Tety's grave was a smaller tomb of the lady (his wife?) Set-net-Pepy, and next to that the tomb of Pepy-yema, also of stone. On the south stood the smaller (eight meters square) mastaba of Nefer-shu-ba ("The Ram Is Fair of Shade"), surmounted by a shrine with limestone false door (see sidebar 3.2 and figs. 3.15 and 3.16). Toward the periphery of the cemetery mud-brick replaced stone. The city is far removed from the source of limestone, and the royal subvention required was usually lavished on the tombs of favorites at court. To the immediate east of the temple stood the impressive mud-brick mastaba of the priest Aha-pu-ba ("The Ram Is a Support"), Nefer-shu-ba's father, identified by his limestone false door,

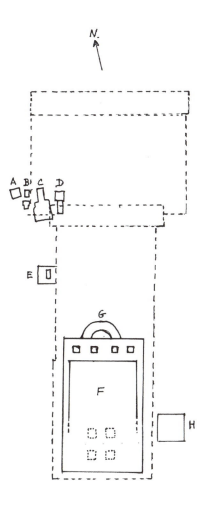

Figure 3.14 (above). Limestone mastaba of Ishtef-Tety.

Figure 3.13. The Old Kingdom temple and adjacent mastabas (broken lines indicate the placement of the New Kingdom temple): A—mastaba of Ishtef-Tety; B—mastaba of Set-net-Pepy; C—mastaba of Pepy-yema; D—unknown; E—mastaba of Nefer-shu-ba; F—Old Kingdom temple; G—Bastion (*wnṯt*); H—mastaba of Aha-pu-ba.

while on what must have been the edge of the ancient area of occupation, 150 meters to the east, mastaba tombs continued to cluster in ever-increasing numbers, the streets and alleys separating them clogged with poorer burials and occasionally dwellings of the poor who lived among the tombs. In spite of the absence of stone, these brick-built sepulchers are nonetheless large (8 × 10 meters on average) and well appointed.

As protector of his people in death the Ram became in truth the Lord of the Abiding Place, *Neb Djedet*, a phrase which eventually entered the toponymy of the region as "Mendes," the name by which the Greeks much later called the city. There were Abiding Places also at "Pillar-City," where the sun was worshiped at the apex of the Delta, and at *ʿAneza*, the Pasturage, one day's journey to the southwest. All three cities enjoyed the

Figure 3.15a–3.15b.
False door of Nefer-
shu-ba, 6th Dynasty
(see sidebar 3.2).

a

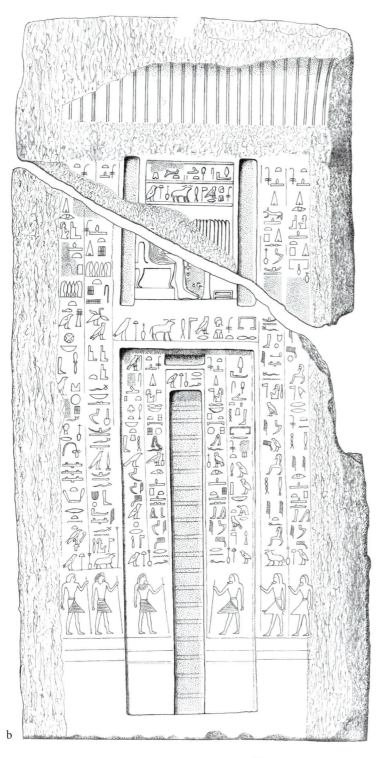

b

3.1 Domestic Arrangements to the Cemetery

The *Baugeschichte* of the late Old Kingdom cemetery can be reconstructed using several lines of evidence.

I. The earliest of the tombs may be established on the basis of (a) onomasticon, (b) location, and (c) building material. The four mastabas of Ishtef-Tety, Set-net-Pepy, Pepy-yema, and the unknown satisfy all criteria. The names of their occupants point to a period no earlier than the first half of the 6th Dynasty; they occupy a prime location on the north, on a rise; alone they incorporate a considerable amount of limestone in their construction.

II. They must be followed by the tombs ranged behind them, that is, to the south, namely the tomb(s) destroyed by the construction of the Ramesside Second Pylon and the mastaba in AK-Y belonging to Nefer-shu-ba.

III. Tombs lying in less optimal locations would naturally be placed next in the sequence, including the mastabas in AJ-E/P to the west and rear of the temple and the mastaba of Aha-pu-ba to the east. The mud-brick mastabas spreading far to the east would belong to this period also.

IV. Uncontrolled access to the burying grounds militates in favor of a period of weak administration. Dating to such a period are the tombs that out-front the stone mastabas to the north and the vaults inserted between the mastabas in AJ-E.

Thus, one can date period I to the middle of the 6th Dynasty, periods II and III to the reign of Pepy II, and period IV to the 8th Dynasty and early First Intermediate Period.

Where the tombs of the 4th and 5th dynasties are to be sought is anyone's guess. But it remains a distinct possibility that in those days of higher centralization the "elite" members of the administration were not Mendesian at all but "Residence men," of Memphite origin, sent out for a term of duty then recalled to the capital. Such individuals would be buried in the Memphite area, not at Mendes.

link of names derived from the same root and indicative of similar function; but it was with 'Aneza that 'Anepat had the closest association.

The Pasturage and its divine denizen, 'Anzata, the Shepherd, were rapidly falling under the influence of another cult in the Pyramid Age. In Egypt, in contrast to the lands north and east of the great sea, the ubiquitous food-stocks which air, soil, and river provided unceasingly were rationalized in the form of a spiritual essence, single and male. Whether under the identity of "Life," or the "River," or "Young Grain," this primordial pleroma intruded into the consciousness of the human community until, in the expanding world of parochial numina, it dominated all else. The paramountcy of Life found a parallel in the hierarchy of mankind in the person of the leader of the commu-

3.2 False Door of the Priest Nefer-shu-ba

Unique Friend, Controller of the Two Thrones, Bishop [lit., Overseer of Priests] Nefer-shu-ba. [Right side, outer.] An offering which the king gives, and an offering which Anubis gives for [good] burial, and that he might cross the firmament and mount up to the great god as a revered one, praised of his father; an offering which the king gives and which Osiris gives that invocation offerings go forth [to] the revered one, beloved of god and praised of the king, the one who makes the offering—oh may he attain the state of reverence!—Nefer-shu-ba.

[Left side, outer.] An offering which the king gives and an offering which [Anu]bis, pre-eminent one of Zepa, gives in all his cult places, that he might attain burial, cross the firmament and mount up to the great god. An offering which the k[ing] gives, and an offering which Osiris, pre-eminent one of Busiris and Lord of Abydos, gives, that he might proceed in good order on the holy roads of the West, Nefer-shu-ba.

The inner columns repeat the mortuary wishes and provide additional titles of the deceased, including "Lector Priest," "Royal Protégé," "Controller of Every (Royal) Kilt," and "He Who Sees the Great One," a title of the high priest of Heliopolis. While Nefer-shu-ba's main titles point to service at Mendes—his father, Aha-pu-ba, buried on the east side of the temple, was also a priest of the Ram—some of the functions he displays seem to indicate a claim of having participated in a royal jubilee.

nity; gradually an ineffable link was sensed to exist between the Chief and the essence. In life the Chief shepherded the community, his flock, and led it to prosperity and fulfillment; in death he united with the earth and the river, and his *bai*, or individual presence, mounted upon the air. Forever he was to be identified with his monumental place of interment, his house of eternity. Under the alias of the identity of his great sepulcher, the "Seat of the Celebrant" (or *st-ir*), he lived on for all time as a transcendent force of fecundity. Mounting up from the torpor of death, the *st-ir*, or "Osir(is)," graduated to the status of a primordial *anthropos*, filling earth and heaven and the underworld, a divine power in its own right. He was in the earth: the grain and the tree grew from his corpse, and the river came into existence from the effluxes of his flesh. He was on the earth: the flocks and herds multiplied at his behest. He was under the earth: in the submerged "dawning land" he presided over the continuation of community life. He was above the earth: he was breath and Life itself in the nostrils of the living. Yet his power was latent and his deportment passive. As the young grain he was buried, then scythed; on the threshing floor he was crushed and winnowed; in the river he was drowned; in the desert he was murdered. He was a personal monad, yet present everywhere. He was weak and unable to help himself, yet in what he was he proved irresistible. His passion evoked

Figure 3.16. 'Anzata, the "shepherd," of Busiris, later identified with Osiris.

Figure 3.17. Osiris.

3.3 Mendes in the Pyramid Texts

"Worthy of Praise" (i.e., the uraeus-serpent) upon her djam-*scepter, the king's Tefnut whom Shu uplifted, may she expand his seat in* Djedu, *in* Djedet, *in* Djedut; *may she erect the standards before the Great Ones, and open the waterway for the king in the Field of Reeds!* [PT 288–89]

Raise thyself, O Osiris, thou son of Geb, his first-born, before whom the Two Enneads tremble! The shrine-keeper attends thee, the Horus-eye acts for thee, that thou mayest make the monthly appearance. Forward to the lake, that thou mayest voyage to the Sea, because thou art indeed one that stands and never grows weary in Abydos, made glorious in the Horizon, and abiding in Djedet! [PT 1259–61]

May Horus not come in this hostile coming of his, when thine arms are extended to him; so let that name be said to him "Him whom the Shaaw have blinded"! Hie thee to 'Anepat, *get going to* Netjery! [PT 1268]

Horus loved his father in thee, he never allows thee to suffer, Horus is never far from thee. For Horus has championed his father in you, living as the "Living Scarab." Mayest thou endure permanently in Djedet! [PT 1633 (to the king)]

an immediate and emotional response: men must help the god because in the truest sense Osiris was their very Life.

Hypostaseis of this great god, crystallizations of his omnipresent essence, appeared in the guise of existing gods or new creations everywhere along the great river and its Delta. In Abydos, where the first kings had been buried, he was the dog, the "First of Westerners," the leader of the dead. At Dendera he was the Young Grain, Nepri; in the desert cemetery west of White Fort, his avatar was the falcon, Sokar. South of White Fort he united with the bull, Apis. In the environs of the Pasturage he adopted the character of the Shepherd, ʾAnzata. And finally he came to ʾAnepat.

The Ram, Lord of the Abiding Place, lent himself to a curious identification. Through homophony the common noun "ram," *bai* in Egyptian, found a like-sounding parallel in the word for "soul, personality, idiomorph," also pronounced *bai*. By wordplay an essential reality was revealed: the ram, *bai*, was also the quintessential soul, *bai*, and by virtue of that fact a special aura began to cling to the city. This sense of sanctity defied explanation, was ineffable, and people everywhere capitalized on it. Beatifications for the dead resound with the new faith that "my *bai* is in the Abiding Place," and that "my *bai* is mine, he through whom I ejaculate; the Abiding Place belongs to me: what I say is what will be done!" The "tomb-chamber is in ʾAnepat," and the "living soul is in the Abiding Place." As the great archetypal essence, Osiris was "pure in the Abiding Place," and the Ram was revealed as his "manifested Soul," his *bai*.

But the notion that the Ram could be the visible avatar on earth of invisible elements was too pregnant with potential to be confined to a single identification. If Osiris, fertility-through-water, could be manifest in the Ram, Lord of the Abiding Place, so could that other great life force, the Sun; and the Ram thus became the "Soul of Re," the sun-god. As Osiris is powerless, Re is powerful; as Osiris is latent force, Re is active force; as Osiris is infernal, Re is supernal. Both represent life force as antithetic modes of reality. Each may be posed at an opposite pole, but each needs the other: latent fertility must meet solar power, and only in their union will life energy be produced. For the Egyptians that union took place in the Abiding Place of ʾAnepat, in the shadow of the House of the Ram: Osiris "entered into the Abiding Place and found the Soul of Re there, and so they embraced each other." The entry was glorious and resembled that of a chieftain of old: "O ye lords and people of ʾAnepat! Avert ye your gaze, lower your staves when Osiris passes by you!" But the Ram, Lord of the Abiding Place, loomed larger than a two-dimensional representation: his capacity exceeded sun and water, and in fact encompassed the very elements of the cosmos. He was also the "Soul of Air" (*Šw*) and the "Soul of Earth" (*Gb*). And so this sacred ram now conveyed more to his worshipers than the pastoral numen of a parochial farming community. In his earthly presence he encompassed the four basic elements, the climatological determinants of Egyptian thought, imputed to the cosmos: water, light, air, and earth.

3.4 Osiris and the Deceased in Mendes

[*Osiris is*] *the living* bꜣy *which is in Mendes.* [*CT VII, 38*]

I have come to you, O Osiris, that I might clothe you with your clothing, that you may be pure in Mendes. [*CT IV, 278*]

"I am his double bꜣy *which is within his two fledglings!" What is that? . . . [T]hat is Osiris when he entered Mendes and found the* bꜣy *of Re there; then they embraced each other, and there came into being his double* bꜣy. [*CT VI 404*]

O ye Anpetite lords! Cover ye your heads! Lower ye your staves when Osiris passes by you! [*CT I 249*]

I am a w'eb-priest of Busiris on the day of elevating that which is to be elevated, I am a prophet of Abydos on the day of the jubilation of the land, I have seen the mysteries of Rostau, I have recited the festival-book of the Ram in Mendes. [*CT VI, 292*]

Says Osiris: "Let my son have free passage before any god, in your offices, in your duties or(?) in your honors, to the sacred room and the coffin in 'Anepat.*"* [*CT VI, 74–75*]

I am that aged one who is wept at the time of mourning. My bꜣy *is mine and I ejaculate by means of him. I am a Mendesian: what I say is what they do. I have not released what my corpse holds in. . . . I am that aged one, my* bꜣy *is in Mendes and Herakleopolis: I cannot be held back by those on earth!* [*CT IV, 95*]

During the Time of the Residence 'Anepat enjoyed perhaps the greatest prosperity of its long existence. The several meters of occupational strata datable to this period mutely witness to a city which was constantly renewing itself; its wealth is reflected in the vast tract of occupied terrain, stretching over one hundred thousand square meters north, east, and west of the shrine of the Ram. The latter, thanks to excavations in the 1990s, is now beginning to come to light.

But at first our investigation was surrounded by uncertainty. The Thutmosids and the Ramessides had both contributed to the rebuilding and extending of the temple, and we could not be sure they had not obliterated earlier remains in their renovations. It was not even certain that the later temple had been built over the site of the earlier one. Possibly the latter should be sought elsewhere, perhaps in a more southerly location on the mound.

In order to introduce a degree of precision into our investigation about the spatial

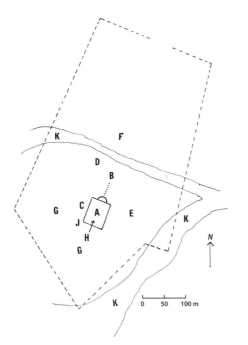

Figure 3.18 (above). Plan of the Old Kingdom city in the late third millennium B.C.: A—Old Kingdom Temple; B—bastion; C—AJ-A (deep sounding); D—mastaba of Ishtef-Tety and Pepy-yema; E—mud-brick mastabas; F—vaulted tombs (TA) of twenty-first century BC; G—houses; H—entry to temple (putative); J—food preparation; K—waterways.

Figure 3.19 (below). Plan of Unit AJ-A, due west of the Old Kingdom temple podium, showing rooms, hearths, and a burial, all dating to the 4th or early 5th Dynasty.

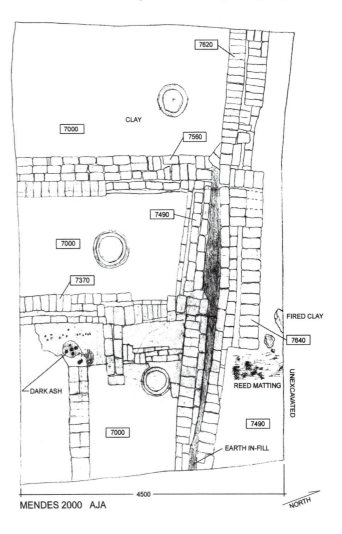

extent of the early temple, five excavation units were laid out within the later temple court, approximately forty meters north of the point at which Amasis in the sixth century B.C. had sunk the deep foundations for his naos-court. At the point of excavation the flooring of the later temple had been stripped away in antiquity, and it proved relatively easy to dig through the foundational sand that the architects had laid down. Although the architects of the later temple, in sinking these deep foundations for their renovations of the shrine, had swept away most of the remains of the preceding centu-

Figures 3.20–3.21. The initial sondage, undertaken in 1996, to uncover the pre-Ramesside levels. The curvilinear structure uncovered defied explanation at the time.

ries, they had fortunately not penetrated deep enough to destroy the *soubassement* on which the temple of the Time of the Residence had stood, which replaced the small shrine of prehistoric and Archaic times, alluded to above.

The new construction was a complete break with the past. In a foundation trench sunk approximately 50 centimeters into the underlying strata a brick podium was constructed to a height of nearly 3 meters; its width east-west was a little over 41 meters, a dimension which in subsequent rebuilds would govern the width of later temples on the site for all time. Its north-south length could not be determined because, at a point in our excavations approximately 31 meters south of the north face of the podium, the architects of Amasis in the sixth century B.C. nearly two thousand years later had sunk their great naos-court. Our excavations east and west of the naos-court, however, had proven the existence of substantial Old Kingdom perimeter walling, which suggested that the podium had originally also occupied the space later usurped by Amasis. This would have yielded an overall measurement for the podium of 60 × 41 meters, the longer axis being north-south. Its southern extent cannot be determined nor described at

Figure 3.22 (left). The mud-brick podium on which sat the temple of the Old Kingdom. The rectilinear depressions in the surface must indicate the placement of component parts (piers?) of the now lost structure. The section in the background clearly shows the sand foundation laid in by the Saite architects, capped by the destruction level of the Middle Ages.

Figure 3.23 (right). The northern façade of the podium, showing the large, "royal" size of brick. The wall on the right is a later attempt, during the First Intermediate Period or early Middle Kingdom, to shore up the ruins.

present, but remains of the corner of a substantial temenos wall just outside the southwest corner of the naos-court suggest that it was slightly wider than the space occupied by the later court. The podium was constructed of large, sun-dried mud-bricks, $42 \times 21 \times 11$ centimeters, and stood over 2.9 meters in height. Its northern face, the only one to be exposed at present, shows a very slight batter and seems to have been plastered.

Our excavations have found some evidence pertaining to what once stood on the podium. At a distance 13.55 meters south of the northern edge a lateral (east-west) wall had been built, enclosing something to the south. At a certain point before the close of the Old Kingdom this wall had been demolished and a new construction built over top of its denuded remains. Over the latter a sand foundation fill, approximately 35 centimeters thick, had been laid to accommodate a massive new wall, 12.35 meters thick north-south and still standing to a height of over 2 meters. This northern wall may have been matched by a similar southern wall, now swept away in Amasis's later building project; what this walling system once enclosed and why this thickness was required are questions at which we can only guess. The open swath, 13.55 × 41 meters extending to the northern edge of the podium, showed rectilinear indentations in the brickwork, suggesting the original plan featured piers as part of a colonnade surrounding the building. No access from the north was in evidence, and the presence of mastabas to the west and the food-production unit to the east preclude an approach from these directions. We can only conclude that the Old Kingdom temple was oriented toward the south.

The date of the construction of the podium can at present be estimated only by recourse to the pottery. Both in the foundational makeup and in the strata through which the podium cut the ceramic content pointed to the high Old Kingdom, 3rd and 4th Dynasties. Matt Adams has plausibly theorized that the decision to replace the earlier shrine with a grandiose podium-supported temple was taken in the 3rd Dynasty, after the violent termination of the Archaic Period. In any case podium and temple were clearly in use over an extended period of time, as several occupational surfaces abut against it.

The architectural remains described above present us with features as unusual as they are unexpected. The podium may well have had the practical purpose of elevating the shrine to a safe height above the annual inundation, a provision that adequately accounts for the elevation of all later construction in the area, but the temple that stood upon it can only be reconstructed by educated guessing. Presumably it was a relatively simple affair enclosed within the massive mud-brick walls described above, with doorjambs, lintels, and columns of stone. If the theology of the quadripartite nature of the manifestation of the Ram already dominated priestly thinking, we may imagine some such arrangement of the cella in the shape of four shrines or naoi, foreshadowing the construction of Amasis. It must be admitted, however, scanty word-descriptions of the cult from this early time make no mention of such a configuration of the Holy-of-Holies. Equally puzzling is the means of access to the temple, as no staircase or ramp was found at the point along the northern axis where it should be expected. Excavation both east and west of the podium failed to find an entry, leaving us only the south (now destroyed by Amasis) as the direction wherein the entry was located.

Like most other major settlements in the Land of the Flood, 'Anepat fit well within the framework devised by Pharaoh. By the time of the mighty Snofru and his son Khufu, builder of the Great Pyramid, the "Priest of the Ram of 'Anepat" appears in the titulary of the highest officials of the Memphite residence of "White Fort." Men bearing personal names incorporating the "ram," thus suggesting an origin in 'Anepat, begin to turn up in the pharaonic administration. One Ny-onkh-ba in the 6th Dynasty even attained the office of grand vizier. Through the wiseman Imhotpe, whose mother hailed from 'Anepat, the city could boast a native son who had revolutionized architecture by introducing widespread use of stone (in place of mud-brick and wood) and had created the first "Step-Pyramid." The Ram extended his aegis over landholding in the region, and numerous farms and plantations bear designations compounded with his name.

Now the Land of the Flood had lost all semblance of independence and had fallen fully under the thrall of the Memphite Residence. Unlike the valley to the south, where several townships throw up the phenomenon of the "Great Chief" of the district, a manor-born local bigwig of modest means, the Land of the Flood knows only that sort of township administrator sent out by the king and responsible to him alone. Sources of production are either in the hands of "Horus' men" or subject to their imposts.

Princes and favored courtiers receive local plantations within the Mendes township as part of their mortuary endowments. The local inhabitants either pay taxes in kind on cattle, flocks, grain, fish, fruit, vegetables, aromatics, and wine or discharge their obligation to the state by laboring on dykes, canals, and construction projects or in the fields. While the monarch's government, now entering its eighth century of existence, is beginning to suffer a diminution of revenue and landed property in the South, its property in the Land of the Flood to the north seems only to grow. The eastern Delta transforms itself into a transit corridor by which expeditionary forces march into Asia to undertake punitive campaigns or engage in trade, and river mouths into points of departure and arrival for fleets in quest of Lebanese cedar. While revenues and booty were destined solely for the Residence, the districts through which the ships and caravans passed en route could only prosper from the exaction of transit dues and the proffering of services.

3.5 Osiris and Life

I am Air, born of the All, my raiment is the breath of life. . . . I am he that makes the light of heaven after darkness . . . my effluxes are the tempest of heaven, my sweat is the twilight storm. The length of heaven is for my wanderings, the breadth of earth is for my settlings. I am the bai *of Air whom the All created: I am destined for the eternal seat! I am eternity!*

I am "Life" the lord of years, living for eternity, possessed of everlasting, whom the All, the eldest, made in his power. . . . "Life" is my name, the son of the god of the Primordial Ones . . . whom the All made as the Young Grain, when he sent me down to this earth to the Island of Fire, when my name became Osiris, son of Earth. [CT II, 80]

Whether I live or die, I am Osiris! (To Osiris) I have entered and gone forth through you, I have been fattened in you, I have fallen in you, I have fallen on my side. Through me do the gods live, (for) as the Young Grain do I live and grow—I cover the Earth. Whether I live or die, I am barley: I have not perished! [CT IV, 330]

Chapter Four

The Collapse

....

The city and cemetery at Mendes reached the apogee of its splendor probably around the middle of the 6th Dynasty, or approximately 2300 B.C.; thereafter a sure decline may be detected. Pharaohs Tety and Pepy I, the first members of the dynasty, after whom Ishtef-Tety and Pepy-yema were named, maintained a prosperous court and a well-functioning state Center. Even though this Center was finding it increasingly difficult to mediate meaningful favors, wealth, and opportunity to the Periphery, the latter unconsciously exhibited, under the guise of a provincial imagination, a continued loyalty toward and idealization of the pharaonic administration at Memphis. The provincials realized their entire being within the pharaonic framework: without it (they firmly believed) they were nothing.

All this began to change with the advent of a boy-king, Pepy II, second son of Pepy I, around 2310 B.C. We know little about the personality of this man, destined to enjoy (or suffer!) a reign of ninety-six years, the longest in recorded history. Folklore later spun tales to the detriment of his memory, which may be revealing, if they do not tax credulity. Was he really in the habit of paying nightly visits to a bachelor friend, a general in the armed forces? And did his courtiers really party continually while justice was denied to the petitioner? The managerial qualities of the head of state in Ancient Egypt were a decisive factor in the successful running of both government and the economy: Pharaoh was in fact a divine CEO. And if Egypt was to avert disaster it could scarcely afford a century of the same incompetent manager, divine or otherwise.

But Pepy II's managerial style may have finally proven irrelevant, for there was little anyone could do in the face of ecological disaster. There is evidence that as the third millennium drew to a close, the northern hemisphere of the globe experienced a relatively sudden decline in temperature with the expected concomitant effects on world climate. In northeast Africa the Nile discharge began to diminish. A lessened rainfall in the Abyssinian highlands caused dessication to set in in northeast Africa, and a series of low Nile floods robbed Egypt of its fertility. This was the beginning of the time of "sand-bars" and "health of heart," both euphemisms for famine. It would not be long before the lament went up: "Why, it's a fact! Grain has run out everywhere! . . . [E]verybody says 'there is nothing!' The storehouse is stripped bare." The man who husbanded grain and distributed it in time of need had verily an occasion for boasting: "I caused this grain to hasten. On the south it reached Wawat (Lower Nubia), on the north it reached the Thinite township. Now the entire South was dying through hunger, and every man was devouring his (own) children"; "I ferried over(?) the House of Amun during difficult years"; "I measured out Upper Egyptian grain and sustained the entire city." To compound the state's difficulties the pharaonic administration had for generations been in the habit of issuing decrees of immunity from taxation and forced labor to favored temples and landed estates. This ill-conceived and shortsighted policy had now resulted in depriving the treasury of a taxation base.

The effect on the material culture attested in archaeological remains is striking. Dated texts cease after year 67 of Pepy II. Large decorated mastaba tombs, such as had surrounded the pyramids of the kings of yore, are no longer built; to replace them there is a return to the small mud-brick tombs of remote antiquity. None can afford the expense of skilled craftsmen to adorn their sepulchers, and consequent thereto a decline sets in in the standards of art of the age.

If Pepy II's presence had imparted a semblance of order in the face of imminent disaster, his passing seems to have triggered something akin to anarchy. The twenty-odd years following his death witnessed a succession of as many short-lived rulers amid indications of palace conspiracies and reprisals, "shogun"-like appointments and decrees of desperation. Obviously nothing was working. Civil war broke out in the Valley, and taxes could not be collected. We hear of "mounds being turned into cities and cities into mounds. One estate will destroy another." No longer is the Residence able to keep up the eastern border fortifications, the purpose of which was primarily to bar access to Asiatic transhumants. The abandonment of forts results directly in the expected ingress: "the bowman is ensconced . . . the desert pervades the land . . . foreign bowmen are come to

4.1 A Royal Decree of Exemption

Year of the "Union of the Two Lands," fourth month of shomu *(harvest). . . . My Majesty [Pepy II] has commanded to exempt and protect the priests, the mortuary priests, the houses, fields, work-houses, towns and serfs of [the king's mother] . . . from doing any construction work or providing any tax [except for that] which is incumbent upon [them] viz. priestly service, monthly service and the performance of divine service, in the temple of the king's-mother in the course of eternity [on the responsibility of the King of Upper and Lower Egypt] may he live for ever and ever!*

(Sealed in the presence of the king).

[*H. Goedicke,* Königliche Dokumente aus dem Alten Reich *(Wiesbaden, 1967), Abb. 15; c. 2300 B.C.*]

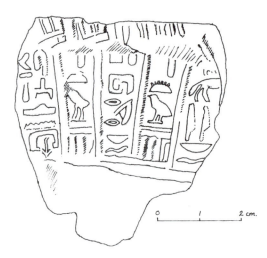

Figure 4.1. Sealing of an official (name lost) of Pepy II, found in the layer of abandonment of the food production unit. The titles read from the right, "[Dig]nitary, [be]loved of his lord, . . . who adjudicates well in the law-suits of the King's House."

4.2 Occupation at Mendes at the Close of the Old Kingdom

The sequential changes in occupation and distribution of economy at Mendes at the close of the Old Kingdom can be convincingly fitted into a relative chronology. For this the fields represented by (I) the storage area AJ-A/B/U, and (II) the food production unit AJ-E/P/Q/R are of paramount importance. (I) has given us the sequence of six "building" phases from the 1st Dynasty through the First Intermediate Period—Phase 2 is anchored by a sealing of Nefer-ir-ka-re (undoubtedly the first of the name, 5th Dynasty) as a *terminus post quem*—while (II) has contributed a rather tight chronology.

End of the Old Kingdom: Stratification

Type of Occupation	AJ–A, etc.	AJ–E, etc.	AL–K	AB–E
Abandonment	X	X	X	X
Squatter	X	burials between tombs at random	burials over mastabas in two levels at random*	—
Occupation between mastabas	—	vaulted tombs between mastabas	occupation between mastabas	—
Mastaba cemetery	—	mud-brick mastabas	mud-brick mastabas in streets(?)	—
Abandonment	—	X**	—	—
Food production unit	X***	X****	—	—

* Carbon-14 dating yields 4200 B.P.
** Sealing of Pepy II.
*** Sealing of Neferkirkare.
**** AJ-Q pottery resembles that at Deshasheh (Dynasty 5).

Egypt . . . the entire 'Land-of-Swamp' is no longer hidden . . . foreigners are (now) skilled in the livelihood of the Land-of-Swamp."

The end of an era is well mirrored in the archaeological record in the Abiding Place. The food-production unit to the west of the temple was left derelict and fell into abeyance soon after the beginning of the 6th Dynasty. Ominously Pepy II felt constrained to place Mendesian affairs in the hands of a legal authority whose sealing was found on site in the abandoned *pr-šnꜥ*, identifying him as "praised of his lord . . . [scr]ibe of the Broad Hall, beloved of his lord . . . who renders sound judgment [in] every case of the King's-House." Why was such a senior magistrate needed in Mendes? What was going on?

When, in 1996, we sank our first probes beneath the floor level of the later temple, we found that our trenches had come down upon the faces of what we at first took for two small, mud-brick mastabas preserved to a height, at the balk, of just over one meter. The sides were not vertical but sloped at a steep batter, and the line of one wall described a very slight, outward curve (see figs. 3.21 and 3.22). Further clearance to north and south proved that we were not dealing with mastabas at all. For what we had by chance intercepted was a strange, semicircular protuberance, approximately 7.5 meters long and three meters thick, which had been added to the north face of the podium, previously described, on which the temple stood. This protuberance consisted of a core of rubble

Figure 4.2. View looking south of the bastion (called *wnṯt* in Egyptian) attached to the northern façade of the podium, and partly excavated to reveal the strut walls.

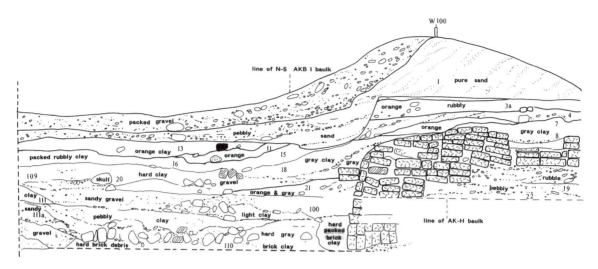

Figure 4.3. Section through the bastion, facing south. The surface associated with the bastion is that on which loci 100 and 111 rest. The alternating stria of orange (brick), gray clay, and gravel constitute the violent destruction of the installation.

and earth, intersected internally by strut walls and lined externally with a "skin" of mud-brick; it gave the appearance of a hastily constructed bastion. The surface on which it sat was lower by about one meter than the ground to the north, and the difference was accommodated by a slightly battered curvilinear retaining wall. The sunken, semicircular court thus created was entered not from the north (the axis) but by a postern opening east of center and a flight of three steps. Such rounded bastions with fosse-like depressions are well-known from the third millennium B.C., when they were widely used in defensive architecture. Had that been the intent of the Mendesian builders?

At some time no earlier than the last quarter of the 6th Dynasty the city had experienced a conflagration. The mud-brick mastabas east of the temple show signs of firing penetrating into the brickwork to a depth of two millimeters. The Temple of the Ram itself and its bastion had suffered destruction in the fire. Stria of orange and black bricks, colored deeply by the fire, cascaded off the tops of the standing brick down into the sunken, semicircular court, especially north and west of the protuberance. The fire had been accompanied by wanton destruction. Bricks had been disarticulated, plaster had been ripped off the walls, and pots and jars had been smashed or dumped unceremoniously inside the temple forecourt. Over the stria, but also mixed in among them, were small fragments of limestone, very likely the remnants of smashed funerary stelae. Highly dramatic was the discovery within the semicircular court of the skeletons of over thirty-five individuals, sprawled in death. Most were clustered on the east side. An old woman lay upon an old man, who in turn had fallen on a younger person. Two adult

Figure 4.4. Bricks, fired in the conflagration, strewn over the floor of the semicircular depression surrounding the bastion.

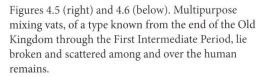

Figures 4.5 (right) and 4.6 (below). Multipurpose mixing vats, of a type known from the end of the Old Kingdom through the First Intermediate Period, lie broken and scattered among and over the human remains.

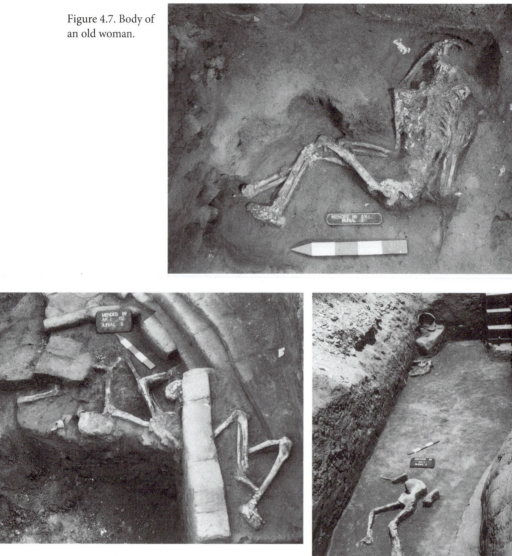

Figure 4.7. Body of an old woman.

Figure 4.8 (above). Two men under a collapsed wall.

Figure 4.9 (right). Fallen sub-adult, sprawled in front of the bastion.

Figure 4.10. Bodies of man and pig.

Figure 4.11a and b. Clusters of bodies in the depression along the central axis.

a

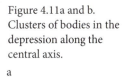

b

males lay sprawled over the retaining wall, part of which had collapsed upon them. A teenage male had collapsed (in flight?) in front of the bastion, clutching a rat in his hand. Half a dozen or so human crania, many fragmented and smashed, were found strewn among the debris on the west side of the court, evidence certainly of desecrated burials. Further to the northeast, still within the confines of the court, two adult males and a child lay with the body of a pig lying between them. Finally, on the east side of the fore-court were four skeletons, three on top of each other, sprawled as they had fallen in death. Curiously, one corpse showed fragments of a crystalline substance adhering to the bones beneath the waist, as though some object of this material had been shattered over the body either before or after death.

What had happened here? The unmistakable evidence points to a violent end to life and the intentional firing of property rather than to accidental destruction. Whether or not the firing had been local—there is evidence that the eastern and western extremities of the necropolis had escaped destruction—it nonetheless was intentional; and desecration and murder had been concomitants. We are left to wonder who the murdered were, who effected the carnage, and why? Certainly the atmosphere must have been one of hostility in the extreme: no survivors returned (or were allowed to return) to retrieve the bodies for proper burial. No one came back to remove the debris and restore the ruined shrine. The firing and destruction proved final, an horrific closure to nine centuries of prosperity.

Whatever the specifics of the local scene (which are probably lost to us forever), the situation in the Abiding Place mirrors strikingly the descriptions of social and political conditions in Egypt during and after the collapse of the Residence of White Fort. At

4.3 From the "Instruction for King Merikare" (c. 2070 B.C.)

Generation shall oppress generation, just as the ancestors prophesied about it: "Egypt shall fight [even] in the necropolis!" Do not destroy tombs, do not [even] destroy remnants [of tombs]. I did that, and the same thing happened as befalls anyone who makes that kind of transgression, through the hand of god! . . .

Behold! A bad thing happened in my time: the district of Thinis was devastated and it happened, in fact, through what I had done. I knew of it [only] after it was done. Behold! My retribution came out of what I had done. Destruction is a bad thing. It does not profit a man to build up what he has laid waste, to refurbish what he has ravaged. Be careful about that, [for] a blow is repaid in kind; everything that is done has a consequence!

[W. Helck, Die Lehre für König Merikare *(Wiesbaden, 1977), 41ff, 74ff]*

a time when oral and belletristic creations abounded that we moderns would dub "prophecies," the dire straits in which the land found itself were supposed to have been foretold: "Egypt shall fight (even) in the necropolis!" The hacking up of tombs and the reuse of dismembered masonry became so common that even the king might own up to having done it. The statues of the noble ancestors were being neglected and their tomb chapels were falling to ruin so that their names and offices were drifting into oblivion. The dead are thrown out of their tombs and the river now becomes both embalming house and cemetery. In view of the centrality of the mortuary cult to the economy of the land, such wholesale disruption could only mean anarchy and cultural amnesia.

The end of the Abiding Place followed within a century. Initially some attempt was made to retrieve the situation by building slight walls in front of the podium to stabilize the ruins, although the destruction debris was not removed. The storage facilities west of the temple which, as we have seen, had been largely abandoned by the reign of Pepy II, were transformed into mortuary space, shrunk to a reduced strip flanking the temple temenos. Here two small brick mastabas were erected, apparently family owned, the corpses being laid away at the same time(!) in nine oval cavities in the brick or let in from the top later. In the narrow corridor between the mastabas and the temple temenos a series of small vaults of mud-brick was subsequently constructed, each to cover a single burial. No interment was accompanied by a show of wealth: almost all were covered only by a mat and grave goods were conspicuous by their absence. One intrusive burial contained two wine-jars; a woman went to her final rest with a bronze mirror covering her face. Another type of tomb in this latest phase of the Abiding Place is represented by the vault. Abutting on the southern end of the mastaba of Nefer-shu-ba a double vault was unearthed, well constructed with four superimposed courses of flat bricks. Over the whole had been strewn a scatter of water- and beer-jugs as a final offering. A similar complex of graves was uncovered situated on a mound about 150 meters north of the temple (Unit T-A). Here four parallel and bonded vaults of mud-brick, 9.5 meters in overall width, had been sunk into earlier strata in a north-south alignment. All were backed on the south by a sinusoidal wall, on the other sides by straight walls. The vaults had been intended for multiple burials and, indeed, eight individuals had been laid away at the same time. Later, however, the vaults had been reopened and three additional cadavers thrust in at awkward angles. Most of the original burials had been accompanied by a wine-jar and a bowl, but in the case of one interment sixteen vessels clustered about the body. With one of the intrusive burials came a cache of seventy-three vessels, strewn unceremoniously down into the vault from a hole in the roof.

Among and over the abandoned tombs two levels of brief squatter occupation indicate the presence of the poor, huddling together close to the ruined shrine in the only place of sanctity and protection they know. Many burials are found in these levels, all over the site. All corpses are laid away supine in shallow graves and covered with reed

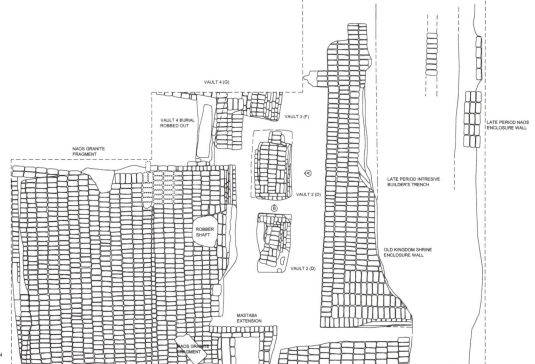

VAULT 4 (G)

VAULT 4 BURIAL
ROBBED OUT

VAULT 3 (F)

NAOS GRANITE
FRAGMENT

LATE PERIOD NAOS
ENCLOSURE WALL

LATE PERIOD INTRESIVE
BUILDER'S TRENCH

VAULT 2 (D)

ROBBER
SHAFT

OLD KINGDOM SHRINE
ENCLOSURE WALL

VAULT 2 (D)

MASTABA
EXTENSION

EXCAVATION PLAN
AJE I-VII / AJF I-II

NAOS GRANITE
FRAGMENT

Figure 4.12 (above). Plan of Unit AJ-E/F, showing the larger of two mud-brick mastabas, erected in the early First Intermediate Period. The large wall on the right represents all that remains of the enclosure of the Old Kingdom temple in this sector. Between this wall and the mastaba poor vaulted burials had been inserted.

Figure 4.13. Unit AJ-E/F under excavation. In the foreground is the food production unit. The mastaba in the background, with nine oval burial cavities, has intruded into the stratification after the earlier building was abandoned.

Figure 4.14. Vaulted tomb with part of the plaster removed to show the brickwork and hole into the interior on the north.

Figure 4.16. Unit AJ-F. Bronze mirror found over the face of a woman in an intrusive burial (early First Intermediate Period).

Figure 4.15. Unit AJ-E: vaulted tomb with superstructure removed to show the mode of burial (highly flexed) under a reed mat.

Figure 4.17. Unit T-A, facing south (First Intermediate Period). Each vault had been intended to receive two interments, but preservation was very poor. The wall in the background belonged to the Ptolemaic *mammisi*.

Figure 4.18. Secondary use of T-A vaults, showing the cache of pottery inserted into one of the vaults.

Figure 4.19. Four examples of wine-jars.

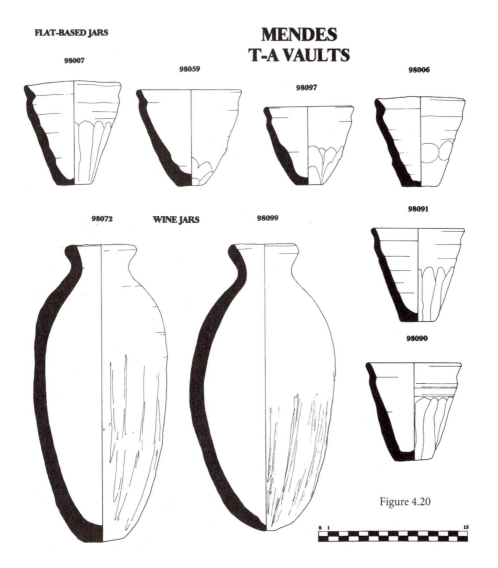

FLAT-BASED JARS

MENDES
T-A VAULTS

98007

98059

98097

98006

98072   WINE JARS   98099

98091

98090

Figure 4.20

0 1   15

JUGLETS

T-A VAULTS

FOOTED CUPS

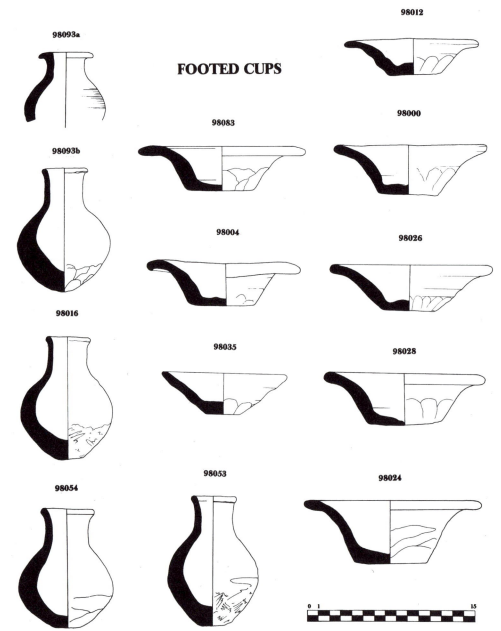

Figure 4.21

Figure 4.22. Cleaning a multiple burial under a single mat, Unit AJ-E (First Intermediate Period).

mats. Only a very few carry with them pottery vessels containing provisions for the hereafter. In one case four bodies were found covered by a single mat, two of them, a boy and a girl, locked in each other's embrace.

Elsewhere infants are in evidence. Analysis of the dental enamel of a wide selection of cadavers from this period shows a significant reduction in enamel hypoplasia, suggesting markedly poor nutrition, a discovery consonant with the ubiquitous famine reports from this period.

The discharge of the local branch of the Nile was declining. The lateral watercourse that had protected the temple promontory on the north began to recede, and human habitation began to encroach on what had been a waterway. The very axial arrangement of the shrine was affected by the ecological changes and, when next we see the Temple of the Ram, it will be approached from the north.

And thereafter silence. The great cemetery was wholly abandoned, even by the living. The inundation itself seems not to have seriously affected the site, as there is minimal deposit of silt above the last graves. While the shrine of the Ram would survive, never again would this erstwhile necropolis be a major City of the Dead. All that remained was the name, *Djedet*, the Abiding Place.

Chapter Five

The Mysterious Centuries

THE MIDDLE KINGDOM

The reader will have observed that, up to this point in the story of ancient Mendes, little archaeological evidence has been brought forward on the domestic quarters of the city. We have discovered the temple and the necropolis and defined their size and nature, but where are the houses of the living? Where, in fact, is *Anepat*?

There is, of course, no lack of ruin mounds in which to search. The tell stretches five hundred meters north of the northern edge of the Old Kingdom tombs and nearly six hundred meters east. To the south of the Temple of the Ram over nine hundred meters of ruins stretch away toward what in ancient times was a swampy tract. It must be that in one or all of these sectors the city of the living from the time of the Residence of White Fort awaits the archaeologist's trowel and hoe; but to date few if any domestic levels have been detected.

What is true for the Old Kingdom is equally true for the periods following the collapse of the Residence. Some slight traces—squatter huts and a suggested granary—may date to the late twenty-second century B.C., but apart from this we have been unable to find the city dating from what broadly speaking is called the Middle Kingdom, 9th through 13th Dynasties (c. 2150–1550 B.C.). That a city existed cannot be doubted, as it is mentioned frequently in the extensive corpus of texts which has survived from the six centuries covered by the Middle Kingdom. Of course it may await excavation in one of the untested sectors described above, but it is curious that surface survey has failed to detect any of the characteristic pottery from these dynasties.

One of the bodies of text in which the site is mentioned is called (by modern scholars) the Coffin Texts (see sidebar 3.4). They have received this appellative through their having been written in ink on the interiors of the large, boxlike wooden coffins characteristic of the 11th and 12th Dynasties; but these clearly constitute secondary copies of papyrus originals kept in sacred archives of the temples. The Egyptians referred to them under the general rubric of *sꜣḫw*, or "beatifications," a term which conveys their basic purpose of transforming the deceased into a glorified spirit. The value they had for an Egyptian facing death—there is some evidence they were deemed efficacious for the living as well—lay in the magic of the individual spells which would provide him with the knowledge of the afterlife, the gods and demons that were there, and what man had to face after death. Anyone in possession of this magico-mystical information was deemed a "well-equipped glorified spirit." Numerous sites, their cults, and gods find a place in this large corpus, and *Djedet/'Anepat* is among them. Some ten passages allude to the site, mainly with respect to Osiris' being there and the connection of the Ram with the *bai* or soul of both Osiris and the individual devotee. But the passages are not specific to the time period in which they were written. The Coffin Texts are usually considered a reuse and redaction of the earlier "Beatification Spells" called the Pyramid Texts found in the Pyramid chambers of the twenty-fourth and twenty-third centuries B.C., and specifically a reflection of the beliefs and interpretation of the later First Intermediate Period and the 12th Dynasty. The overall picture, however, may be much more complex. The Pyramid Text corpus, wrongly considered by some to have been exclusively for royal use, may have begun evolving toward the Coffin Texts before the Residence collapsed and the Old Kingdom came to an end. In fact mortuary texts found within the mastaba of Pepy-yema at Mendes itself, and firmly dated *before* the end of the Old Kingdom, are suspiciously close to the Coffin Texts. In short, nothing contained in the ten passages referring to the site in the Coffin Texts need necessarily derive from the cult or belief system of the Ram contemporary with the post–Old Kingdom period.

The anarchy which attended the dissolution of the Residence of White Fort was limited by the rise of a new power center some ninety kilometers to the south. At Herakleopolis (ancient "Plantation-of-the-King's-Offspring") a local ruler, Akhtoy by name, assumed power and proclaimed himself Horus-of-the-Living, the King of Upper and Lower Egypt. While insistent upon its legitimacy as successors to the defunct Residence, the House of Akhtoy (9th and 10th Dynasties) never enjoyed the whole-hearted support of the entire country, and shortly a challenge to its supremacy was hurled by the seven southernmost townships in the Valley, terminating in Aswan at the First Cataract. Here, in Thebes (ancient "Township of the Scepter"), one Antef enclosed his name in the official cartouche-oval and raised the standard of rebellion. The ensuing civil war dragged on for over four generations, neither Herakleopolis nor Thebes being strong enough to dompt the other. Eventually a mutual agreement to suspend hostilities was agreed to—it was to prove temporary—and for a brief season the land knew peace. The House of Akhtoy prided itself on the truce, which it viewed as its own achievement. No longer need we fear the South, was the general feeling: they have been cowed and now willingly send their tribute. It is the north, the Land of the Flood, that is our natural and manifest destiny to exploit.

The Delta was both a blessing and a concern. Its potential as a source of food was proverbial, yet Asiatic barbarians lurked on its frontier as a constant threat to the farmer. One of the scions of the House of Akhtoy elaborates on the problems and rewards for the benefit of his son and heir apparent.

Everyone who succeeded to power in a town did so with his heart distraught over the Land-of-the-Flood, that is <from> the "Tree-Plantation-Town" opposite its southern boundary [as far as] the Rekhty-water. I pacified the entire West (scil., of the Delta) as far as the maritime beeches: (now) when she (i.e., the West) labors for her(self), she gives *mrw*-wood; when juniper-wood appears, she gives it (also). The East has a lot of bow-people (barbarian nomads), but (now) they labor upon. . . . The "Central Islands" (in the Delta) have come back with every man within them, and the civil administration has expanded in my time(?). Behold! [the land] which they(?) destroyed is (now) made into townships with many and varied townspeople [therein]. The domain of one man is (now) in the possession of ten. Let a magistrate be appointed with labor-tax obligations, assigned all sorts of tax quotas; let the priest be provided with a farm, and it's as though a whole gang were working for you! That means no disaffection among them. The Inundation will not fail you by not coming. The labor-taxes of the Land-of-the-Flood are yours! (For) look! the freedom to moor which I have effected on the East extends from Hebenu (in Middle Egypt) as far as the Way-of-Horus, (the whole) being provided with towns full of people of the best of the entire land. . . !

This is a noteworthy claim to success. The king characterizes the period before his ascension to the throne as one of barbarian inroads, poor production, sparse population, and sectors beyond government control. But now! What a difference! He has won back the Northland from the Asiatic nomads and reorganized it with an efficient civil service. The results are dramatic: a tenfold increase in population, new towns, more farms, greater agricultural production, and effective tax collection.

In spite of a note of boastfulness, the king sounds genuinely elated over an historical reality. Times were getting better in the Land of the Flood, and Mendes, located within the tract described above as the Central Islands, must have experienced a degree of betterment. When, around 2050 B.C., a reunification of the war-weary country was forcibly effected, albeit by the Theban Montuhotpe I, its situation must have improved again. Whether the northern towns suffered in this final phase of the civil war we do not know, but all the town headmen made haste to do obeisance to the new conqueror.

Peace finally came shortly after the turn of the millennium when a new family of Theban origin, later labeled the 12th Dynasty, usurped power from the ineffectual successors of Montuhotpe. The founder of the house, Amenemhet I, after some initial indecision, decided to move his residence back to the Memphite region clearly in emulation of the "Time of the Residence of White Fort." To this end he established a new palace city thirty kilometers south of Memphis, which he dubbed in honor of his military and

5.1 Prophecy of the Coming of Amenemhet I

A king shall come, of the south; "Ameny the triumphant" his name! He is the son of a woman of Nubia, born in the home counties. He shall take the white crown and elevate the red crown, he shall unite the double diadem, he shall placate the Two Lords (Horus and Seth). . . . Rejoice ye people of his time, (for) a gentleman's son shall establish his reputation for ever and ever. Those who had fallen into bad practices and counseled rebellion, have curbed their (own) mouths for fear of him. The Asiatics shall fall to his slaughter, and the Libyans shall fall to his flame. . . . "the Fort of the Ruler l.p.h."* shall be built, and the Asiatics shall not be permitted to come down to Egypt that they might ask for water in begging fashion to water their flocks. And ma'at shall come into its place, and wrong be cast out!

* *Life, prosperity, and health.*

[*W. Helck*, Die Prophezeiung des Nfr.tj *(Wiesbaden, 1970), 49ff.*]

political triumph *'Imn-m-ḥȝt-it-tȝwy* (lit., "Amenemhet-Is-the-Seizer-of-the-Two-Lands"). For three and one half centuries the land was ruled in an ever-tightening administration from this central point. So closely associated with power and governance did the name *'It-tȝwy* become in the Egyptian language that long after, when native Egyptians, now second-class citizens in their own country, had to speak of Alexandria, they called it "the *'It-tȝwy* of the Greeks."

While the 12th Dynasty moved slowly and circumspectly toward centralizing its control of the Valley, its hold over the Land of the Flood was complete from the start. Even as early as the *floruit* of Montuhotpe the post of "Palace Chamberlain, Governor of the Land of the Flood," had been instituted, and a sequence of these officeholders can be traced for well over three centuries. As part of its program of restoration the new regime undertook to resurvey the cities, towns, and farms of the entire country, and the result was a land cadaster, portions of which still survive. In the section devoted to the Delta, the sixteenth township appears identified by its ancient appellative *Djedet*, the Abiding Place, with a north-south extension from just north of Bubastis to the sea and an east-west demarcation by the Central branch and the Mendesian branch of the Nile. The city was governed by a mayor (probably of local birth) and a "controller" with civil and police duties. Once again, as in olden days, the ruling royal family began to take cognizance of the city: the reigning king would display the epithet "beloved of the Ram Lord of *Djedet*," and royally sponsored cults were introduced. One of the latter was that of the popular crocodile god at home originally in the environs of the Fayum, Sobek, whose administrator is attested for Mendes under the title "Steward of the Divine Income of Sobek of *Djedet*." While to date we have been unable to shed much archaeological light on this period, chance finds of sarcophagi and offering tables suggest that at least a part of the ancient necropolis continued in use.

The temple was to a certain extent refurbished before the accession of the 12th Dynasty, at least to judge by the flimsy support walls built over the Old Kingdom rubble; but for some reason the latter was not removed. Refuse continued to accumulate among the undulating mounds of ruins. In contrast to the relative frequency with which the name "Mendes" turns up in the Coffin Texts, divine service at the site must have been carried on on a modest scale.

All this changed some time during the reigns of Amenemhet I and his successor, Senwosret I (1990–1925 B.C.). The ruins in front of the ancient podium were filled in and the ground level brought up to the surface of that structure. While no trace of the 12th Dynasty temple has survived, it undoubtedly occupied the same space on the podium as had its vanished precursors. The surface in front now became a courtyard for sacrifice: bones of sheep and cattle have been found. Occupying the space of the later naos-court on the south side there probably stood some kind of structure. A surviving section of Middle Kingdom wall was found in excavation flush with the southern edge of the naos-court. Outside this continuous margin wall were found small rooms of domestic purpose, with pottery of early 12th Dynasty date. On the east side of the naos-court the massive brick fill which Amasis's architects had prescribed was found to have cut into a much earlier wall made up of bricks about 34 centimeters long (in contrast to the 42-centimeter variety of Amasis). Although ceramic evidence was lacking, this could easily have been part of an installation of Middle Kingdom date (or even earlier).

In spite of high Niles, a thriving economy, and an efficient administration, the Middle Kingdom suffered an inevitable decline. Following the long and prosperous reign of nearly fifty years of Amenemhet III (1842–1797 B.C.), a lengthy period of gradual "downsizing" began, in which Dynastic succession was suspended, a welter of kings followed each other in rapid succession, and construction projects fell off in size and number. In the north commerce, which during the 12th Dynasty had been largely in pharaonic hands, became the initiative of foreign traders from the coast of the Levant. While Mendes lay directly in the path of such Asiatic trading initiatives, it was not at this city that the alien merchants chose to locate. A temple city thirty kilometers southeast, which had been founded by Amenemhet on the easternmost branch of the Nile, attracted the Asiatic ships to a far greater extent; it was here that an emporium dubbed the "Plantation of the Desert Tract," or *Avaris* in Egyptian, was established at least as early as the eighteenth century B.C. With an increasingly foreign population Avaris proved a magnet for an immigration the central administration seemed unable or unwilling to stem;

Figure 5.1. Surviving wall of the Middle Kingdom temple, later built into the circumvallation of the naos-court (sixth century B.C.).

Figure 5.2. Chambers (perhaps magazines) along the south side of the Middle Kingdom temple (destroyed by the naos-court in the background). The "skin" of flat bricks in the foreground, a stabilizing feature introduced by the sixth century B.C. architects, originally extended over the remains of the Middle Kingdom.

Figure 5.3. First
Intermediate Period
bread-pot, with
whitewashed exterior.

a

Figures 5.4a–5.4c. Pottery from the
chambers south side of the temple.

c

b

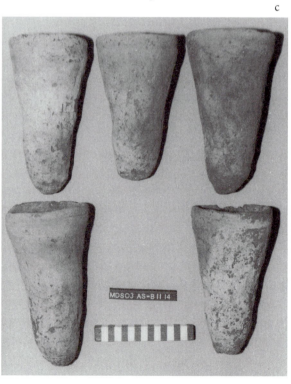

and when, around 1660 B.C., a Canaanite warlord from somewhere in Palestine or southern Syria descended in conquest upon the Land of the Flood, Avaris became a natural residence for this new regime. The native pharaonic administration at *'It-tȝwy* disintegrated and its surviving remnants retreated south, leaving the Delta and the lower Valley to the new "Foreign Rulers," or *Hyksos* in Egyptian.

Figure 5.5. Map of Egypt, illustrating the Second Intermediate Period and Middle Kingdom. The broken lines represent desert transit corridors.

Mendes cannot have remained unaffected by the new power at Avaris, but at present the record is virtually silent. We know that the Hyksos kings considered the *La-ḥaḥta*-water as their northern frontier, and shell samples submitted for C-14 analysis have proven that in the seventeenth century B.C. this broad, shallow lake lapped at the edge of the city. Excavation at the northeast corner of the New Kingdom temple proved that the latest occupational debris, at the moment when the Ramessides built their pylon, was of the 13th Dynasty (late eighteenth century B.C.). It is conceivable that, in the subsequent Hyksos age, that is, the late seventeenth to the early sixteenth centuries, the site had suffered partial abandonment. It is clear, in any case, that the city lay on the forgotten edge of the Hyksos domain. Its position must have exposed it as few other Egyptian cities to the natural effects of the explosion of Santorini; but to date no evidence of the catastrophe has been retrieved. From every standpoint the seventeenth to sixteenth centuries B.C. constitute the lowest point in the history of the City of the Ram.

Chapter Six

Mendes under the
Empire Pharaohs

....

Beginning around 1550 B.C. the Black Land, the domain of the pharaohs, embarked on five centuries of triumph, the memory of which lives on even to the present. The Hyksos regime was thrown out of the Land of the Flood, and follow-up campaigns led ever deeper into Asia. Military expeditions which had begun as retaliation for past outrages graduated to the status of preemptive strikes, and then, as the inherent value of expansion began to be appreciated, as conquest for conquest's sake. With the acquisition of the Levant in the north and the northern Sudan up the Nile, Egypt sat over an empire which stretched from Karoy, three hundred miles north of Khartoum, to the banks of the Euphrates, a stretch of the earth's surface over two thousand kilometers in extent. Wealth in the form of tribute, taxes, manpower, and trade goods poured into the pharaonic state to the extent that, by 1400 B.C., the proverb was circulating, "in Egypt gold is as (plentiful as) dust!" POWs, merchants, and mercenaries descended on the Nile from Nubia, Canaan, Cyprus, Anatolia, and the Aegean, exerting a detectable influence on Egyptian religion, the minor arts, and even the Egyptian language. In the realm of art and architecture conquests were celebrated by the introduction of new types of temples, a new military art, and lavish use of colossal statuary. It was the age of Horus-the-Mighty-Bull, son of Amun, the larger-than-life god-on-earth, who acts with his own arm and before whom millions flee. It was the age of "Sesostris," the quintessential conquering pharaoh.

What was happening at Mendes during the early Empire period, the 18th Dynasty, can only be inferred at present. Being in "occupied territory," the inhabitants took no part in the war of liberation in which the Hyksos were expelled. The city did not lie directly on the military route whereby, in subsequent generations, Egypt's armies made their way into Asia; nor, in all probability, did the fleet make use of the Mendesian branch which flowed past the site. Like other Delta townships the sixteenth, or Mendesian, township must have experienced the land redistribution effected by the new native pharaohs of the empire and the gift of parcels as rewards for the kings' henchmen. Some, like Nefer-khau, the treasury scribe and tax collector, donated statues of themselves to be set up in the ambulatory around the shrine of the Ram.

The reign of Thutmose III (1504–1451 B.C.) witnessed the greatest expansion of the empire in Asia. From his twenty-second to his forty-second year the king campaigned almost yearly in Canaan and northern Syria, confronting Egypt's great rival in Asia, Mitanni, on the banks of the Euphrates. Although this frontier could not be maintained, Egypt did succeed in retaining control over Palestine and central Syria for over three hundred years.

During the final decade and a half of his reign Thutmose set on foot the first major program of temple rebuilding in the north. The roster of gods benefiting from construction work reflects a comprehensive list of Delta deities: Sopdu of Saft el-Henne, Horus of Letopolis, Hathor of Yamu, Edjo of Buto, Osiris of Busiris (the old 'Anzata), Horus of Athribis, Bastet of Bubastis. While Mendes is not mentioned—there are, however, several lacunae—we now know that the city was not omitted by the king. A list of townships, inscribed in the Theban temple at Deir el-Bahari and dating from the regime of Hatshepsut, gives prominence to Mendes and its neighbor Hermopolis Parva. It may be that the pattern known from Buto is to be applied also to the City of the Ram. At Buto the temple was restored and refurbished with statuary, the calendar of festivals (dating from the 6th Dynasty) with their offerings reinstated, and a triumphal stela erected. The text of the latter, conveying news and inculcating attitude among the populace, is typical of the type of encomium favored by the new imperial regime. The king is described as "the Perfect God, son of Amun," and continues with the following hymn.

> The southerners are in his grasp, the northerners are under his authority, the Two Banks of Horus are in awe of him,
> All lands and all foreign lands lie together beneath his sandals,
> They come to him with head(s) bowed, groveling to his might;
> The foreign chiefs of each and every land say: "He is our master!"
> It is he they serve through fear of him! There is no land he has not trod to extend the boundaries of Egypt
> In might and power! Myriads and millions are of no concern to him;
> He is an active king who makes great slaughter in battle among the nomads all together,
> Who makes the chiefs of Retenu to a man bear their labor-taxes,
> Taxed with an annual labor-quota like serfs of his palace;
> He is more effective [than] a multitudinous army of millions in his van, a unique fighter,
> A brave for whom no-one else comparable has come along in any land
> Among his (own) troops, the foreign rulers or the southerners and northerners.
> He is a king deserving of praise commensurate with his strength.
> Egypt is strong since he came (to the throne)—no country is a concern to her;

(Now) she never has to attend on the southerners or pay court to the northerners

In the full knowledge that her champion is like Min with-uplifted-arm

The King of Upper and Lower Egypt Menkheperre, the bowman of Montu

Who sets his frontier at the Horns of the Earth, on the highland of Min!

Kush is like his serf, directing to him her labor taxes

Of numerous and endless gold, ivory and ebony!

There is no king who has done what he has done, among any of the kings who ever
      have been!

Figure 6.1. Ethnic groups of the Egyptian empire: (a) Canaanite from northern Jordan valley; (b) headman from northern Syria; (c) and (d) Canaanites from Palestine; (e) Canaanite woman; (f) Philistine; (g) Shasu (bedu) from the Negeb.

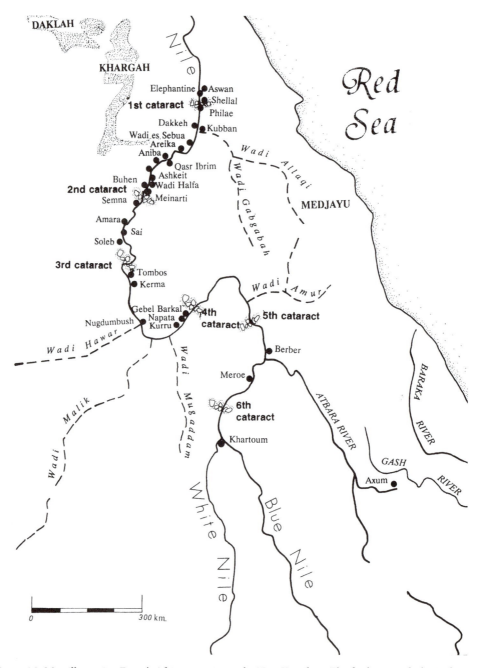

Figure 6.2. Map illustrating Egypt's African empire in the New Kingdom. The farthest south the 18th-Dynasty pharaohs raised their frontier was between the Fourth and Fifth cataracts.

In addition to this propagandistic news dissemination, Thutmose introduced a statue of himself into the temple that would become the object of a cult in commemoration of the accomplishments of his reign. He further decreed that the temple staff was to enjoy a holiday on the anniversary of his accession to the throne.

It is not at all unlikely that Mendes also was favored with the setting up of a triumph stela and the founding of a royal cult. That the Temple of the Ram did, in fact, enjoy restoration at this time is indicated by the discovery during the excavations of the 1960s of a disturbed foundation deposit, apparently of Thutmose III, some forty meters to the north of the putative site of the older shrine. If the deposit had originally been inserted at approximately that point, we might well surmise that the king had *expanded* the Old and Middle Kingdom temple to the north, perhaps by adding a court to the original simplex.

This, in fact, our excavations (2003, 2004, and 2007) have now demonstrated. Thutmose cleared the detritus in front of the Middle Kingdom temple and dug a deep pit disturbing in part some of the Old Kingdom mastabas. He then proceeded to expand the temple toward the north so that it covered 125 meters north-south, albeit retaining its 42-meter width, and fronted it with a mud-brick façade. (The Ramesside act of piety [see below] in preserving some of the dislodged bricks of this façade has preserved the identification of the builder as Thutmose III.) Presumably the exterior face of the façade was plastered and whitewashed in an effort to make it resemble a limestone pylon; but it was a "pylon" with a strange configuration. A gate, later replaced by Ramesside builders, must have pierced the center as would be expected and may have attained a width of ten meters or more; but the remainder of the external massif was not left uninterrupted. *Four additional* apertures, arranged symmetrically, two on the left and two on the right, pierced the façade at intervals. Each aperture, separated from its fellow by a tongue-wall 2.5 meters wide, measured 3.9 meters in width and was founded in the underlying Second Intermediate Period strata. Each showed a gravel foundation at the point of entry, presumably to support a granite threshold, and a square "slot" in the brickwork above for a door post. Immediately inside the door semicircular indentations marked the reveals on both sides, perhaps to receive engaged columns. Processional temples from the New Kingdom onward are usually organized around a single axis. Thutmose's rebuild follows suit but introduces the quadripartite complement, as if cognizant of the theological tenet of the "Ram with Four Faces." Should we reconstruct four lateral axes, each leading straight to a naos in which one of the four avatars of the god was worshiped? Certainly the arrangement was deemed sacred enough to prevent its later demolition. Even though the later Ramesside pylon blocked up the apertures on the north side, and in spite of Saite renovations, the four passageways remained standing, though filled in with foundation sand.

In terms of its wealth and power, though perhaps not its organization, the empire reached its apogee during the reign of Amenophis III (c. 1412–1375 B.C.). This king, whose sobriquet was the "Dazzling Sun-Disc," enjoyed a thirty-eight-year reign of rela-

Figure 6.3. Western balk of excavation Unit AJ-A Extension showing, at bottom, the top of the Old Kingdom side wall of the temple. This is capped by debris of the First Intermediate Period, with evidence of ephemeral rebuilds. The wall at top is probably of Thutmosid date, reused throughout the remainder of the structure's history.

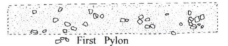

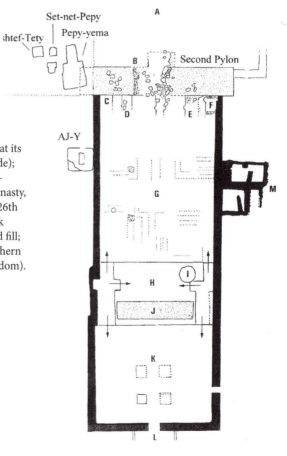

Figure 6.4. The Temple of the Ram-god at its greatest extent. A—first court (Ramesside); B—line of bricks (Menkheperre); C–F—apertures in mud-brick façade (18th Dynasty, Middle Kingdom); G—central temple (26th through 29th Dynasties); H—mud-brick platform (18th Dynasty); I—pit; J—sand fill; K—naos-court (26th Dynasty); L—southern entry; M—side chambers (Middle Kingdom).

Figure 6.5. East reveal of the easternmost aperture through the Thutmosid façade.

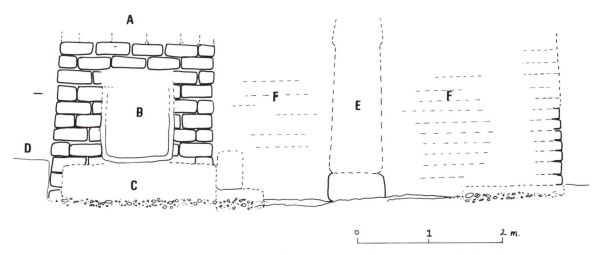

Figure 6.6. Reconstruction of east reveal: A—thickness of façade; B—rectangular indentation in brickwork; C—putative granite threshold; D—foundations of Ramesside pylon; E—column; F—side walls of aperture.

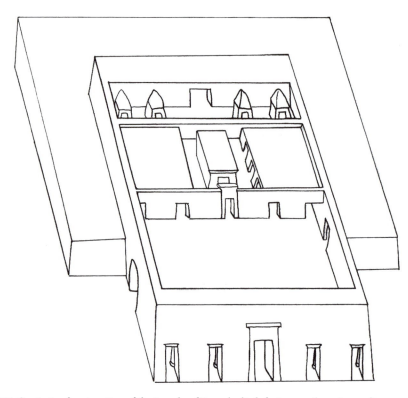

Figure 6.7. Conjectural restoration of the temple of Ba-neb-djed, facing south, as it may have appeared in the 18th Dynasty. The presence of a façade with four apertures (exclusive of the central gate) seems to be confirmed by excavation and lends credence to a restoration of four separate axes leading to four naoi. With the exception of the barque-shrine, the internal arrangements pictured here cannot be confirmed.

tive quiet throughout his vast domains and set about to celebrate the might of the pharaonic throne by erecting ever larger temples and more colossal statuary. Most of the surviving buildings of this king are to be found in the Valley, but to a lesser extent the Delta also received his favor. The cities chosen to receive new or refurbished temples were in many cases the birthplaces of his favorites: Athribis, hometown of his famous minister of manpower, Amenophis son of Hapu; Heliopolis, with which his brother-in-law was connected; Bubastis, whence came a favorite, Khamwese, colonel and governor of the northern lands. In a grandiose honoring of Sakhmet, the "Powerful One," the goddess who brought plague, the king singled out over ninety local avatars of the goddess for commemoration by sculpting life-size seated statues for inclusion in the temple of "The Mother," Mut, goddess of Thebes. While several Delta forms of the goddess are represented, the king seems to have bypassed Mendes, although the neighboring town of Hermopolis Parva is mentioned.

Similarly, the momentous events of the reign of Amenophis IV, alias Akhenaten, son and successor of Amenophis III, seem to have left Mendes unmentioned, though scarcely untouched. In his denial of the gods, and the very notion of the plurality of deity, Akhenaten promoted one god only, the sun-disc, with the cumbersome name "Re-Harakhte, He-Who-Rejoices-in-the-Horizon-in-His-Name-of-Light-Which-Is-in-the-Disc." This monotheistic revolution, for that is what it was, had the immediate effect in everyday life of focusing all attention on the king and centralizing the economy of the state in the royal city of Akhetaten (modern Amarna), which Akhenaten built for his sole god. All the older temples everywhere in Egypt were simply ignored in the New Order, their priestly staffs disbanded or recruited into the new sun-cult, and their incomes diverted across the board into the coffers of the new "House of the Sun-Disc," as the earthly estate of god was now called. Again: although some northern cities occur in the admittedly fragmentary lists from Akhenaten's reign, Mendes is not one of them. We can only surmise that some Mendesians must have been included in the 1,573 "men of Lower Egypt" whom the heretic pharaoh transplanted to the south as factors in the new sun-cult. It is also very likely that an altar and offering table to the sun-disc were introduced into the Temple of the Ram, pursuant to Akhenaten's directive, early in his reign, to make offerings to the sun-disc in every shrine "from Aswan to Sam-behdet."

The revolution of the sun-cult, associated as it was with Akhenaten, scarcely survived his death. The ineffectual boy Tutankhaten who, after confusion in the Dynastic succession, inherited the throne, was constrained to abandon the new city and monotheism alike after three years, and the court returned to Memphis. In spite of the effort to re-open temples and placate the gods, military disaster followed. War in Asia involving the new Hittite empire in Asia Minor issued in defeat for the Egyptian forces, who were forced to cede territory to the expansionist regime of the northerners. Dissension in the Egyptian administration resulted in a factional split at court: in spite of the risk, the dowager queen, widow of Tutankhaten, appealed to the Hittite king for a Dynastic marriage, only to see her Hittite fiancé murdered before she could marry him. In the aftermath the queen disappeared and the Egyptian army took over. The octogenarian Ay, lieutenant-general of chariotry and sometime amanuensis of Akhenaten, seized the throne and appointed Horemheb, a fellow general who had distinguished himself under Tutankhaten, as his heir apparent. Reform and retrenchment were the watchwords of the day. Now for the first time the temples to the sun-disc were closed, their walls dismantled, their staffs disbanded. Reliefs and paintings depicting Akhenaten and his family and coterie were hacked out and their statues smashed. People associated with the heresy were dismissed from office; others, who had incorporated the word *itn*, "the sun-disc," in their official appellative, changed their names. Akhenaten became a non-person, "that rebel of Akhetaten," anathematized forevermore. Etiological folklore grew up around the recollection of the "Amarna Period," distorting its events and subjecting the memory of its principal figures to pejoration.

Mendes shared in the post-Amarna restoration. Probably late in the reign of Tutankhamun one Ibaba (of unknown parentage) was appointed "first prophet of the Ram, the Lord of *Djedet*." Deferring to the new regime, he dedicated a kneeling statue of himself in the reopened sanctuary of the god, dutifully inscribed with the cartouche of his overlord, Pharaoh Ay.

In 1317 B.C. Egypt stood on the threshold of a new era. Horemheb had chosen as his successor a comrade in arms, a general and fortress commandant named Paramesses. The latter was an old man when, in that year, he succeeded Horemheb on the throne; but he was not about to select *his* heir apparent from any but his own family. Dynastic succession had been reestablished: a new dynasty, the 19th, had begun, ushering in the "Ramesside Age."

Egypt experienced a new lease on life under the new regime. Military operations were conducted in all the traditional spheres of Egypt's political interest: Libya, the Sudan, and Asia. The transit corridors across the Sinai were freed from the risk of Bedouin raids, and brigands along the "King's Highway" in Transjordan were punished and dispersed. The intermittent war with the Hittites was prosecuted with renewed vigor and, in spite of the dramatic though temporary setback at the abortive siege of Kadesh on the Orontes, Egyptian arms generally triumphed. Gradually, throughout the 1280s, the Egyptian forces pushed ever deeper into the lands of Amurru and Nukhashshe (central and northern Syria) until it appeared that Pharaoh was about to win the day completely. Major powers beyond the river Puratti (the Euphrates), Asshur (Assyria), and Karduniash (Babylon) turned cool toward the Hittites, who risked diplomatic isolation. By 1284 B.C. the Hittite king had had enough and made overtures to Pharaoh. In that year the war ended, as Egypt and the Hittites signed a treaty of "brotherhood" and mutual assistance. And so began half a century of peace during which international commerce thrived as never before.

6.1 Statue Inscription of Ibaba

An offering which the king gives to the Ram, the Lord of Djedet, *the Living God, the "Ejaculating Bull" who mounts the beauties, that he may give life, prosperity, health, a sweet disposition and joy every day . . . (and) an offering which the king gives to Hathor, Lady of* Hetpet *and Mistress of the Two Lands, that she may grant a good and prosperous lifetime in serving her, while I behold her [for ever]!*
[*J. Vandier, "La statue d'un grand prêtre de Mendes," JEA 54 (1968), 89–94, pl. xv–xvi*]

Though the causes of the prosperity of this fifty-year period are probably more complex than we can divine today, there can be no denial that the personal energies of the members of the Ramesside 19th Dynasty played an important role. The family first sprang to prominence during the reign of Akhenaten when one of its members, a colonel named Sety, functioned as a district commissioner in Canaan. (It was his son Paramesses who, as Ramesses I, succeeded Horemheb as king.) Unlike the 18th Dynasty, which was Theban in origin, the 19th hailed from the eastern Delta, not far southeast of Mendes. It was here, on the outskirts of the old Hyksos capital at Avaris, that they established a new royal residence called, with clear allusion to their triumph, *Per-Ramesses-ʿaȝ-nakhte*, "The House of Ramesses Great of Victories." While they could scarcely turn their backs on 18th Dynasty traditions and spurn the great Amun-re, "King of the Gods," who had guaranteed and underwritten the empire, they could and did show special favor to northern gods. Temples in the Delta were restored and northern deities took their place beside Amun-re as protectors of army divisions. The very personal names the Ramessides favored in their own family were compounded with the divine infixes "Re," "Seth," and "Ptah," indicating a focus on the sun-cult and its cultic satellites along the axis Memphis-Heliopolis to the northeastern frontier.

It would be strange if Mendes, lying so close to the new residence and center of power, did not share in the reconstruction of the Ramesside Age. Already in the immediate aftermath of the Amarna debacle Horemheb had honored the city by restoring a gate in the temple, and "the *Djedetite* Ram, the precious god," is invoked along with Osiris and Ptah-Sokar, god of the Memphite necropolis, in private devotion. Mendesians begin to filter back into the royal administration at various levels. The son of Ramesses I, who later acceded to the throne as Sety I, had during his earlier years occupied the vizierate and the rank of fortress commandant of Sile, and had also functioned as "Festival-Director of the Ram, Lord of *Djedet*, and Lector-Priest of Edjo." While the latter priestly role is associated with the cobra-goddess of the north Sinai, west of the border fort of Sile, his service to the Ram places Sety squarely within the cultic functions of the 16th township, the Fish-township.

But the prosperity of Mendes under the Ramesside kings owes most to the activity of Ramesses II, the son and successor of Sety I. This king, the victor in the Hittite war and signatory to the treaty, used his remaining forty-six years to set on foot the most extensive program of temple construction Egypt was to witness for nearly one thousand years. The militarist organization of Ramesses' reign had issued in the conscription of 10 percent of the population of the vast temple estates, perhaps 25,000 to 30,000 men, mustered initially to prosecute the Hittite war. With the cessation of hostilities this manpower was shifted to peacetime duties and put to work on building operations. There is scarcely a single major city in Egypt that does not show, even today, marked signs of this building boom, either in the form of walls and pylons or in the decorative statuary used

6.2 Sety, as Vizier, Visits Seth, Lord of Avaris

There came the Hereditary Prince, Overseer of the City and Vizier, Fan-Bearer on the King's Right Hand, Battalion Commander, . . . Overseer of the Fortress of Sile, Chief of Police, King's-Scribe, Overseer of Horses, Festival Director of the Ram, Lord of Mendes, Lector-Priest of Edjo who judges the Two Lands, the Overseer of Prophets of all the gods, Sety, deceased; son of the Hereditary Prince, Overseer of the City and Vizier . . . Paramesses, deceased; born of the Chorister of Pre, Tiya, deceased. He said: "Hail to thee, O Seth, the son of Nut, great of strength in the barque of millions, felling the enemies at the prow of Re's boat with a mighty roar! . . . [mayest thou grant] me a good lifetime in service to [thy] ku."
[D. B. Redford, "Textual Sources for the Hyksos Period," in E. Oren, ed., The Hyksos: New Historical and Archaeological Perspectives (Philadelphia, 1997), p. 19].

to adorn existing structures. The final extent and layout of a surprising number of temples was achieved under Ramesses II, and was never exceeded or modified during the subsequent course of Egypt's history. Since the power configuration of first millennium Egypt was more conducive to structural preservation in the backward south, most of the standing monuments of Ramesses II are in the Valley and Nubia. But this, at face value, gives a distorted picture of the distribution of his effort, for Memphis and the north were as much favored as the Thebaid.

The Temple of the Ram at Mendes grew to its maximum length, approximately 165 meters, under Ramesses II (see fig. 6.4). The building took the form of a processional temple, laid out along a central axis stretching north from whatever had once stood on the site of the later naos-court. On the summit of a low rise made up of the destruction debris from the 6th through 13th Dynasties, Ramesses built the front pylon of large limestone blocks, laid upon a foundational fill of sand. The presence of shellfish throughout this sand may indicate that it was brought from the seacoast. Each massif of the pylon measured approximately 28.5 × 5 meters, and they were separated by an entrance about four meters wide, yielding an overall width of over sixty meters. (The height can only be estimated on the basis of preserved parallels in Upper Egypt at perhaps fifteen meters.) While at present only about thirty-four of the blocks once composing the masonry of the structure lie scattered over the surface, several of these show the expected angle of batter at which the exterior face would have risen. Whether this outer face was decorated with scenes of battle remains speculative, but a band of text at the bottom mentions Meren[pt]ah, son of Ramesses II. A block that may have constituted one of the reveals of the gate contains the cartouche of both Ramesses II and Merenptah, the latter added below the name of his father. Most pylons of the New Kingdom were provided with flag-staves from which pennants fluttered, and our excavations revealed several fragments of bronze sockets used for the securing of such staves.

Behind (i.e., south of) the pylon a court thirty-five meters long was laid out immediately on top of the ruins of the First Intermediate Period. This may have been designed as a peristyle with a floor of stone flags, but no evidence of this arrangement has been found. Excavation along the east side of the court revealed the line of the retaining wall connecting to the front pylon, although all that remained was the sand foundation fill. This wall had been pierced by a lateral gate, approximately 3.5 meters wide, permitting access from the east. Its threshold, probably of granite, is now missing, but the underly-

Figure 6.8. Section through the foundation trench of the first pylon, showing sand *soubassement* and earlier trenching of Edouard Naville.

Figure 6.9. Pylon block with part of the name of Merenptah; east massif, first pylon.

ing layer of pebbles and sand is still in situ. The approach from the lower ground to the east may have involved one or two steps. The court just described was backed on the south by a second pylon of limestone, the foundations of which were sunk two meters below the then surface and measured ten meters wide. Even allowing for batter and a reduced thickness aboveground, this second pylon would have been thicker than the first. In the center, along the main axis of the temple, was fitted a door whose jambs were of diorite, carved with a vertical column of glyphs giving the cartouches of Ramesses II. But again, this monarch is not the only one involved in the construction. One of the jambs of the lateral gate was unearthed, having been pushed into a shallow pit, and on one surface the worn, but unmistakable, cartouches of Merenptah appear. The same king added his alternating vertical cartouches as a granite dado on the reveals of the entryway. More surprisingly, he is also represented by two foundation deposits, discovered, anomalously, flanking the second pylon and flush with its northern face. Both deposits contained miniature pottery vessels, small faïence miniatures of offerings (a haunch of beef, a bull's head, a goose), and a stone "brick" with the prominent prenomen of the king. One of the deposits also contained a real haunch of beef, secreted under the other objects as an offering. The unusual position of these dedications—foundation deposits are always found *under*, not *beside*, the foundations—casts light on the history of the building. Undoubtedly the two pylons and the forecourt were designed and brought (nearly?) to completion under Ramesses II, but late in his reign. Upon his death Merenptah, his successor, left with the task of adding finishing touches, made bold enough to add his text to the front pylon and the lateral gate, and to commemorate himself in the foundation deposits of the second pylon. But since the latter was already standing, he was forced to place the deposits beside the structure.

Beyond the first court to the south there stretched the 18th Dynasty temple, probably constructed of a combination of mud-brick and limestone. It is unclear whether this "nucleus" shrine had been altered in any way by Ramesses, although his practice elsewhere in Egypt was to leave existing temples as he found them, while merely fronting them with his own construction.

The builder of the 18th Dynasty temple was, as we have noted, Thutmose III, and the bricks of the façade, and perhaps an outwork at the gate, were stamped with his cartouche. The Ramesside architects in their siting of the Second Pylon were obliged to remove part of this earlier façade, but they did not treat the dislodged bricks as unwanted refuse. Instead, at intervals of five to six meters, these bricks were laid in their hundreds in lateral stacks across the width of the pylon foundation trench, each brick leaning diagonally upon its neighbor, to a height of over a meter. The care with which this arrangement was effected militates in favor of interpreting the whole as an act of piety.

Presumably the 18th Dynasty builders had planned and erected some type of columned hall at the front of their temple; but which type of column was used in the hall is un-

Figure 6.10. Foundation trench of the eastern lateral wall of the first court, as it leaves the Second Pylon; the rubble foundation of a postern gate appears on the right. In the lower right is one of the jambs of the gate (see fig. 6.13).

Figures 6.11a–6.11b. Gate of the Second Pylon under excavation. The blocks of granite, diorite, and quartzite were of no interest to later pillagers, but the limestone of the wings of the pylon has been completely robbed out. The gate has undergone at least two rebuildings in the course of its fifteen centuries of use.

Figure 6.12. Jamb of the postern gate, showing the vertical cartouches of Merenptah.

Figure 6.13. Part of the reveal of the gate of the Second Pylon, showing the repeated cartouches of Merenptah as a dado along the base. At some point in its history the block suffered the carving of a rectangular depression (for unknown purposes), which, again later, was filled in with plaster that received a very lightly inscribed cartouche, unfortunately illegible.

Figure 6.14. Foundation deposit of Merenptah, north face of eastern massif, Second Pylon.

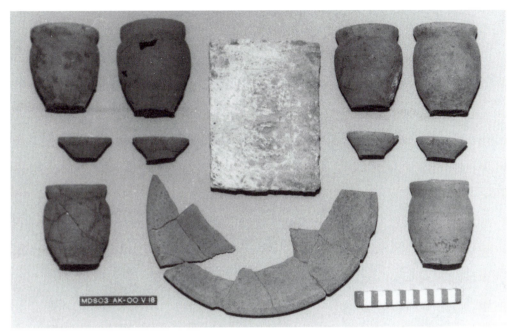

Figure 6.15. Vessels from the foundation deposit.

Figure 6.16. Stone "brick" from the foundation deposit, with Merenptah's nomen.

Figure 6.17. Haunch of beef as a sacrifice under the deposit, in situ.

Figures 6.18a (above)–6.18b (right). Bricks of Thutmose III, laid ceremoniously across the foundation trench of the western massif of the Second Pylon.

Figure 6.18b

known, as to date no fragments have been found. It is a fair guess, however, that it was probably the papyrus-bundle column that was favored by the early New Kingdom architects.

This hypostyle hall would have given access to the cella and surrounding storage rooms, presumably dating from the Middle Kingdom, and may have been renovated several times in the millennium that preceded the Ramessides. But today it is idle to speculate on what form they took, as the Saite reconstruction has totally obliterated in this sector any structure before the mid-sixth century B.C.

There was undoubtedly some sort of ambulatory around the shrine. Here, in close proximity to the cult-seat and image of the deity, statues of royalty and laity would have been placed to partake in the offerings to the Ram and to guest gods. Apart from Ibaba (see sidebar 6.1), only one such New Kingdom statue has survived, but it probably reflects the Ramesside veneration of the town, for it belonged to the highest official under the king, the grand vizier Paser, who functioned in the first three decades of Ramesses II's reign. Paser prays for offerings from the state gods Amunrasonther and Re-Harakhte, but also from Thoth and Ma'at, the daughter of Re. Another worthy who may also have had his statue included in the shrine was the scribe and priest of Thoth, Nehemaway, who prides himself on being the "spokesman who brings calm in the townships of the north." This hint of strife resonates with the titulary of another official at the site, one Hery, deputy high priest of the Ram, who was also a shield-bearer.

There is no doubt that the temple was an impressive building; but it is a curious fact that it stood in isolation. From about 2100 B.C. the great necropolis of *Djedet* had been almost wholly abandoned, and not even houses had subsequently encroached on the area. Some attempt had been made to provide an approach to the temple by adding a dromos on the north, presumably leading from a canal connecting with the Mendesian branch; but this, too, as far as we know, ran over the ruins of the Old Kingdom now buried and out of sight. Just where the city of the living lay is at present a matter of conjecture, as no traces have so far been unearthed in the excavations. It is a fair guess, however, that the domestic quarters lay south of the temple, extending several hundred meters and encompassing most of what today constitutes Tel er-Rub'a.

Although no longer a burying ground, the northern part of the site was still considered to be a sacred temenos and therefore had to be walled in. About two hundred meters east-southeast of the Ram temple a much denuded temenos wall, probably of Ramesside date, was laid bare, built on the same axial alignment as the temple. Although its east and west faces were totally destroyed in the fourth century B.C., it probably measured between six and ten meters in thickness when first constructed. It was built of alternating courses of purely alluvial mud-brick and courses of mud-brick with a substantial component of limestone powder. How far north this wall ran is unknown, but a plausible conjecture would have it describe a right angle due east of the Ramesside pylon, then proceed west to connect with the eastern massif.

At the point where this old temenos was first detected, in excavation Field AL east of the temple, the ground sloped down markedly toward the east. It is very likely that here the tell ended and, as in later times, a body of water (perhaps a harbor) lapped at the edges of the settlement. It was on this slope, enclosed and protected by the temenos wall, that we found, over a length in excess of twenty-five meters, hundreds of pottery vessels laid carefully on their sides in rows, at some points two to three deep. In the main the vessels belonged to two types, beer- and water-jugs and wine cups, datable on stylistic grounds to the latter half of the Ramesside Age. It appears that none had been intentionally smashed, although the weight of superimposed deposition had taken its toll. In five of the better preserved were fish bones, and faunal remains of the same kind were found scattered through the deposit, all coming originally from immature specimens of the *schilby*-fish. In one case the fish had been wrapped in linen sealed by a clay bulla impressed with a Ramesside-type seal. To date we have been unable to find either the upper or the lower terminus of this tightly packed swath of vessels along the slope of the mound; consequently the focus and context of the cache remain conjectural.

It is not without significance that the species of fish that seems ubiquitous in this deposit is the *schilby*, the fish sacred to the tutelary goddess of the township, *Ḥ3t-mḥyt*, "She-Who-Is-Foremost-of-the-Inundation." The origins of this goddess go back to prehistoric times when clearly fishing was a mainstay of the early community of *'Anepat*;

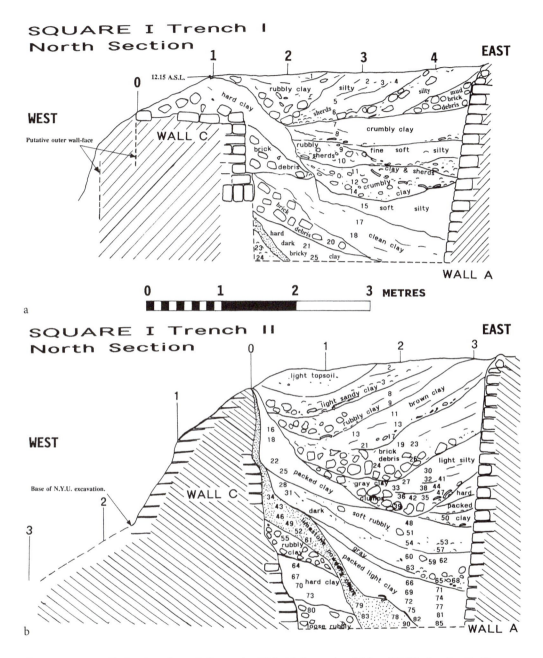

Figures 6.19a–6.19b. Sections through Excavation Unit AL-I, trenches I (a) and II (b), showing the New Kingdom temenos Wall C denuded on the west, and destroyed on the east by the foundation trench of Wall A (Nektanebo, early fourth century B.C.).

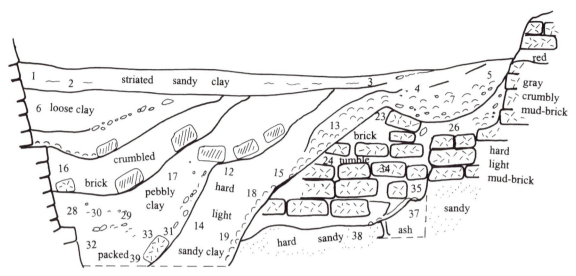

Figure 6.20. Section through Unit AL-I, trench III facing south, New Kingdom wall on right.

Figure 6.21. New Kingdom temenos wall, cut away by the Nektanebo foundation trench, showing alternating courses of alluvial and whitish bricks.

but her person and her cult are difficult to trace in historic times. We know of no extended mythology that might have surrounded her, and she herself remains a cipher.

In the AL deposit, however, we may have our first clear evidence of a cult of the fish-goddess. The immature fishes bear all the earmarks of votive offerings by the inhabitants of Mendes to Ḥȝt-mḥyt and undoubtedly indicate that the slope of the tell, above the then margin of the harbor, was sacred to her. The lower part of the slope was later occupied by the burial chamber of Neferites I, which cut deeply into the tell and may have destroyed part of the jar-deposit. Neferites' architects, in their siting of their master's tomb, may well have destroyed other installations as well, specifically structures the masonry of which they recycled into the fabric of the royal tomb. One type of object that they put to such use was a round-topped stela, about 30–35 centimeters tall, which must originally have been freestanding, as it is inevitably found to have been inscribed on both front and back. Over thirty of these have come to light in the excavations, mostly in fragmentary condition and often with the plaster still adhering which Neferites' builders applied in their reuse. All share a single decorative theme: they are inscribed with numerous representations of *schilby* sacred to Ḥȝt-mḥyt. Sometimes a large "mother-fish" will dominate the upper portions of the stela, with a welter of "baby" fish below; sometimes the field will be divided by a vertical lotus-plant separating the fish into two schools. Again, on occasion, a ram will be carved in the upper curved portion of the field, relegating the lower parts to the fish. In all cases the inscribed surfaces are devoid of texts: we are left to wonder precisely what was the intent of the sculptor/devotee.

While the truth behind the practice of giving ex-voto offerings and erecting dedicatory stelae will probably always elude us, evidence exists from a later period of Egypt's history which is undoubtedly germane. The non-human biological world always exercised a curious but irresistible attraction on the ancient Egyptians. Almost every deity was conceived by the Egyptians to be associated with some species, less often an inanimate "fetish," to be seen in the familiar world of everyday life. Not always is the relationship clear. Sometimes the animal or plant is the usual avatar of the deity, sometimes only an occasional embodiment. Sometimes the animal, plant, or object will enjoy a cultic existence of its own and be revered in its own right. In cases where an animal species was deemed to be related to a god in a special way, a single member of the species might be selected and worshiped as the immediate incarnation of the god, and the cult would prescribe what special marks (coloration usually) would identify the specific animal in whom the god had chosen to abide. In life the animal would be housed and treated with the reverence befitting a god; and in death it would be embalmed and buried in a specially prepared tomb. During the Late Period of Egypt's history—the roots of the practice may be traced much earlier—vast animal cemeteries begin to appear in the archaeological record, in which thousands of members of the same species are embalmed and interred. The custom evokes the accusation of crass animal worship, and was so inter-

Figure 6.22. Votive vessels in situ.

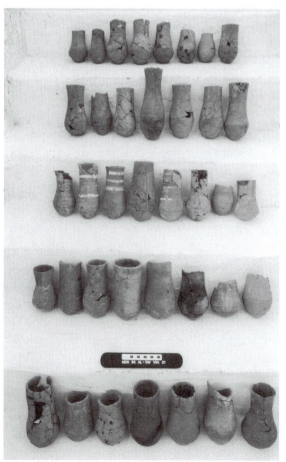

Figure 6.23. 20th-Dynasty wine-jars.

Figures 6.24a–6.24c. Fish-stelae.

preted by the later Greeks. But what in fact was the rationalization in the mind of the ancient worshiper?

Certainly the basic motivation must be piety. Men of high rank are proud to acknowledge the expense they incurred in embalming and burying myriad dead animals. They thus curry divine favor in this life and god's grace in the next. The very species itself, however, and not simply a single incarnation has now achieved the untouchable status of a taboo. And this is specifically stated to derive from the fact that the animals themselves are "images" of the deity. And so, from a concept of the divine essence coming to earth and dwelling in a single beast, Egyptian thinking has gravitated to the position of viewing the terrestrial species as a collective reflection of a great divine archetype. That this thinking already informs the cultic practice we have detected in the jar-deposit of Field AL is a most attractive hypothesis.

The evidence militates consistently in favor of the thesis that Field AL, in the vicinity of the later tomb of Neferites, was considered sacred to *Ḥꜣt-mḥyt*. One might speculate that it may well have been this sanctity that prompted the king to choose the area as the site for his tomb. It would not be without parallel that in executing his design his architects destroyed an existing shrine to the goddess that was considered old-fashioned and out-of-date.

The date of the putative shrine and deposit of ex-voto offering jars can be pinpointed accurately. In the destruction debris coming from the tomb of Neferites, but clearly a piece already found in the area and reused, there came to light a fragment of a sandstone stela in hieratic, the cursive form of the hieroglyphic script. Although less than half of the original inscription has survived, the cartouches of the king under whom it had been carved were clearly preserved: they belonged to Ramesses VI (c. 1156–1148 B.C.). The text appears to record, inter alia, dedications to the cults of the region, although neither the Ram nor *Ḥꜣt-mḥyt* appears in the surviving fragment. That it was Ramesses VI specifically that chose to bestow his patronage on the site and its fish-goddess is more than coincidence. Elsewhere on a stela from his reign he is depicted worshiping "The Ram, Lord of *Djedet*," and in her tomb at Thebes his mother, queen Ese, is shown offering braziers to the same god. Could this singling out of the Ram for special devotion indicate a closer relationship? Is it possible, say, that queen Ese hailed originally from Mendes?

One additional discovery puts the Ḥat-meḥyet "shrine" in an international context. In our 2004 season a vessel was unearthed among the votive pots which is clearly un-Egyptian. In fact it is modeled on a Late Helladic IIIc form of a beer-jug with strainer spout, well-known in the eastern Mediterranean in the outgoing thirteenth and early twelfth centuries B.C. Similar forms occur among "Philistine" pottery from the south coast of the Levant and are associated with the "Sea Peoples." Our pot most closely re-

Figure 6.25. Fragment of hieratic stela of Neb-maʾa-re, beloved of Amunrasonther.

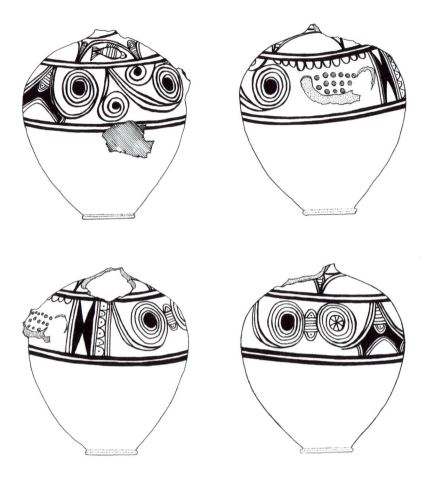

Figure 6.26. Late Helladic IIIc strainer spout beer-jar, with Cypriot overtones.

sembles a Cypriot version of the form, and one is reminded of the prominent role Cyprus played at this period, not only during the movement of the Sea Peoples but also in the new trading patterns that emerged afterward. Ramesses III indicates that captives from the enemy hosts were settled in camps and strongholds to serve as "mercenaries" (better, "impressed warriors"), and one wonders whether this might explain the presence of the beer-jug. Or is it one of the first harbingers of a foreign trade in which Mendes was to play a major role?

Chapter Seven

The Great Chiefs
of the Meshwesh

The two generations following the death of Ramesses II witnessed a social and demographic upheaval on an international scale, the like of which the ancient world had never before experienced. Foreign lands were "agitated in their limbs," "migrating and scattering through the war of the countries at one time." They came on "their faces set towards Egypt, their hearts confident in their (own) arms . . . their fighters trusted in their (own) plans coming with confident hearts: 'we shall conquer!' Their intent in their inmost being: 'we shall act!' (for) their hearts were full of violence."

During the last half of the thirteenth century B.C., for reasons that are still hotly debated, the coastal communities along the south and west littoral of Asia Minor and the tribal enclaves of Libya begin to display migratory tendencies. Many of these peoples had earned a deserved reputation for piracy ever since the time of Amenophis III, and those from Asia Minor were known throughout the Mediterranean as expert seafarers. Highly skilled swordsmen from Sardonia (northwest Asia Minor) had even entered Pharaoh's service as auxiliaries. But in the brave new world which was dawning after the passing of Ramesses the Great, it was not only the pirate ships in ones and twos that set out, Viking-like, to plunder coastal shipping. Now entire communities were uprooting themselves and setting forth to settle elsewhere. The ancient world was quite familiar with the forcible transplanting of large dissident populations within an imperial context: the Egyptians, Hittites, and Assyrians all practiced shifting communities of thousands to other parts of their empires to preempt uprisings. In the present case, however, the migrations were voluntary, and all had the same goal: to settle in Egypt.

Western Asia Minor and eastern Libya produced communities of markedly different economic and cultural bases. The coastal location of settlements in the former zone imposed maritime interests and economies on the inhabitants. Poised as they were between the Mycenaean cities of Bronze Age Greece and the Hittite empire in the mountains to the east, the cities of the Ionian coast partook of a hybrid culture. Their helmets, body armor, and bronze long-swords reflect the great advances in metalworking of contemporary

Figure 7.1. Sardonians ("Shardana") from the west coast of Asia Minor, in the employ of the Ramesside pharaohs.

southeastern Europe; their ships compare favorably with those of Greece. Willy-nilly they lived within a Hittite sphere of influence and had either to kowtow or to risk rebellion and resistance. As the thirteenth century drew to a close it was the latter course that these communities chose. We hear of a coalition of twenty-two cities from Wilusa (Ilion, i.e., Troy) to Lycia that waged war with the Hittite king. Eventually a coalition took shape to descend upon the Nile, but at first this was in concert with the Libyans.

To the Egyptians Libya had long seemed to be a backwater. The inhabitants, whether settled or nomadic, were few in number and rarely posed a threat. Blond and blue-eyed in some cases, the Libyans wore feathers, long ringlets, and cutaway gowns. Some tribes lived in houses and practiced limited agriculture; all were tied to a cattle-rearing economy, and their herds were highly prized by the Egyptians. Egyptians seldom caught sight of Libyans: except for the few that came to trade or joined the Egyptian armed forces, they had generally kept to themselves. But they did, in spite of the landlocked nature of their lifestyle, enjoy an opening into Mediterranean trade: a transit corridor through the Sahara oases to the coast brought African products via Mersa Matruh into the Cypriot, Phoenician, and Aegean trade routes.

But now, with the death of the great king, the Libyans too set their sights on migration. Whatever the reasons—the prospect of a rich and defenseless land coupled with local drought?—a great coalition of Libyan tribes headed by the Labu and the Meshwesh began to move on Egypt in the fourth year of Ramesses' son and successor, Merenptah. With them came members of the Aegean coalition: Sardonians, Shekelesh, Eqwesh, Lycians, Taruisha. The oases were cut off and the Delta penetrated. The Egyptians looked on in consternation as Libyan tents began to sprout on the banks of the canals and Nile branches. In spite of a defeat at the hands of Merenptah's army in his fifth year, at a cost of six thousand casualties, they refused to leave Egyptian soil and settled down to stay.

Figure 7.2. Libyan tribesmen, as depicted in the tomb of Ramesses III.

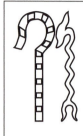

7.1 The Libyan Menace

(Ramesses III speaks): See, I shall inform you of other matters which happened in Egypt under (former) kings. The Labu and Meshwesh settled in Egypt after having seized the towns along the western edge (of the Delta) from Memphis to Karbana. They reached the Great River on both its banks, and it was they that ruined the towns of the Xoite township during the very many years they were in Egypt.

[P. Harris 76:11–77:2; see P. Grandet, Le Papyrus Harris I *(Cairo 1994)*]

Egypt was ill equipped to mount a successful defense. Sixty years of peace had taken its toll on the military and an increasing reliance on foreign auxiliaries now becomes discernible. The successors of Ramesses II fell to feuding over the rule in the wake of the death of the decrepit Merenptah; and the untimely death of a grandson of Ramesses, Sety II, opened the door to a cabal. Veiled allusions in contemporary records hint at a bid for power by a Canaanite-born chancellor, a self-made man called Beya, which seems to have raised native ire. A palace coup quickly followed: Beya disappeared and a general, Seth-nakhte, assumed rule. The 20th Dynasty had been inaugurated.

The triumph of the new house was realized by its second member, Ramesses III, son of Seth-nakhte. By reorganizing the army and administration and taking inventory of state and temple treasuries, the new king aimed at nothing less than destroying the hostile coalitions and restoring the empire to its former greatness. In his fifth year a pretext was found to reopen hostilities, and the Libyan forces were engaged in the western Delta. It was a resounding Egyptian victory: over twelve thousand Libyans were left for dead upon the battlefield and a route carried the remainder back into the western desert. Although the Labu were now broken and their coalition disbanded, the Meshwesh tried again six years later, only to suffer defeat again with a loss of over two thousand men. In the meantime Ramesses had met a more grievous threat from the west as a coalition of the piratical Sea Peoples from Asia Minor and the Aegean islands descended on Egypt via Syria and Lebanon. It took an intense effort on the part of the Egyptian army to repel this mighty force, and success came only with a firm defensive stand on the eastern fringes of the Delta itself. Exhausted though the country must have been, Ramesses could in fact claim to have restored the empire.

How did Mendes fare during this time of crisis? To date few remains have been recovered from the excavations, but it is safe to say that the town escaped unscathed from the marauders from Libya and Asia Minor. In fact in one respect the town continued to thrive. Yet to judge by the history of the 20th Dynasty and its aftermath, the Mendesians of the outgoing second millennium must have lived in anxious times. Within fifty years of the death of Ramesses III the empire in Asia was lost, and another fifty years saw the withdrawal of the garrison of Kush as the Sudanese province followed suit. The return of a sequence of low Niles meant a loss of agricultural revenue, and it is conceivable that the purpose behind the Ḥat-meḥyet votives was an attempt to lure back the "Foremost of the Flood" and with her the high inundations she stood for. To add to the country's problems, trade with Asia suffered a drastic curtailment and the Nubian gold mines slipped out of Egyptian control. Unable to meet its payroll, the state suffered from increased labor strikes. As inflation struck the commercial sector the inhabitants of the major cities, Thebes in particular, took to tomb robbing; and temples succumbed to petty thievery from the very priests assigned to celebrate the cult.

An added problem for the inhabitants of the north was the continued presence of Libyans. Incredible as it may seem, the repulses they had suffered at the hands of Merenptah and Ramesses III had not deterred the tribesmen from the North African coast. They continued to enter Egypt in family groups and clans, moving here and there, occasionally trading with the inhabitants, often hiring themselves to the authorities as paramilitary personnel. Their independence and non-sedentary tendencies were a concern to the Egyptian government, who found them also to be destructive of the agricultural landscape. They had long since devastated the western townships of the Delta as far east as Xois, and even Memphis and Heliopolis had not been spared. Now they were trekking about in the very heart of the Land of the Flood, and the vizier was upset. "Come quickly," writes the vizier to a chief of police, "with all the magistrates' people and the police who are in Pi-hboye (mod. Behbit el-Hagar, a few kilometers west of Mendes) . . . and do not let any of them be missing, (for) by their names which are with me in writing shall I check them! And come when you have ascertained the movements of the Meshwesh. . . . Do not neglect your duties! See to it, and do it!"

Gradually the Meshwesh bands and a smaller contingent of Labu began to settle down, often in encampments on the outskirts of towns. Most Delta cities, Mendes included, would have become familiar with such faubourgs filled with foreigners who spoke a foreign language and wore strange clothing. It is difficult to establish the degree to which the Libyans became, or even wished to become, acclimated to the Egyptian way of life. In spite of attested intermarriage with the Egyptians, their distinctive names are easily spotted in the onomasticon and continued in use throughout the period of their hegemony. Ramesses III claims to have tried to arrange for their instruction in the Egyptian language, but it appears they preferred to keep their own language. While often appearing in Egyptian dress, they never relinquished the characteristic feather worn horizontally upon the head. As late as four centuries after the close of the New Kingdom empire they could still be castigated for lack of cleanliness and failure to follow Egyptian dietary laws. While these criticisms may be biased, the racial motivation behind them suggests the Libyans by and large remained an unassimilated lot until the very close of their rule in Egypt.

One decision taken by the government early in the eleventh century B.C. proved symbolic of the final demise of the New Kingdom. "The House of Ramesses-Great-of-Victories," which had served Egypt as a royal residence from the beginning of the 19th Dynasty 220 years earlier, fell upon hard times. The river on which it was located began to diminish in annual discharge and its harbor to silt up. A new site, free of ecological problems, had to be chosen speedily, and one was found closer to the Mediterranean on a stronger branch thirty-five kilometers northeast of the House-of-Ramesses. Here, close to the desert edge, on windswept flats known as the "Field of the Storm" (*sḫt ḏ'*), a new city, *Ḏ'nt*, "Storm-Town," was planned. No quarries adequate to the task of supplying masonry to erect a new royal city were closer than two hundred kilometers; the House-of-Ramesses was thus systematically dismantled, temple by temple, and the blocks shipped downstream to the new site. *Ḏ'nt*, or Tanis as it came to be called, took shape in the early years of the last Ramesses, no. XI, as a Thebes *redivivus* with temples to Amun, Mut, and Khonsu, and priesthoods reminiscent of those of Thebes far to the south. And while suburbs of the House-of-Ramesses continued to be occupied, most of the city was abandoned and fields began to encroach on the once busy thoroughfares. A new era, the "Tanite," had begun.

Ramesses XI (c. 1099–1067 B.C.) had the misfortune to experience other setbacks, more serious than the extinction of his ancestral seat. He gained the reputation of being a weak executive and was treated with contempt by his officials. In his early years he could not adequately control the south, and a civil war broke out there, the repercussions of which eventually affected the north as well. In a desperate effort to bring order the king was constrained essentially to cede authority to three special appointees, "troubleshooters" we might say, with virtually dictatorial power. All had obscure backgrounds and may well have "come up through the ranks." An oracle of Amun confirmed their appointment, and a new era, called the "Renaissance," was dated from that event. Piankhy and his colleague Herihor, who were given the southern command at Thebes with responsibility for the Valley, were products of the military, and they took up their post with the grandiose titulary "Great Courtier in the Entire Land, High-Priest of Amun-re King of the Gods, Field-Marshal of Upper and Lower Egypt, Duke." The appointee for the north brings us back to the topic of this book, for he was undoubtedly from Mendes. His name, Ny-su-ba-neb-djed, "He-Who-Belongs-to-the-Ram-Lord-of-the-Abiding-Place," points to the city which, from our archaeological discoveries, seems to have enjoyed a prominence of more than cultic proportions at the end of the New Kingdom. A Dynastic marriage and a key post ensured for Ny-su-ba-neb-djed a position of power in the political vacuum

a

b

c

Figures 7.3a–7.3d. The ruins of Tanis; (c) shows the headquarters of
the high-priest of Amun.

d

7.2 "Hit-Men" and Anarchy: Pharaoh Derided

The General of Pharaoh to the scribe Tjaroy of the necropolis, to wit: "I have heard all the matters about which you wrote me. Now as to what you said about the matter of the two Nubian policemen, that they have made these statements, you shall co-operate with Nodjme and Pai-shu-uben, and they shall send and have these two policemen brought to my house, and finally put an end to their words. If they find it to be true, they shall put them into two sacks and cast them into the river at night, without letting anyone know of it. And as for Pharaoh (Ramesses XI), how can he ever be effective in this part of the country (Thebes)? Of whom indeed is Pharaoh the master? . . . do not be concerned about what he might do."

[P. Berlin 10487; J. Černý, Late Ramesside Letters (Bruxelles, 1939), 36]

which followed the demise of Ramesses XI in the second quarter of the eleventh century B.C.; it should come as no surprise that he used his power base as a springboard to the monarchy. In the official king-list he becomes the founder of the 21st Dynasty.

The first royal house to rule from Tanis, the 21st Dynasty, had three major roots. It was, of course, by virtue of the curious ecological features of its foundation, the daughter of the House-of-Ramesses-Great-of-Victories, and self-proclaimed heir to the greatness of Ramesside Egypt. But it was also a child of Amun-re, a kind of Thebes of the north, with temples to Amun-re, Khonsu, and Mut (in her Canaanite guise). The other root was Mendes, a few kilometers across the *Laḥaḥta-water to the west. Not only does the personal name Ny-su-ba-neb-djed figure prominently in the onomasticon of the brave new Tanite world, but one of the early archbishops and military commanders in the city was called Un-djeb-en-djede, who continued to hold a Mendesian office. Time would prove the close link between the two cities.

7.3 The Tribulations of One Caught in the Civil War

I was wronged although there had been no accusation, deprived although no crime had been laid against me; I was thrown out of my city and my property seized piecemeal, I was greatly ruined . . . my wife who had approached them was killed and her [sic] children scattered. . . . I was ejected from my previous office, and made to wander about in harsh journeyings, while the land was engulfed in the flames of war including south, north, west and east. I joined the crew of a boat which was not mine. . . . I traveled around the country, skimming along the river and hastening over its depths; I got to the north on it, to Chemmis, I wound my way eastward through the hillocks of the marshes and circled through their water channels. . . . I wandered through villages on foot for my horses had been stolen and my chariot seized.

[P. Pushkin 127, cols. 2–3; R. Caminos, A Tale of Woe (Oxford, 1977), passim]

7.4 Favors to a Mendesian in Royal Service

[Inscription on a gold vase]
Given as a royal favor to the Steward of Khonsu-in-Thebes-Nfr-Ḥtp, Priest
of Khonsu, General of the Army and Leader of All Pharaoh's Battalions,
Archbishop of All the Gods, Priest Un-djeb-en-djede of the House of Osiris,
the Lord of Mendes.
[*P. Montet, Les Constructions et le tombeau de Psousennes I à Tanis (Paris, 1951),*
p. 84, fig. 31]

Throughout the course of the 21st Dynasty the Libyan presence in Egypt continued to increase. Five generations after the founding of the dynasty the enclaves of the Meshwesh were scattered over the Delta and in the Fayum; a smaller component of the Labu were settled around Sais in the northwestern Land of the Flood. The Great Chief of the Meshwesh, or the Me, as the name came to be shortened, was ensconced in Herakleopolis just south of the Fayum. This city had provided a military headquarters of elite troops and had been equipped with a fort from at least as early as the reign of Ramesses II, and the surrounding countryside had been thickly settled by army veterans. Not entirely at ease with the presence of a semi-autonomous chiefdom in the lower valley of the Nile, the government had implanted a series of forts on the east bank of the river slightly upstream from Herakleopolis. From this vantage watch could be kept on this large settlement of suspicious aliens.

But there was a certain inevitability in the Libyan rise to power. The Egypt over which the 21st Dynasty ruled was essentially divided. The high priests in Thebes, while related by marriage to the ruling house, maintained a semi-independent regime over the "House of Amun," that stretch of the valley between Asyut and the First Cataract. By locating their residence at a northern extremity of the natural Egyptian realm, the successors of Ny-su-ba-neb-djed had created a geographical and political vacuum. While the Tanite residence was well situated to serve the 21st Dynasty's commercial interests in western Asia, Middle Egypt and the upper Delta did not represent the vital interests of the administration and fell prey to the Libyans. The latter made themselves indispensable to the Egyptians through filling the armed forces with competent fighters; by approximately 950 B.C. the Great Chief of the Me had risen in status to become commander in chief of Egypt's armies.

The holder of this rank at the time was one Sheshonq, son of Namlot, a mature man with obvious ambition. He had succeeded not only in aggrandizing his own office but also in placing his sons and daughters in key positions in the state: one son inherited his tribal chiefdom, another assumed the high priesthood in Thebes, and a third was married to a daughter of Psousennes II, the contemporary king in Tanis. When the latter died without issue, Sheshonq found it a simple matter to supplant the line of Ny-su-ba-neb-djed and mount the throne himself as founder of a new house, the 22nd Dynasty.

The first century of Libyan rule is a somewhat confused period. While Tanis remained a residence, some of the early Libyan kings seem to have elected to live elsewhere. Sheshonq I and his son Osorkon I may have favored the old capital of the House-of-Ramesses (or what was left of the abandoned town); neither was buried at Tanis, as far as we know. Yewepet, son of Sheshonq I who became high priest of Amun, established his headquarters in Middle Egypt and became more a military commander than a cleric (although in this he was only aping the ways of his immediate predecessors in office).

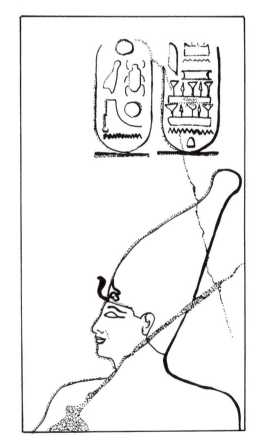

Figure 7.4. Sheshonq I from a relief on the Bubastite portal, Karnak.

Needless to say, the Libyan regime was not universally liked. For a few years Thebes refused to acknowledge Sheshonq's kingship, preferring to refer to him by his old title, Great Chief of the Me. The personal policies of the 22nd Dynasty kings may have contributed to the disfavor into which they soon fell. There is evidence of heavy taxation on the one hand and neglect of certain parts of the country on the other; and Libyan potentates soon earned a reputation (whether deserved we know not) for quick tempers and public rages. By the reign of Osorkon II (c. 868–839 B.C.), when a royal jubilee was in the offing, the king felt it expedient to make gestures toward Thebes, that part of the country where disaffection was most rife. "I have exempted Thebes," declared the king in his twenty-second year, "in its length and breadth; it is purified and given (back) to its lord (i.e., Amun). There shall be no interference with it (Thebes) by the inspectors of the king's-house, (for) its people are exempted for an aeon in the official name of the Perfect God." Tax relief, however, was not enough. Suddenly, in about 829 B.C., Thebes broke into full-scale rebellion. "Although the sky had not swallowed the moon (i.e., there had been no lunar eclipse as an omen) an uproar came about in this land like [that which had never been(?)]. The children of rebellion spread civil strife in south and north." The insurrection was eventually put down, but not before it had weakened the regime irretrievably. Within a generation of the restoration of order several of the largest cities in Egypt declared their own kingships and, in the Delta, Libyan clansmen took to themselves the title "Great Chief of the Me." Gradually the 22nd Dynasty, now permanently resident in Tanis, was offered lip service only.

During the period of Libyan rule Mendes, like other Delta cities, fared better than might have been expected. While it may well have suffered during the Theban rebellion—Ny-su-ba-neb-djed, the Great Chief of the Me, speaks of "damage" done to the Temple of the Ram (see below)—nevertheless, with the weakening of the Tanite kings it began to enjoy virtual independence. By the beginning of the eighth century B.C. the Delta boasted three kingships, one princedom, and eight chiefdoms, each centered on a major town and its territorium. The rulers of these principalities were kings in all but name, free in their own opinion to arrogate unto themselves royal titulary, insignia, and mythology. Combining the roles of district governor and military dictator, they commanded the allegiance of the Libyan soldiery within their districts.

As one of the more important of the chiefdoms, Mendes controlled the land between the Mendesian branch and the "Great River" (i.e., the modern Damietta branch), on the south as far as Leontopolis and on the north to the shores of the sea. The Mendesian branch now ran immediately east of the city, and Hermopolis Parva eight kilometers to the west across open terrain could be added to the Mendesian jurisdiction. In the generation following the Theban rebellion one Eskheby had appeared in Mendes with the title Great Chief of the Me. His origins are obscure: a fragment found by us in later fill mentioning a "[Great] chief [of the Me] She[shonk]" may provide a clue to his ancestry. Since his son refers to himself as a descendant of priests, a sacerdotal function may have been involved from the beginning. In any event, at least eight generations of successors (possibly his descendants) followed Eskheby in the city in uninterrupted succession. By the time of Eskheby's grandson, Ny-su-ba-neb-djed, the family had secured the three basic ranks that ensured its hereditary power. Each leader now boasted the status of Great Chief of the Me, which designated him as the clan leader of the local community of the Meshwesh; but to this he had added the title of High-Priest of the Ram, Lord of the Abiding Place. The title conferred a prebend encompassing the temple estate of the Ram and his priesthood, an oversight in fact of the substantial real estate and wealth in kind which the Ram was gradually accumulating. Under a certain Tachos in the late eighth century the office graduated to a true bishopric, an "Overseer of the Priests of the Ram," which involved a substantial emolument. The Great Chief of the Me appeared in solemn quasi-cultic scenes in which a local dignitary donated land to the god, retaining usufruct as long as he lived, and celebrated the pious donation undoubtedly receiving a consideration for his intermediacy. The third rank reflected in the chiefdom's standard titulary is that of "leader" or *dux*. A military title originating in the outgoing New Kingdom, *dux* indicated the command of the local militia, in the present case Libyan in ethnic makeup.

Mendes had now become the permanent residence of the chiefdom. Sheshonq III, the king who followed the great rebellion on the Tanite throne, added relief scenes to the sanctuary of the Ram, and the Great Chiefs prided themselves on refurbishing the rest of the temple, but it had changed little since the days of Ramesses II, 450 years before. For that matter, the city itself remained in its extent and appearance very much the same settlement as would have greeted the gaze of a traveler in the twelfth century B.C. The Temple of the Ram fronted the city on the north, probably communicating with the Nile by means of a canal. The houses of the people lay to the south of the temple, bounded in turn by a watery tract to the south. Although farming activity in the last century has drastically reduced the ninth and eighth century B.C. levels in this sector (in search of fertilizer), we were able to retrieve evidence of the sub-floor basements of the houses (cf. fig. 7.7).

One probable addition to the ancient topography was the palace of the chiefs. To judge by other "rest-house" palaces associated with temples (cf. the Ramesseum, Medinet Habu, the Karnak temple), this structure would have lain to the east of the Temple of the Ram, on the left of the main axis when one faced the sanctuary. Today two mounds in this position greet the visitor, the smaller of the two immediately adjacent to the eastern wall of the temple, the larger about twenty meters to the east. Our excavation has proved the smaller mound to be an excavation dump, probably belonging to Edouard Naville, and we were quite prepared for the discouraging discovery that the larger was his

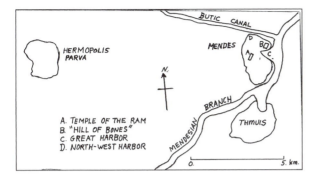

Figure 7.5. Map showing the position of Mendes, Thmuis, and Hermopolis Parva in relation to the Mendesian branch and the Butic canal.

Figure 7.6. A Great Chief of the Me(shwesh) "offers the field" in a scene from a type of record called the "Donation Stela," in which a landed endowment is given over to a temple.

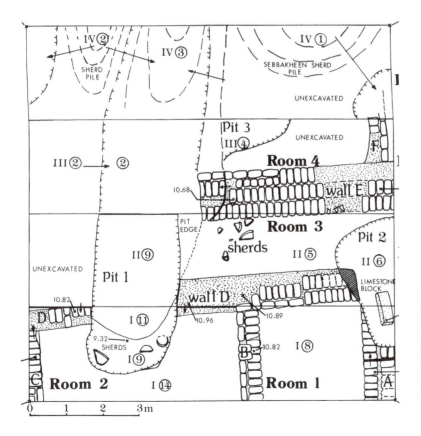

Figure 7.7. Excavation Unit HF, south of the temple. The walls and rooms date from the First Intermediate Period. The pits descend from overlying buildings of the Third Intermediate Period, now lost through farmers digging for fertilizer.

7.5 Land Donation

Regnal year 22 of Pharaoh Sheshonq (III): bequest to Harpokrates residing in Mendes, through the agency of the Great Chief of the Me and Dux Hornakht, son of the Great Chief of the Me Es-kheby—ten aruras of land (c. seven acres) which the Flautist of Horus Onkh-horpokrates son of the Chief Flautist of Ba-neb-djed Gemnef-horbak gave, they to remain his property for ever and ever. (As for) the one who shall take them from him, may a donkey copulate with his wife and his wife with <a donkey>. Ba-neb-djed, the great living god, Hat-mehyet and Harpo-krates shall decapitate him, not allowing his elder son to succeed him. (But) the one who shall seek its (the bequest's) benefit, he shall abide in the land, and the gods shall put his son in his place.
[K. A. Kitchen, "Two Donation Stelas in the Brooklyn Museum," JARCE 8 (1969–70), 59–68[

also. Imagine, therefore, our surprise when, within minutes of setting pick in soil, mud-brick walls began to emerge! After two seasons of excavations a large, rectilinear building had been unearthed, about thirty meters east-west and of larger (though as yet unknown) dimensions north-south. The walls were thick, in some cases over one meter, as though designed to sustain a second story. The northern side where an entry was to be expected had been eroded, and a road now passes over the western side where undoubtedly a passage connected with the main temple. (In fact the doorjamb of Ny-su-ba-neb-djed probably came from here.) Today a doorjamb block rests on the summit of the mound, bearing the unmistakable outline of the figure of a Libyan chief (fig. 7.9).

The pottery associated with this building suggests that it was built in the eleventh century B.C. and remained in use through the Saite period. The south side of the complex, downwind of the rooms for habitation, was given over to food production as ovens and hearths attest. Domestic use of rooms was signaled by the presence of a curious ceramic ratio: three or four jars, one or two hole-mouth storage jars, and a large number of conical drinking cups that stood, in relation to everting bowls, at a ratio of three or four to one. The final function of the building, after its ultimate destruction at the hands of the Persians, was as a place of pottery preparation and storage for some nearby kiln.

In spite of their foreign roots, the family of the Great Chiefs of the Me in Mendes had entered into the spirit of the town and its divine patron. On the reveals of one of the gates which the family built connecting the palace described above with the temple, two generations of chiefs inscribed records of themselves. The Great Chief of the Me Ny-su-ba-neb-djed described how the Ram "had chosen him out of his kinsmen, and had appointed him to be master of his sanctuary, since he perceived his heart and recognized he would prove excellent in performing benefactions for his house." He proceeded to address the god: "I am thy servant, active for thy *ku*, a son of thy servants of former times(?). I was marked(?) with thy *ku* upon my birth-stool, I was conceived(?) in order to create

Figure 7.8. Excavation of the "Libyan Palace" (mound AK-E), east of the temple.

Figure 7.9. Doorjamb from the palace, showing the head of a Great Chief of the Me(shwesh), with characteristic feather lying flat.

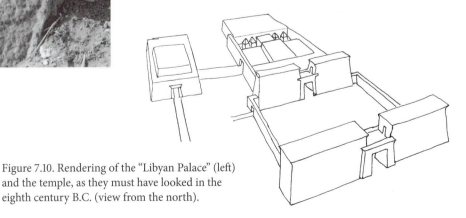

Figure 7.10. Rendering of the "Libyan Palace" (left) and the temple, as they must have looked in the eighth century B.C. (view from the north).

thy monuments. I spent (every) day seeking [ways to embellish(?)] thine entire sanctuary, commensurate to the damage thou (hadst suffered) which I found therein. I never tired in amassing property (simply) in order to donate it to thy majesty." His son, Hornakht II, made a triumphal entry into his patrimony upon his father's death.

> His father appointed him to take possession of his bequests (as) great heir of his dwelling place . . . he being like unto Horus in the seat of his father, having felled him that seized sinfully (i.e., Seth). They jubilated to the breadth of heaven, both men and women, and lo! they said . . . : "A Son-Whom-He-Loves on the seat of his father through what [the Ram, Lord of the Abiding Place] the great living [god] has ordained for him, who has been brought in peace to the district(?) of *Djedet*!" And those who were in *Djedet* were at ease and happy. Then he approached the temple . . . and placed himself on his belly groveling(?) in his presence, and he said: "O my lord! Mine eyes see the light, mine ears hear speech, [my] stride is free in movement, mine arms are strong after the weariness of the years which have passed. . . . Peace be to thy heart! Mayest thou remember me as one who petitioned god. Thou didst bring me to thy city, while mine arms [were active(?)] through the command which issued from thy mouth; for thou didst perceive my heart and recognized that I would be excellent in performing benefactions for thy house. Mayest thou drive off mine ignorance(?). . . . What thou dost ordain is that which comes to pass, thou art a wall of bronze. . . . Thou abidest firm for ever! I have enlarged thy house and embellished thy temple with everything thy heart lovest, so hearken, O my protector!"

These texts are brimming with piety. At one moment the speaker masquerades as a common suppliant, prostrating himself before the god, craving his protection, protesting his devotion, and recording his benefactions. At the next he is donning the guise of the dutiful son, the Horus who champions his deceased father, Osiris. Much of this smacks of the jargon formerly used by kings to describe their intimate relationship with the divine, but now arrogated generally unto themselves by power-wielders in a more parochial setting. The family clearly enjoyed several generations of uninterrupted descent from father to (eldest) son, yet the legitimizing fiction of *selection* by the Ram is still maintained. The fine line between the pharaonic monarch, the Horus-of-the-Living, and the man-made potentate is blurred, and it would take a reformer to reestablish the dictum: "Men make a king, (but) it is Amun that makes (the true king), [namely,] the one that no dukes can ever make!"

The Great Chiefs of the Me in Mendes may well have refurbished the temple proper and seen to their own dwelling, but there is evidence of administrative neglect in the rest of the city. The New Kingdom temenos wall, which had at some unknown date suffered a fire and destruction and had been poorly rebuilt, was now in complete dilapidation. The poor used the slump of collapsed mud-brick as a burying ground, and lower-class extended burials are rather common.

Chapter Eight

Egypt in the Time of Troubles

If the strength of a river-valley civilization is measured in the absolute and uncontested power of the Center over the Periphery, then Egypt of the mid-eighth century B.C. was rapidly developing into a political vacuum. Under its final scion, the 22nd Dynasty was no more than a primus inter pares: in contemporary opinion its advisors looked foolish. Its effective jurisdiction was increasingly confined to the city of Tanis. No other Delta principality, however, commanded the military strength to supplant Tanis, nor the imagination to rally and unify the country. All displayed a disquieting preoccupation with matters parochial, to the exclusion of a greater good. Intestine feuding abounded. Some of the phrases used in the gate inscription of Hornakht (II) (see above), although seeming allusions to the Osiris-Seth mythologem, could easily be veiled references to actual events of civil unrest and attempted coups. Ny-su-ba-neb-djed (II?), the Great Chief of the Me at Mendes referred to above, has left cryptic allusions to his own squabbles which, unless they point to engagement with *foreign* forces, can be read as symptomatic of the times. He refers to "all them that are loyal to him, so great was the love for him . . . at the head of the army" and to himself as "leading it (the army) to battle when the rearguard had fled [. . .] on the day of battle; making carnage among his enemies." (Yet in the same breath he claims to be "beloved of men and gods, well-spoken"!)

There did exist, on the other hand, a Power that was broad enough in scope and sufficiently endowed with vision to exert an irresistible force for unification; but it was exclusively spiritual. The god Amun had twice, from his Theban redoubt, championed rebellions which had issued in the reunification of a divided land; and even if the third attempt, against the Libyan 22nd Dynasty, had failed, the god's stature remained undiminished. Amun had emerged from the New Kingdom as father and mentor to Pharaoh, the king of the gods, the primordial one of the Two Lands, the hidden force of the cosmos. His omnipotence and universal dominion, couched within terms of an Egyptian nationalism, are succinctly conveyed in the invocation: "certainly, thou hast made every land and every foreign country know that thou art the power of Pharaoh, l.p.h. [life, prosperity, health], thy child, over every land and every foreign country. Thou it is that hast championed the land of Egypt, thy land alone—there is no soldier's hand at all in this, but only thy great power!" But since the abortive rebellion of Thebes in the ninth century Amun sat over an estate drained of political might. The high priesthood had declined as an office wherein power-seekers might fulfill themselves, and none of the other ancient posts in the bureaucracy offered themselves as a stepping-stone to political influence. The god's continuing spiritual prestige, it is true, attracted the daughters of northern potentates and warlords, at their fathers' behest, to assume the status of hierodules in Thebes; and it became customary for a royal pretender to attempt to cement his ties to the religious capital of the south by appointing his daughter "Divine Worshiper of Amun" with cartouches and reginal epithets. As a sort of "queen of the south," the divine worshiper was surrounded by a veritable court in which her majordomo loomed large. She was, however, still beholden to her father and blood family withal, and the principal effect of her presence was to turn Thebes into a protectorate.

At the close of the third quarter of the eighth century B.C. a power-seeker appeared who attempted to tap into latent power in Egypt, but identified the latter as having an essentially Delta base. Tefnakhte, Chief of the Labu in their enclave in the environs of Sais, set out to increase his power base and subvert his neighbors undoubtedly with the broader goal of reuniting the principalities of the north in a new centralized state. By methods we can only guess at he had extended his direct control over the townships on the western side of the Delta as far inland as Xois; even Memphis acknowledged his ascendant authority. With the expiry of the 22nd Dynasty at Tanis, fifteen principalities of the Delta hastened to throw in their lot with the rising power of the upstart as "dogs at his heels," in the jargon of Tefnakhte's detractors. Under Tefnakhte's leadership a coalition took shape. As the united militias moved upstream beyond Memphis fortress after fortress welcomed the advancing host until a tract extending as far as Hnes (near modern Minya) had been secured. Tefnakhte installed his son in Tehneh as commandant of the fortress. Only Herakleopolis held out under its "king" Peftjaudibast, and was promptly put under siege by the northerners.

At this point a second aspiring conqueror with a mission made his appearance in the Nile Valley; but unlike Tefnakhte, his situation and cultural background capitalized on a more potent ally than the Delta chief could ever hope to win over. This ally was none other than the god Amun, and the rising star belonged to Piankhy the Kushite. Beginning perhaps as early as the turn of the ninth century B.C. the autochthonous Nubian communities around Gebel Barkal in the northern Sudan had begun to evolve into a complex society finding expression in a nation-state. By the mid-eighth century Egypt had supplied the only monarchic model the incipient kingdom, Kush, could copy; and the erstwhile chieftain now called himself King of Upper and Lower Egypt and adopted the pharaonic panoply. Because of the temple and cult of "Amun of the Holy Mountain," a sacred transplant from the early New Kingdom at Napata (Gebel Barkal), the Sudanese kings shared a community of worship with the Thebans and the "original" Amun.

Around 740 B.C., if not before, Thebes formally accepted the new regime from the

Figure 8.1. Amun crowns his Divine Worshiper (Temple of Osiris, Ruler of Eternity, Karnak); late eighth century B.C.

Figure 8.2a. The Divine Worshiper Shepenwepet II (Medinet Habu), seventh century B.C.

Figure 8.2b. The Divine Worshiper Amenirdis I (Medinet Habu), seventh century B.C.

8.1 Tefnakhte

There is a chief of the West, the nomarch and grandee in Sebennytos, Tefnakhte, (also) in the <Western Harpoon> township, in the Xoite township, in the "Nile"-district, in [. . .], in the An-marshes, in Punube and in the Memphite township. He has seized the West in its entirety from the northern marshes to Itj-towy, and has come south with a great army, the Two Lands united behind him, and the nomarchs and sheriffs being dogs at his heels. No fortress has shut [its gates] in the townships of the south. . . . He turned himself to the townships of the East and they opened to him in like fashion. . . . And lo! [he has] surrounded Herakleopolis . . . not allowing those that would go out go out, nor those that would enter enter, all the while fighting daily against it!
[*Report to Piankhy about the doings of his enemy: Piankhy stela 2–5; N.-C. Grimal,* La stèle triomphale de Pi(ankh)y au musée du Caire *(Cairo, 1981)]*

Figure 8.3. A Kushite king libates to Amun.

south as political overlords (the 25th Dynasty), and military garrisons were sent to occupy the Thebaid. Since the geopolitical thrust of the Kushites was northward down the Nile, it was clear that they would sooner or later be locked in a power struggle with Tefnakhte.

It was the siege of Herakleopolis that caused the confrontation. Piankhy sent an expeditionary force into Egypt and later came himself. Tefnakhte at once lifted the siege and moved south with his forces to intercept the Kushites as they came north; but he was no match for the ferocity of the Sudanese and suffered defeats on both water and land. His coalition disbanded and he fled back to the Delta, trusting in the strength of the fortresses he had garrisoned.

Mendes had been a major player in Tefnakhte's coalition. Its ruler, Great Chief of the Me and "mayor" of the town, was called Djed-Amun-efonkh; his lofty status is indi-

8.2 Revere Amun!

Now when you arrive within Thebes, before Karnak, enter ye the water and purify yourselves in the river, and clothe yourselves on the bank. Loose the bow, and release the arrow: do not boast as one all-powerful—the strong have no power without him (Amun) and he makes a broken-armed of a strong-armed—for a multitude can turn tail before a few, and one man can seize a thousand men! Sprinkle yourselves with water from his altars, kiss ye the earth before him and say ye to him: "Grant us a way that we may fight in the shadow of thy mighty arm; (for) the lads whom thou sendest, they gain the victory, and multitudes tremble before them!"

[*Piankhy to his expeditionary force, about to leave for Egypt: Piankhy stela lines 12–14; N.-C. Grimal,* La stêle triomphale de Pi(ankh)y au musée du Caire *(Cairo, 1981)*]

cated by his placement in the list of Tefnakhte's allies, first after the kings in one list, and second (after Sheshonq of Busiris) in another. How he is related to the Hornakhte clan is unknown; he may well have belonged to another family. His son, Onkh-Hor, was general of the army in neighboring Hermopolis Parva, functioning under his father within the Mendesian jurisdiction. Both had accompanied Tefnakhte to the siege of Herakleopolis and had been posted each to his "allotted portion" of the "measured-out" circumference of the city wall. With the subsequent disbanding of the coalition Djed-Amun-efonkh and his son had withdrawn to their hometown to await the outcome of events; and as Tefnakhte's fortresses south of Memphis capitulated one after the other, they clearly began to reassess the overall situation. When Memphis itself fell in a single day and the inhabitants of neighboring townships fled in panic, all the chiefs and mayors of the Delta experienced a change of mind. Dutifully they came before Piankhy to proffer presents, while Tefnakhte himself retreated to his hometown of Sais; and when Piankhy's fleet moored at Athribis in the southern Delta, the two kings and thirteen chiefs and mayors of the Delta assembled again formally to offer allegiance and pay an indemnity.

8.3 Pharaoh Piankhy on the Uncouth Libyans, c. 720 B.C.

Then these (Libyan) kings and mayors of the Land of the Flood came to see the beauty of His Majesty, their legs as the legs of women. They could not enter the palace because they were in a dirty state and ate fish, and that's a palace prohibition. King Namlot (an Egyptian) indeed entered the palace since he was clean and had not eaten fish. Three were kept standing (outside), only one had palace access.

[*Piankhy stela 149–53; N.-C. Grimal, La stêle triomphale de Pi(ankh)y au musée du Caire (Cairo, 1981)*]

Figure 8.4. Nine Egyptian potentates do obeisance to Piankhy (from the vignette of his stela, Napata). Piankhy, later partly erased by his detractors, faces Namlot, king of Hermopolis, who is preceded by his wife and who brings the Kushite king a horse as gift. Beneath, King Osorkon of Bubastis, Awepet of Leontopolis, and Peftjawbast of Herakleopolis perform proskynesis, while to the left the great chiefs and mayors follow suit. Djed-amun-efonkh of Mendes is second in the upper row.

The aftermath of Piankhy's victory remains a puzzle for modern scholarship. Having won what the record on his victory stela would have us believe was a resounding victory, the conqueror failed to penetrate the Delta fastnesses but turned round and retired with his forces to the Sudan! Can his triumph have been as final as he claimed? Might the numerous sieges he undertook have exhausted his troops so that his success was reduced to little more than a Pyrrhic victory?

The withdrawal of Kush left the Northland to its own devices and Tefnakhte undisturbed. He had begun to call himself king with cartouches and formal titulary, and when he passed away a year or two later his son Bocchoris replaced him on the throne. Whether Bocchoris exercised the same authority over the Great Chiefs of the Me as his father had is a point of moot discussion; the fact that the local families of these dynasts, to judge by papponymy, remained undisturbed throughout the late eighth and early seventh centuries B.C. argues that he lacked the power to unseat any of them. Even when in 712–711 B.C. Piankhy's brother and successor, Shabaka, invaded Egypt again on some unrecorded pretext and swept Bocchoris off the throne, the political situation in the Delta remained essentially unchanged. Shabaka executed Bocchoris and united Egypt and Kush under one crown and administration, but he was unable or unwilling to change the political configuration of the north. The Great Chief of the Me in Mendes and his compatriots retained their bailiwicks under the new authority.

If the puritanical, Amun-worshiping Kushites had won the day, both militarily and spiritually, over the native Egyptian North, their presence on the Nile did not terminate the geopolitical struggle over northeast Africa. For half a century prior to Shabaka's conquest

8.4 Shabaka Conquers His Enemies

King of Upper and Lower Egypt, Neferkare, Son of Re Shabaka, given life, beloved of Amun more than any other king who had ever been since the land was established. He overthrew those who had rebelled against him in Upper and Lower Egypt and in every foreign land. The desert dwellers are weakened before him, and fall to his fury; they come of their own volition as prisoners-of-war, each of them having seized his fellow!—because he has done what is good for his father, inasmuch as he loved him!

[*"Toronto" scarab: J. Yoyotte, "Sur le scarabée historique de Shabako: Note additionelle," Biblica 39 (1958), 206–10*]

another foreign power, this one in western Asia, had been pursuing the political goal of imperial aggrandizement in a sort of *Drang nach Westen*. This was Assyria, an aggressive nation-state which had originated in the city of Asshur and its immediate environs. Tiglath-pileser III (745–727 B.C.) had undertaken a major offensive into the coastal lands of the eastern Mediterranean, annexing the Aramaean and Phoenician cities and terminating their independence. With the annexation of Damascus and the reduction of Israel (732 B.C.) the Assyrian forces had appeared in the Philistine plain. A decade later under Sargon II (722–705 B.C.) Israel too was annexed and the Assyrians were in the northern Sinai. While trade with Egypt offered a peaceful incentive for Assyrian involvement in Africa—Sargon in fact built a trading post for that very purpose near Gaza—outright acquisition of the riches of the Nile through conquest lay well within Assyria's capabilities.

The view from Asia must have been promising. That part of Africa closest to the Assyrian sphere of influence, namely, the Delta, suffered from a parochialism inimical to united resistance; and the overlord, Kush, lay one thousand miles to the south. Even the sometime presence of Shabaka's court at Memphis could not compensate, so the counsel might have argued, for the unreliability of the Land of the Flood, the first line of defense. And the asylum offered by Shabaka to a dissident rebel from Ashdod who had fled the Assyrian advance could be presented as tantamount to a *casus belli*, in spite of the fact that he had been extradited in 705 B.C.

If such a broad assessment was ever made by the Assyrian general staff in 712 B.C., it proved to a certain extent wrongheaded and outstripped by events. The following year Shabaka himself had struck first and wrested the rule of the Nile basin from any other claimant. Assyrian temporizing over how to use the Ashdod affair also worked against the interest adumbrated above. In 706–705 B.C. Shabaka, now resident in Memphis, appointed his nephew Shebitku as ruler in the Kushite heartland in the south; the first official act of the regent was to extradite the Ashdod rebel. Sargon's death shortly after this precluded any immediate action on the grounds of any trumped-up charges relating to the asylum. To complicate the situation Hezekiah of Judah used the uncertainty of the early years of the new Assyrian king Sennacherib to fashion an anti-Assyrian coalition involving the remaining Philistine cities and the Transjordanian states. Help was promised by Babylon, and Egypt may have given the impression of sympathy. In any event, when in 701 B.C. Sennacherib and his forces marched down the coast to put down the rebellion, they were met unexpectedly at Eltekeh on the southern plains of Philistia by "the kings of Egypt and the archers, chariotry, and cavalry of the king of Kush, an army beyond counting." The Egyptians and Kushites fought the Assyrians to a standstill, deprived them of success in mopping up opposition, and ensured Egypt and the Levant of thirty years of peace. Shebitku, who, rather than his uncle, must have led the host, commemorated his victory by a triumphal relief in the temple of Osiris at Karnak.

The "kings of Egypt" referred to in Sennacherib's inscription are none other than the Delta dynasts, the Great Chiefs and mayors of the Northland, whom the Assyrians persist in calling *sharru*, "king"; and there can be little doubt that the Mendesian chief was among them. The succession of the local ruling family is somewhat in doubt following the invasion of Piankhy. We have no way of knowing whether Onkh-Hor, erstwhile military commandant in Hermopolis Parva, succeeded his father, Djed-Amun-efonkh, in Mendes, but it is likely that this is the case. A Tachos is attested at about the end of the eighth century B.C. with the titles "Hereditary Prince and Mayor, Great Chief of the Meshwesh, *dux*, and Bishop of the Ram Lord of Djedet" whose son bears the same name as that of the son of Djed-Amun-efonkh, which could be taken as militating in favor of a family relationship. It is tempting to see in Tachos the Great Chief of Mendes at the turn of the century, which would make him a candidate for participation at the battle of Eltekeh.

Whether Onkh-Hor and his son Tachos, named after his grandfather, ever succeeded to the Mendesian patrimony is unknown; but there is no doubt that Mendes, like other Delta principalities, continued to thrive under the "Libyan" Dynastic family long ensconced. The Kushite 25th Dynasty, although strong in domestic and foreign affairs, failed to devise a new system of provincial administration to replace the one it had inherited in the north; and the Delta chiefs proved masters of opportunistic politics. No matter who ruled in Memphis, they were determined to survive. And their ability to perform political acrobatics was soon to be tested.

The success of Kushite arms at Eltekeh, unexpected as it was, proved salutary for the image the 25th Dynasty projected in the world of the seventh century B.C. Shebitku's successor, Taharqa (690–664 B.C.), was able in the first decade of his reign to carry war into Asia and to contest with the Assyrians control over the Mediterranean coast. The result was a sphere of influence encompassing Gaza, Ashkelon, and the Phoenician coast as far north as Tyre and Sidon. While the declining years of an ineffectual Sennacherib

8.5 The "Kings" of Egypt

[Piankhy speaks, c. 720 B.C.]

The one to whom I say: "you are king," he functions as king; the one to whom I say: "you are not king," he never functions as king. . . . the one to whom I say: "accede to the throne," he accedes to the throne; the one to whom I say: "do not accede to the throne," he never accedes to the throne. . . . Gods make a king, men make a king, [but] it is Amun that made me, viz. the one whom no dukes have ever made!

[Gebel Barkal no. 26; G. A. Reisner, "Inscribed Monuments from Gebel Barkal," ZÄS 66 (1931), 76–100]

must have contributed to the Egyptian victories, the Egypto-Kushite forces under Taharqa—their speed and élan on the battlefield became legendary—represented a military power not seen in Egypt for six centuries. In any future clash of arms with Assyria, so the conventional wisdom of the day must have had it, the outcome was by no means foreordained as another Assyrian victory.

And such a test was not long in coming. In 681 B.C. Sennacherib was assassinated and, after a short civil war, his son Esarhaddon won the throne. In retrospect history must characterize this man as being fixated on the war with Egypt. A pretext was not difficult to find: broken oaths and treaties by erstwhile vassals in Phoenicia and Philistia offered themselves. By 674 B.C. Esarhaddon had justified a renewal of hostilities and had prepared his army for an attack. Nevertheless he met defeat. On the frontiers of the Delta Taharqa's troops met the invaders and threw them back in a battle which has achieved naught but a laconic statement in the chronicles of the time. Three years later, however, the Assyrian returned, and this time the invasion was much more carefully planned. The Phoenician allies of Taharqa were reduced, stores laid in for the desert march, and Bedouin tribes won over to supply the expeditionary force.

The result was complete surprise. The Assyrian army appeared suddenly out of the Sinai desert, not exhausted but fresh and well supplied, and hammered the eastern edge of the Nile Delta. Taharqa recovered as best he could and mounted a fighting withdrawal during which he appeared constantly in the thick of the fight, being wounded five times. But it was no use. There had been no time to construct a defense in depth (if it had even occurred to the defenders that one was necessary), and Memphis the capital fell to the Assyrian battering rams within a single day. Taharqa fled south, abandoning his family and court to the Assyrians, and holed up in Thebes. It appeared that all was lost.

Certainly by the autumn of 671 B.C. the Delta and lower Middle Egypt were in Assyrian hands. Esarhaddon convened a conclave in Memphis to which the Delta dynasts trooped to offer submission. The principalities of the Delta were given Assyrian names

Figure 8.5. Taharqa, shown in typical "Nubian" cap with double uraeus, which the kings of the 25th Dynasty often wore.

8.6 The Prowess of the Kushite Troops

Taharqa begins to speak: "There is no coward among my troops, no weak-armed one among my recruits!" The king himself journeyed to the highlands to view the excellence of his army, [and th]ey [moved] as blows the wind, like kites flying with their wings, the household troops included, sure-footed—there was no distinguishing between them! The king himself was like Montu, having no equal among his troops. He was intelligent and strong in every activity, a second Thoth! The king himself was mounted on a chariot to view the running [of] his army, (but then) he ran with them over the desert of Memphis (beginning at) the ninth hour of the night. They reached the Fayum lake at the hour of dawn, and returned to the capital at the third hour of the morning. Then he singled out the best of them, and had them eat and drink with the household troops . . . and rewarded them with all sorts of things. Now His Majesty had a love for the art of war that his god had given him.

[*Dahshur stela of Taharqa: A. Moussa, "A Stela of Taharqa from the Desert Road at Dahshur,"* MDAIK 37 (1981), 332–37]

and governors appointed; but it turns out, from surviving fragmentary records, that the old ruling families were simply reconfirmed in their ancestral positions. It would seem that Mendes received the Assyrian name Asshur-massu-urappish, "Asshur-Has-Expanded-His-Land," and was assigned a governor with an Egyptian name, Ṣiḫurru. But this is merely the contemporary vocalization of "Tachos," and it is more than likely that this individual is the same scion of the family mentioned above, Tachos son of Onkh-Hor!

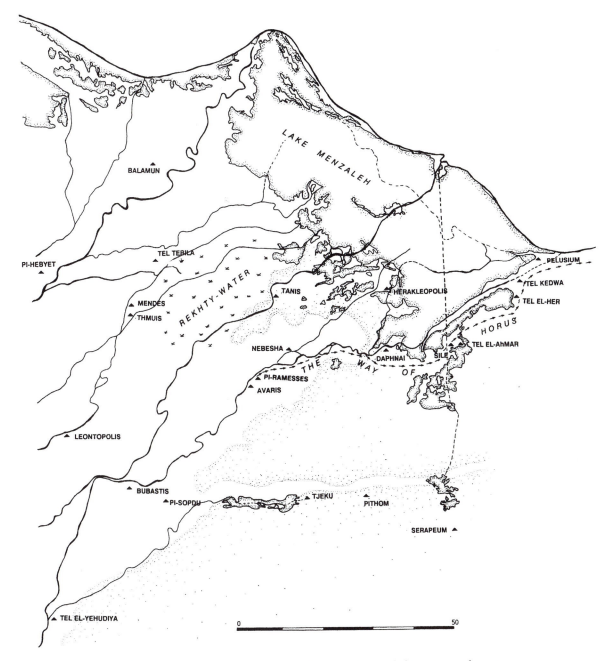

Figure 8.6. The eastern Nile Delta, showing the disposition of border forts intended to intercept the routes leading west from Asia.

Any pretense at permanent control on the part of the Assyrian victors was fated to be illusory. Kush was still too strong and Assyrian provincial administration too weak to prevent a riposte in the form of a military challenge. No sooner had Esarhaddon and the bulk of his forces withdrawn into Asia than Taharqa mustered his scattered forces and marched north to retake his lost territory. The Assyrian records claim that the Delta chiefs fled at the return of Taharqa, but it is much more likely that most of them came over to him and reaffirmed their allegiance. In Mendes a certain Payom was now the mayor, but his origins are obscure. Was he an Assyrian appointee as the Assyrians claimed or a protégé of Taharqa? In any event, to judge by the uninterrupted family trees of the Delta families, he most likely belonged to the old Hornakhte family. In any event he may well have been summoned, with his local militia, to contribute to Taharqa's defense force assembled to repel Essarhaddon's return (669 B.C.). But the Assyrian king died en route to Egypt, and the invasion plans were temporarily shelved until his successor, Ashurbanipal, could reactivate them. In 666 B.C. the expeditionary force was on the move again. In an apparent repetition of the events of five years before, Taharqa beat a retreat from Memphis to Thebes, enticing the Assyrian army to follow him. This they did, only to have the entire Delta flare into open revolt in their rear. The Assyrian garrison left behind in the north was able to quell the insurrection; and in spite of continued Kushite attempts to return, Ashurbanipal was able to sack Thebes itself in 663 B.C.

Assyrian reprisals against the Delta took a form well-known elsewhere throughout the empire, but not hitherto suffered by Egyptians. The local chiefs and mayors who had plotted the uprising were rounded up and packed off to Nineveh. Most of them, it is claimed, were executed. Only Necho, mayor of Sais and son of the ill-fated Bocchoris, was allowed to return as a governor-general on behalf of the Assyrians. The principal cities wherein the conspiracy had taken shape were singled out for especially vicious treatment. The Assyrians "put to the sword the inhabitants, young and old, of the cities of Sais, Mendes, Tanis, and all the other towns which had associated with them in the plot; they did not spare any among them. They hung their corpses from stakes, flayed them, and covered the city walls with their skins."

On the northeastern periphery of the mounds that make up the city of ancient Mendes there lies a bizarre and isolated elevation known locally as the "Hill of Bones." Burials abound on its summit, dating mostly from the Ptolemaic and Roman periods. But at a certain depth a level of burning and destruction can be detected, and unburied skeletons lie sprawled over the sometime surface. Assyrian retaliation was always swift, hard-hitting, and merciless. But as is the case with all such military revenge, the action serves only to steel the victims' will to resist.

The end was not yet. Mendes could not be finished off by the hand of man. Under its god, the Ram, it was destined to rise once more to heights it had never before attained.

The Time of Troubles, extending from the Kushite through Assyrian invasions, was to inform a broader folklore of heroic legend in which Mendes occupied a prominent place. The invasion of Piankhy in particular, in the form it took in the famous stela from Gebel Barkal, which must have lived on in a lively oral tradition, was used as a backdrop and springboard for plot action. The Kushite conqueror is transmogrified into Moses/Hermes who gets the honor of besieging Hermopolis and marries a Kushite princess (Artapanus; Num. 12:1). In the Demotic Saga, *The Fight for the Armor of Inaros*, the townships of Egypt and their dynasts are remembered much as they are reflected in the Piankhy stela and the Assyrian records. A hostile view is taken of Mendes in this epic, whose prince Urt-Amun-no (a likely corruption in Demotic of the Djed-Amun-efonkh of the stela) has wrongfully secreted the precious armor of the legendary hero Inaros in his castle "the Mount of Re" (a distortion of another toponym in the Piankhy stela) on the north of the Mendesian township. At the head of the combined armies of Tanis, Mendes, Natho, and Sebennytos, said to be "the strongest in Egypt," Urt-Amun-no does battle with a coalition of other townships from both Delta and Valley, and is defeated. The Mendesian family of the Great Chief of the Me is remembered as "the clan of Hornakht son of Smendes," and Djed-Hor the son of Onkh-Hor also figures prominently. The population of the Mendesian township, "which is very numerous," became fixed in folk memory: Pharaoh Vaphres (Apries?) sends twenty thousand men from Mendes to Jerusalem to help Solomon build the temple (Eupolemos).

Chapter Nine

The Ram, Lord of Djedet

··

In the Late Period the city, formerly called Djedet, had long since come to be identified with its foremost resident, the Ram. Indeed the common name of the site, appearing already in the New Kingdom, was "the House of the Ram, Lord of Djedet," in Egyptian Pindidi. Thence came the name by which the city was ever after to be known, namely, Mendes, derived by way of the Greek.

Everywhere in the city the Ram was celebrated. His temple, scarcely larger than it had been during the reign of Merenptah, occupied prime real estate on the north side of the town, whence came the cooling breezes of the prevailing north wind. Its basic plan, pylon backed by open court, hypostyle, and sanctum, had not changed since Ramesses II designed it. It was called variously "the House of the Ram," "the God's-Mansion," "the Residence of the Ram," and "the Seat of the Ram." Unlike other Delta temples such as those at Sais, Buto, and Pi-Sopdu, which represented local Delta traditions in their layout and orientation, the Mendes temple conformed to the most common type dating in origin from the early New Kingdom, namely, the Processional Temple, in which the layout accommodated the ceremonial progress of the god at festival time. To this end the structure possessed a "shrine" (*iwnn*) or "naos" (*kꜣry*), sometimes called "the Great Seat," and a "barque-block" (*tntꜣt*) whereon the portable barque-shrine of the god rested when not in use. It is most likely that an ambulatory ran laterally on both sides of the shrine, giving access to side rooms wherein statues of "guest" gods and private devotees were placed. Fragments of four naoi, each estimated to be between two and three meters in height, were unearthed in the destruction debris over top of the Old Kingdom podium. These certainly come from the Late Period and, if they were not for guest gods, may constitute evidence that the four avatars of the Ram were honored by individual shrines (figs. 9.1a–9.1e).

At a distance of about fifty meters north-northwest of the temple pylon lies a ruin mound of modest proportions (see fig. 11.4). Here, thanks to the treasure-hunt of Edouard Naville, a swath of shattered limestone and granite blocks has been exposed, which has yet to be fully explored. The presence of worked surfaces—pilasters and architraves seem to be in evidence—suggests that this is the site of a formal structure, undoubtedly sacred, rather than a secondary pile of debris. Mud-brick enclosure walls of Ptolemaic

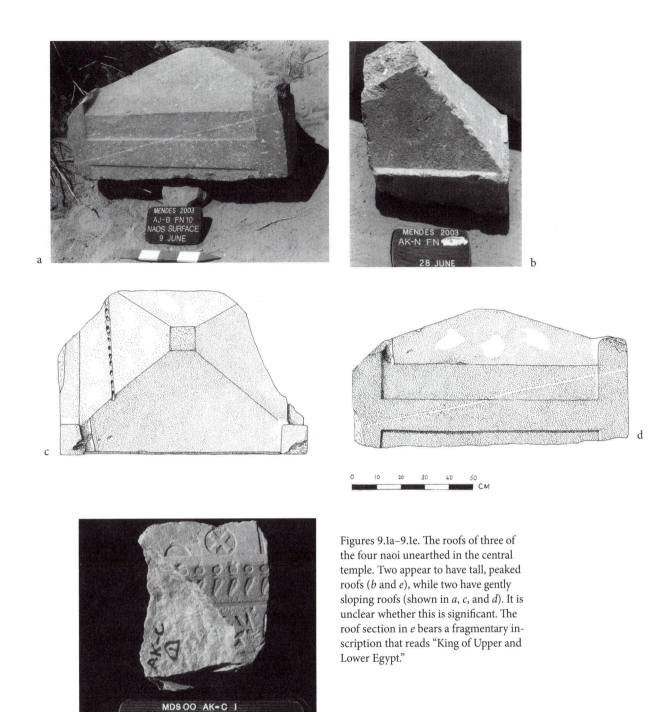

Figures 9.1a–9.1e. The roofs of three of the four naoi unearthed in the central temple. Two appear to have tall, peaked roofs (*b* and *e*), while two have gently sloping roofs (shown in *a*, *c*, and *d*). It is unclear whether this is significant. The roof section in *e* bears a fragmentary inscription that reads "King of Upper and Lower Egypt."

date on the east side, running over the T-A vaults (First Intermediate Period) described above, confirm the formal nature of the building. It seems ideally situated to qualify for a *mammisi*, or "birth-house," a shrine commemorating the birth and nurturing of the young god, common to many Late Period temples. If so, it is tempting to identify this structure with the "birthing-house" (*msḫnt*) mentioned by the Great Chiefs of the Me in their eighth century B.C. inscriptions.

As in other animal cults throughout Egypt, the specific member of the species in which the god had chosen to abide was housed in splendor within the temple. He had been "discovered" on the death of his predecessor somewhere in the Mendesian township and identified on the basis of certain body colorations which signaled the god's spiritual presence within the animal. A typical record of the new avatar's appearance is given in Ptolemy's Mendes stela (third century B.C.).

> Then one arrived to tell His Majesty: "Lo! the living Ram has come forth in the farmland on the west of Mendes—(that's) the place where he was found on the First Occasion!—and he is now in 'The-Mound-of-the-Shearing' until Thy Majesty can install him in his seat. Let the staff of the House-of-Life come to see him." Then His Majesty sent to the temples of Upper and Lower Egypt to have the [staffs of the House-of-Life] and the priests of the townships come . . . and after the staff of the House-of-Life had seen him, they realized that his form corresponded to the (prescription of) the Festival-book.

We have yet to identify the cultic installation designated by "The-Mound-of-the-Shearing," though it may well be one of the unexcavated tumuli within the broader complex of the site. Inscriptions refer to it as under the patronage of *Ḥȝt-mḥyt*, the local fish-goddess, and housing guest cults of several other gods. Of some significance, in light of the role of the Mound-of-the-Shearing in identifying the young avatar according to written prescription, may be the priestly title at Mendes "Scribe of the God's-Book of the Ram . . . [in] 'The Shearing.'"

Like all the other town gods of Egypt, the Ram enjoyed feast days which brought him into contact with the populace. In the Cairo Calendar of Lucky and Unlucky Days (a species of almanac, probably of Middle Kingdom date), the fifth day of the first month of Harvest is designated as Ba-neb-djed's feast day; but one thousand years later (in the Edfu nome-list) it had gravitated to the eighteenth day of the fourth month of Planting. The fifteenth day of the third month of Inundation was also considered sacred to the god, for it was on that day that he had "inspected" something (lost in a lacuna) in "the holy mansion." *Ḥȝt-mḥyt*'s mythological activity also governed the activity of a devout Egyptian. The Cairo Calendar declares the twenty-eighth day of the fourth month of Inundation to be "wholly inimical": "You are not to eat any *mḥyt* fish on this day, nor are you to make offering of them, (for) this is the day when *Ḥȝt-mḥyt* went forth from Mendes in the form of a tilapia."

Figure 9.2. Hathor capital with abacus from a pier in the *mammisi* at Mendes.

The description of Diodorus (first century B.C.) gives a vivid impression of the lavish care showered upon the sacred animal.

> (He is kept) in a sacred enclosure and is cared for by many distinguished men who offer (it) the most expensive fare; for they provide with unfailing regularity the finest wheaten flour . . . seethed in milk, every kind of confection made with honey, and fowl either boiled or baked. . . . They are continually bathing the animal in warm water, anointing them with the most precious ointments, and burning all sorts of fragrant incense before them. They provide the most expensive coverlets and fine jewelery.

Diodorus goes on to describe how the devotees of the animal, at its death, "mourn for it as deeply as do those who have lost a beloved child, and bury it in a manner not in keeping with their ability, but going far beyond the value of their estates." The archaeology of the site illustrates these fabulous obsequies as we shall see in a subsequent chapter.

9.1 Provisions for Sacred Animal Burials (Djed-Hor)

The ritual procedures for beautifying the limbs of the god (the falcon) in the place of embalmment in this temple are undertaken by the masters of the mysteries at the time of their burial. When the burial takes place they are laid to rest in the cemetery on the north of Athribis, called Pirostawtjaw. . . . *On one occasion many falcons were discovered which had not been embalmed in the temple . . . in the chamber "Seventy." They were introduced into the place of embalmment and given (proper) burial with . . . unguent and fine cloth which was in the place of embalmment, and (then) were introduced into the cemetery.* [G. Daressy, "Statue de Zedher le sauver," ASAE 18 (1918), 145]

On a sarcophagus lid from a burial emplacement of a sacred ram, now in the Cairo museum, two figures of Nut, the sky-goddess, extend themselves over the mummified ram, cynocephalos baboons and female personifications of the uraeus lift their arms in adoration, and hieroglyphic texts beatify the deceased (see sidebar 9.2). It is most likely that the majority of ram interments were provided with decorated lids which have either been destroyed or are yet to be unearthed. In keeping with Egyptian cultic conceptions in the first millennium B.C., any sacred, secluded cult installation could be called a "mound" (*iȝt*), in allusion to and identification with the primordial archetypal mound on which the god effected creation and in which the divine power lay buried. In Mendes one of the names of the sepulcher of the sacred rams was "The Mound of the Souls," and here amid a sacred grove stood the holy zizyphus tree.

The priestly establishment over which the Ram presided had grown apace since the Middle Kingdom. It now conformed to the structure of a temple community anywhere in Egypt. Cults of the parochial gods (nome deities) in Egypt often throw up a priestly nomenclature which sounds mysterious but which has reference to mythological identification and roles. The upper grades of the priesthood (the first four ranks in the case of the temple of Amun at Thebes, the first two at Mendes) were singled out for special appellatives: the first prophet of the Ram was called He-Whose-Decay-Is-Hidden, possibly under the influence of Osirian theology, which made much of the life force latent within the decaying flesh of the deceased god. His deputy, the second prophet, was dubbed Commander-of-the-Host, a possible reflex of the socio-administrative hierarchy of the period of the Great Chiefs of the Me when the title was borne by the son of the Chief. In this case the second prophet stood to the first prophet as Horus to Osiris. Another priestly

9.2 To the Ram Deceased

Hail Osiris, the living bai! May thy mother embrace thee as thou liest in her womb and art born like Re every day! Mayest thou enjoy youthfulness on the horizon of heaven, and transform thyself into the living bai! Mayest thou traverse heaven as a "Heliopolitan" . . . on earth like thy father Re in heaven. No eye will ever fail to see thee! May thy mother protect thee like thy father Re, may she conceal thee as Khopry, her arms extended over thee, so that no creeping thing shall go into the cavern in which thou art. The "Mistress" has made thy protection like Re, she has put fear of thee in their hearts! [Sarcophagus lid from Mendes, now in Cairo Museum 29792]

function with Osirian overtones is Son-Whom-He-Loves, again drawn from the Horus-pattern. One of these might also function as Bishop of the Priests of the Ram. Both belonged to that upper echelon of priests designated by the title Prophets (lit., Servants of God) of the Ram Lord of Mendes. Of hereditary stock with unrevoked ancestral claims to functions and perquisites, the "prophets" usually held office in several temples throughout Egypt, drawing hereditary salaries from all with no inescapable obligation to

Figure 9.3. A prophet of the Ram and lector priest, Smendes, "burns incense to his lord."

shoulder the burden of regular service. Beneath them lay the sacerdotal stratum of functioning priests, the *web*-priests, "the pure ones/purifiers," who carried on the daily cult.

Temple activity conformed, as did most divine service in ancient Egypt, to the
model of the functioning of a rich man's house. The god, as lord of the mansion, needed
sleep, purification, meals, clothing, adornment, transportation, and entertainment. The
need to sleep was satisfied by the provision of a naos or sacred shrine within which the
cult-statue, the most precious representation of the deity, provided a means of divine
manifestation. During the night the cedar doors of the shrine were closed and sealed; but
at dawn they were ceremonially opened. This task in Mendes fell to the "Opener of the
Doors of the God in His Temple," performed by a priest called the "Shorn-One in the
Fish-Township," who probably supervised the cleansing and adorning of the statue. The
morning meal which followed was prescribed in an "offering menu," the items of which
were symbolically presented to the statue, then deposited on the offering table. After a
discrete lapse of time they were removed from the table, after the god had satisfied himself, and became part of the daily income of the establishment, to be handed out as sal-
ary-rations to the priests. Each priest had a contract with the temple whereby he received
a certain percentage ("X number of portions") of the daily offerings, the complicated web
of salary arrangements being overseen by the business manager of the temple, the *lesonis*-priest. Offerings and presentations to the god were often accompanied by music. For
the Ram of Mendes a flautist might pipe a tune as the celebrant made the offering, and a
choir sang. Music at Mendes was largely the preserve of women. A priestess shook the
sacred sistrum to quiet the god and drive off baleful influences, while "choristers of the

Figure 9.4. Three priestesses (from the Hieroglyphic Papyrus from Tanis), named *hty.s*, "One-
with-the-Belly"; *hm<t> tknw*, "Servant of Intimacy" (lit., "drawing near"); and *sm3[t]*(?), "She
Who Presents(?)." The name of Mendes is written
above.

Ram" presumably sang hymns. One priestess's epithet was "she that makes hale his soul." Two other mysterious ladies bear strange but suggestive titles: "One-with-the-Belly" and "Servant of Intimacy." What these priestesses did we can only guess.

Like other Egyptian temples, the Temple of the Ram of Mendes hosted a number of guest cults within the city walls. These were partly the initiative of the reigning house at any given period, an unconscious signal and litmus test of the unity and loyalty of the realm, and partly a reflection of natural cultic facts and alliances. In Mendes the long-standing link between the cults of Osiris and the Ram (see above) resulted in the presence of the Osirian cycle, Osiris, Isis "the Great, the God's-Mother," and Horus-the-Child (Harpokrates), all "residing within 'the Abiding Place.'" (Osiris is also designated as "Lord of the Tomb" in Mendes.) Normative Egyptian religion promoted a cultic rationalization of the mythic dismemberment of the body of Osiris, wherein the pieces of the corpse were buried exactly where the grieving Isis found them, thus providing a "foundation mythology" for local cults throughout the land. Mendes housed the relics of Osiris's member and back, the spot of the discovery being marked by the "House of the Dais," a cultic installation yet to be identified. The geographical proximity of Hermopolis Parva (modern Baqlieh) and its political subordination to its larger neighbor resulted in an integration of priestly titulary, which probably reflects some sort of administrative and/or economic union of the priesthoods of the two sites. Certainly Thoth was a guest in Mendes. Mythologically Hermopolis Parva is given a sort of parochial primacy by being spoken of as "the Seat where he (the Ram) settled on the First Occasion," that is, the dawn of time. The principal sacerdotal title at Hermopolis Parva, "Chamberlain-Separator-of-the-Two-Gods," an allusion to Thoth's role in judging the two combatant gods, Horus and Seth, is found also at Mendes. Although it lay much farther afield, Heliopolis and its divine denizens also found representation at Mendes. Re, as supernatural counterpart to Osiris, had long enjoyed an association with the city; and his influence is seen in such titles as "Prophet of the Ram of Re in the Horizon of Re," and "Prophet of the Ram and *Ḥ3t-mḥyt* and the Great Ennead which is in the Abiding Place." An as yet unidentified sector of the town was in fact called the "House of the Ennead." *Ius-aas*, the Hathorian avatar at Heliopolis, and even Hathor herself, were also honored at Mendes. It is unclear whether occasional allusions, in text and statuary, to a lioness-headed goddess are to be interpreted as referring to Sakhmet or simply to Hathor in feline form. Though politically and economically demoted from its former status of glory, Thebes continued to be represented by priesthoods and "branch" cults in the Delta, a survival abetted by the "Theban" nature of the founding of Tanis. The cult of Amun-re King of the Gods, presumably sustained by an endowment of sorts, is still found at Mendes well into the Late Period. But one should not imagine an *administrative* connection with the great temple at Karnak far to the south: in contemporary texts of northern provenience the priesthood at Thebes is a shadowy group, far away and incapable of extended influence.

Figure 9.5. Bronze figurine of Osiris; surface find at Tel er-Rub'a.

Figure 9.6 (above). Figure of Harpokrates, "Horus-the-Child"; surface find, Tel er-Rub'a.

Figure 9.7. Faïence aegis of the feline goddess, probably Bast, from the foundation trench of T-2, the temenos wall of Nektanebo I.

By the outgoing first millennium B.C. the Ram of Mendes had developed a personality, the broad outlines of which are dimly discernible. The sexual proclivity of the animal as the progenitor par excellence had long since come to the fore. The priests ensured that the Ram "enjoyed sexual intercourse according to the demands of nature, for with every animal they keep the most beautiful females of the same genus whom they call his concubines." His epithet "fornicating ram who mounts the beauties" not only underscores the biological function of the male of the species but by its ambiguity carries with it the suggestion of perversion. For the "beauties" in question could be human, and the ancients so construed it. The city gained thereby an equivocal reputation abroad: Pindar refers to "Mendes on the overhanging sea-cliff, at the farthest horn of the Nile, where goat-mounting he-goats fornicate with women." When Herodotus visited the city (mid-fifth century B.C.) he heard report of a recent public spectacle in which a goat had had intercourse with a woman; and according to a mold from the site itself (fig. 9.8), such *coitus a tergo* had become a motif in art and perhaps a staple of cultic mythology.

On a higher and more respectable plane the Ram now entered the mythology of the engendering of the king as a principal avatar of the divine father. The creator says to Pharaoh: "I changed myself into the Ram Lord of *Djedet*, I copulated with thy noble mother in order to procreate thy physical being," and pursuant thereto the queen calls herself "beloved of the Ram," and the Ram himself "the Ram who engendered him [the king]." In the picaresque tale "The Contendings of Horus and Seth" (twelfth century B.C.) the Ram of Mendes is called upon by the divine tribunal to give legal advice on who, uncle or son, should inherit the office of the deceased Osiris, presumably in his capacity as a

Figure 9.8. Figure of "Ba-neb-djed, the fornicating ram who mounts the beauties"; after a mold in the Michaelides collection.

9.3 The Mysterious Link: Osiris and the Fornicating Ram

'Anepat *is what they call* Djedet *(Mendes), the Seat-of-Glory of the "Heart-Weary-One," the restorer to life of "Him-That-Awakes-Whole." He migrated as a bai to Busiris, his horns uplifted; and that's how Hu and Sia wandered into his entourage. They had referred to this god (as) the phallus of the Great God, for whom indeed he ejaculates as the fornicating bai; and they referred to the divine flesh as "the Living One," with respect to the member and the back. Divine entities are upon the* djed, *and a vulva of metal close to it; since the female "sisters" (lie) at the pudenda of the phallus, Shenty and Mer-khetes they are called, as its protection. His lifetime is for ever, and his quiescence eternal.*

[*D. Meeks,* Mythes et légendes du Delta d'après le Paprus Brooklyn 47.218.84 *(Cairo, 2006), xi.9–xii.2*]

kind of archetypal Sire. The same story, by associating the god with the island of Siheil at the First Cataract, points up a predictable linkage in the Egyptian pantheon. By virtue of the close similarity of species, a comparable proximity of traits and functions was postulated of other ovine cults. The Ram of Mendes drew close to three other "Bucks" of essentially the same formulation but of slightly different role: Khnum, the creator, resident at the First Cataract; Arsaphes, the fighter, denizen of Herakleopolis; and Amun-re himself, the great overlord. All in origin were chthonic deities, and aspects of creative power were predicated of them. A universal purview, moreover, attaches itself to the Ram of Mendes. He becomes the Father of the Gods, the Ram of Rams, the King of the Gods, the Manifestation (*bai*) of every god, the Heir of Tatenen (the primordial earth-god), the Unique God with overwhelming awfulness. The nuance of the Absolute inherent in these epithets leads to the perception of the god's power and person being unrestricted in the universe, no matter what superficial manifestation may intervene. Besides his essence as the earth, he is also water "who comes as the inundation that he may bring life to the Two Lands." As the Living One of Re he becomes the source of light and heat "that brightens heaven and earth with his rays"; as the air "he is breath for all people."

One of the most interesting and significant aspects of the god of Mendes, which originated at least as early as the New Kingdom and comes to the fore in the first millennium, is that of the Ram *quadrifrons*, "four faces on one neck." The psychology of language in ancient Egypt conveyed the notion of plurality by the number three, totality by the number four. To refer to all four sides means the *total* perimeter (whether the object is rectilinear or not), to be "four-times pure" means to be *completely* pure, to "recite four times" is to render a text *totally* effective, and so forth. In trying to express the total nature of the Primordial Ocean, the *Nun*, the Egyptians conceived of four hypostaseis of the abstract qualities of this Abyss, each with a nuance of the infinite: (absolute) Darkness (*Kkw*), Infinity (*Ḥḥw*), Fluidity (*Nw*), and Directionlessness (*Tnmw*). It is the same mind-

Figure 9.10. Amun-re identified as "Khnum-re, Lord of the Cataract"; after a figure in the Book of the Fayum.

Figure 9.9. "Arsaphes-re Ba-neb-djed," after a figure in the Book of the Fayum.

Figure 9.11. "Amun-re, Lord of the Lagoon," after a figure in the Book of the Fayum.

set that produced the quadripartite Ram, the latter identified as the great creator, the "Complete One" (*'Itm*). Though the formulation of the concept may be earlier, the New Kingdom yields our earliest evidence of the four avatars of the Ram, the Lord of Heaven, the Great Living One of Re: Light/Flame (Re), Air (Shu), Earth (Geb), and Flood (Osiris). The Ram thus becomes "He Who Rises on the Horizon with Four Faces," the proleptic personification of the four elements of the universe which is to be. When linked to the older concept of the union of dynamic solar power (Re) with latent fertility (Osiris), which we have encountered already in the Coffin Texts, the Creator in his aspects of heat and life is also manifest in the very elements of his creation; with the addition of the embodiment of *national* existence, Amun-re, the result is a primordial deity of unequaled antiquity and immanence.

Like many early peoples, the Egyptians believed that homophony in language was not a coincidence. Since names had been given by the gods at the dawn of time, similarities in structure and vocalization *meant* something. Names signaled the very essence of a person, thing, or action, and similar-sounding words indicated a common essence. The verb *sr* in Egyptian meant "to proclaim (in advance)," "to announce" what was coming in the future, whether or not this was immediately predictable. From here it is but a step to the extended meaning "to foretell, prophesy" by virtue of divine or god-given powers of second sight. In Egyptian the generic term for "sheep" was also *sr*, with a pronunciation approximating *sr*, "to foretell." Small wonder, then, that from an early period Egyptians imputed the powers of prophecy to the gods whose earthly manifestations took the form of the Ram. Khnum of the First Cataract region became famous for his ability to see into the future. Under certain conditions human beings too, especially the sages, could predict "what had not yet happened; and it came to be exactly as they said it."

The prophetic power attributed to Ram-gods is different from oracular power. From an early period the deity, when he appeared in public (rather less often within the shrine), was expected to be able to make determinations that settled disputes or certified selection. Sometimes this involved a modicum of forecasting or revealing ordained fate. But in the main the power of the oracle derives from clairvoyance rather than knowledge of the future.

The prophetic talent of the Ram of Mendes appears at an early date. In the Coffin Texts the devotee declares, in a statement of identification with the god, "My *bai* belongs to me, the one through whom I ejaculate; I am a Mendesian: what I say is what will be done (or what they [will] do)." The Great Chief of the Me Ny-su-ba-neb-djed seems also to have benefited from the Ram's prediction (though the account smacks of an oracle): "he (the Ram) chose him from among his kin, for he had discerned his heart and knew how effective he would be in performing benefactions for his house." Perhaps it was appropriate that a deity able to prophesy what was to come should have eschewed oath-taking, for the very sounding of his name would have compromised a sinful mortal: "I have not sworn by the Ram, Lord of Mendes," avers the pious devotee, "I have not pronounced the name of Tatenen."

Powers of prediction drew the sacred ram into the arena of folklore. Increasingly during the course of the first millennium B.C. foreign invasion loomed as an ever-present prospect in the view of the Egyptians, then as a terrifying reality. Out of the experience of defeat and occupation there arose a type of folktale at once admonishing and reassuring: a prophecy had been uttered long ago that, because of sin or negligence, the gods would some day abandon the land to the vile foreigners who would pillage it mercilessly. But future generations were to take heart, for the prediction contained a happy ending: a deliverer would arise who would unite Egyptians, drive out the enemy, and restore the land to its proper state. The most popular of these tales made the Ram-god the prophet and set the piece in the reign of Bocchoris (717–711 B.C.): in nine hundred years' time foreign invaders will conquer Egypt, desecrate its temples, and cart off the shrines of the gods to Nineveh. Heliopolis, Hermopolis, Per-Hebyet (west of Mendes), and Thebes will be particularly devastated. Finally the Egyptians will unite around a deliverer who will lead them victoriously against the foreigners and restore the shrines to the temples. So impressed are the auditors that they take the Ram's words down in writing and lay them before the king who thereupon decrees a sumptuous burial for the animal. It is clear, although the surviving papyrus is dated to early Roman times, that the historical point of departure is the Assyrian invasions of the seventh century B.C. How the pattern repeated itself, and how the Ram was himself to suffer, we shall see below.

Chapter Ten

The Saite Revival

....

Destructive and morale-shattering as it undoubtedly had been, the Assyrian occupation of Egypt was of short duration. Political problems in other parts of their empire, such as Babylon and Elam, diverted the attention of the Assyrians from northeast Africa; and increasing military resources had to be directed toward quelling revolts in these Asian sectors. Ashurbanipal required a local protégé to govern Egypt in Assyrian interests, and such a person he believed he had found in Psamtek, son of Necho, the headman of Sais. Necho had met a violent end for his role as a species of "quisling," and his son had placed himself under Assyrian protection. When Taharqa died in 664 B.C. his nephew Tanwetamani, legitimate heir to the Kushite throne, laid claim to the kingship of Egypt also as his rightful inheritance and marched north to Memphis. While Ashurbanipal had driven out the Kushites in 663 B.C., the Delta dynasts had already declared for Tanwetamani; a rift soon developed between them and Psamtek, the Assyrian "stooge." Psamtek was in fact forced to flee for his life to the impenetrable fastness of the Delta marshes along the Mediterranean coast.

Because our sources are largely classical, and derived from an oral tradition centuries after the events, the history of Egypt from 664 to 654 B.C. is bedeviled by uncertainty. Later legend spoke of an oracle prophesying Psamtek's victory by means of "Bronze Men" who would emerge from the sea, while king "Tementhes" (Tanwetamani) was for his part warned by another oracle to "beware of the cocks." Both predictions came true: Psamtek encountered some Ionian hoplites blown ashore on the Delta coast and hired them as an effective fighting force, while Tanwetamani learned to his chagrin that the "cocks" in question were those self-same hoplites with their crested helmets. Toward the end of the decade Psamtek found himself in a military position favorable to taking on the Kushites (who were undeterred, apparently, by their defeat at the hands of Ashurbanipal in 663) and succeeded in defeating Tanwetamani's forces south of Memphis. By 660 B.C. the victor was contemplating the administrative reorganization of the Southland (i.e., Upper Egypt) and in 656 B.C. felt sufficiently sure of his power to appoint his young daughter Nitocris to be Divine Worshiper of Amun in Thebes. Tanwetamani might continue to hanker after his "rightful inheritance," or Ashurbanipal to fulminate against a protégé now turned "traitor": it did not matter in the immediate event. All Egypt as far as the First Cataract was now united under Psamtek of Sais, and thus had been inaugurated what history calls the 26th or "Saite" Dynasty.

The accomplishments of the long, fifty-four-year reign of Psamtek (I) earned him the well-deserved epithet "the Great." Whether military, economic, administrative, or social, the problems facing this remarkable king were all overcome with an intelligence and perspicacity that few world leaders ever display. Psamtek reformed the military by hiring Greek freebooters and employing Asiatic contingents from Judah, Syria, and Phoenicia as auxiliaries. The unwelcome Libyan clans, which had heretofore formed the core of the Egyptian armed forces, were forcibly expelled from the country in 654 B.C.; at the same time plans were laid to reconstitute the entire provincial administration.

The Saite administration, probably already within the reign of Psamtek I, excelled in establishing a supremely workable township bureaucracy. Ostensibly its creators looked to the past: the old titles often rendered "hereditary prince" and "count" fronted the list of dignities borne by many a local worthy. But the designation "mayor of (metropolis) X," the latter expression often doing double duty for the township, makes a reappearance at this time, heralding a return to a traditional partition of the country's local administration. The "nomarch" or "commissioner" (i.e., the township CEO) was responsible for agriculture—he distributed seed-corn and oversaw the grain tax—and also presided over a local court, or "leet," which settled disputes within a broadly defined civil, fiscal, and criminal jurisdiction. A tendency, already discernible in the Libyan period, to separate police and local militia from civil administrators now informs local government, and titles such as "head of militia," "chief of police," and "bailiff" make their appearance.

Mendes took a prominent place in the new organization of the Delta. The city recovered remarkably well from the punishment it had received at the hands of the Assyrians and emerged in the early Saite period with most of its ancient families still in charge of local affairs. The township had apparently thrown in its lot with the young Psamtek, and the king did not fail to respond. In 654 B.C. "His Majesty gave a town in the environs of the Mendesian township [to his mother Isis the Great . . . namely] 'The Fort of the Idol(?)' . . . with all its property in field [and fen . . .], its [peo]ple, its cattle and its game, together with 524 aruras (of land; c. 350 acres)." The cult of the Ram began to spread into the eastern and southern Delta to Memphis and endowments established as far away as Tjebu south of Assiut.

Enlightened self-interest dictated subservience to the new pharaoh who had shown himself so politically able. Basa, one of the Mendesian magnates, perhaps the mayor, early in the reign informs us of his loyalty as he invokes the sacred Ram.

O prospering Ba! Mayest thou cause the King of Upper and Lower Egypt to prosper, as the gods of *Anepat* prosper! Mayest thou prosper the hereditary prince and mayor Basa in thy house for ever! O Ba of the red crown! Mayest thou "redden" against thine enemy (and that of) the Son of Re Psamtek! Mayest thou prevent them removing me from thy seats, for I am a "butler" of thy house, and I shall never quit thy house! O Ba of Vacuity! The King of Upper and Lower Egypt Wahibre (Psamtek I) shall not vacate the Seat of Horus, and he who is in thy house shall not vacate! Mayest thou grant me the sweet breath that is in thy nose, (for) I am the son of thy priest! O Ba of Extant Earth! Mayest thou cause the Son of Re Psamtek to exist firm upon the *serekh*, and mayest [thou] cause me to remain firm in the Hat-mehyet township, as thou remainest firm in this township!

The priest Tja-ba-neb-djed-memau likewise submits willingly to the royal directives.

I was one who does what His Majesty likes every day, one free from sloth who seeks the good of his city. . . . one beloved of his lord, [whom he praised every day. As for any task] for which His Majesty [dis]patched me, I performed it in its entirety, and never spoke ill of it (i.e., grumbled). . . . Now as for one who is beloved of His Majesty, he it is that lives, he it is that is hale, he it is that descends to his tomb in the necropolis revered before Ba-neb-djed.

Mendesian families now stood in the forefront of political life, a distinction they were not to lose for three centuries or more. A Harsiese could count himself "an acquaintance of the king," and Keref-er-Ptah, perhaps his son, prided himself in "the abiding favors and permanent love from his lord"; while a Ny-su-ba-neb-djed could boast of his appointment as overseer of granaries. One of the scions of a local family, Ahmose, son of Nes-Atum, rose high in the judiciary and later the army: "I am a royal servant who does good, a righteous man. . . . See! I was not inattentive! See! There was no one whom I expelled from his land, there was none whom I deprived of his paternal property; I committed no evil against [anybody]."

In western Asia the outgoing seventh century B.C. witnessed the final collapse of the much weakened Assyrian empire, as the revivified Babylon, in the form of the Neo-Babylonian empire (c. 624–539 B.C.), expanded westward to the Mediterranean. In what turned out to be a sort of world war, Egypt had adopted a policy of active support of Assyria, an odd bedfellow in light of recent history, against Babylon; and when the last scion of the Assyrian royal house met his end at Harran around 609 B.C. continued the struggle. Egyptian expeditionary forces marched into Syria in 608 and in 605 B.C., on the latter occasion led by the new Egyptian king, Necho II, son of Psamtek I; but Egypt's hold over the Levant was short-lived. In 605 at Carchemish on the Euphrates Necho II was soundly defeated by the Babylonian forces under Nebuchadrezzar II, and forced to relinquish all the territory north of the Sinai. Hesitant about further involvement, Necho sat idle as the Babylonians moved against Ashkelon in 603 B.C. and annihilated the city.

Three years later Nebuchadrezzar crossed the Sinai with his army, and it was only by a desperate effort that he was repulsed on the very frontiers of Egypt. On one of these encounters Ahmose seems to have been in command: "Now [His Majesty] sent me [to] smite (the) Asia(tics), I being commanding officer of his army. When he saw how able I was, then he [praised me]." Ahmose must have impressed the royal administration with his military prowess, for in 593 B.C. Psamtek II, Necho's son, appointed him as lieutenant-general commanding Egyptian forces on their successful invasion of Kush. As the troops passed Abu Simbel on their way to sacking Napata, Ahmose among others left his name scratched into the legs of one of the colossoi of Ramesses II.

Another Mendesian also distinguished himself in the south. Nes-Hor was the "Hereditary Prince and Count, Seal-Bearer of the King of Lower Egypt, Unique Friend and General of the Army" under Pharaoh Apries, son and successor of Psamtek II. In Egypt during the first quarter of the sixth century B.C. resident Greek mercenaries were to be found in considerable numbers. Suspicious of their foreign antics but beholden to them as necessary to the defense of Egypt, Pharaoh assigned Egyptian liaison officers fluent in Greek to each contingent and posted the latter to garrison duty in frontier fortresses. Under Apries one such contingent had been assigned to the southern border fort at Aswan, perhaps in the expectation (unwarranted as it turned out) that the Kushite 25th Dynasty would retaliate for the recent destruction of its capital city. Nes-Hor found himself the liaison officer seconded to this garrison. Possibly disgruntled by the remote posting, the foreign soldiers (who included Phoenicians as well as Greeks) took it into their heads to defect to the Kushites, thereby putting Nes-Hor in a critical position. In an inscription erected at Elephantine he credits the gods of the cataract with saving the situation: "ye saved me in a difficult situation from the battalions of Phoenicians and Greeks who were considering . . . in their hearts to effect a departure (or) to flee to the upland. His Majesty was apprehensive over this evil deed they were going to commit. (But) I changed their minds through my council and did not allow them to flee to Nubia, but made them return to the place where His Majesty was." Once back home in Mendes Nes-Hor set up another inscription on the back-pillar of his statue, wherein the incident takes on embellishment. Nes-Hor was "general of the army on the day of battle, stout-hearted on the day of rebellion, one who soothed hearts which had been enraged, recipient of praise for every task assigned him. . . . I was (so greatly) thanked that those who come into being (in the future) shall hear (of it)."

Although Egypt's frontiers had remained inviolate, the Saite pharaohs had had little success in extending hegemony of any sort in the traditional manner over hither Asia. Psamtek I could count the coast of Philistia and Lebanon loyal to Egypt, but the hinterland could not be held. Necho suffered the loss of the coast, and Psamtek II proved ineffectual in galvanizing the small surviving states of southern Palestine into any kind of anti-Babylonian bulwark. Apries suffered a reversal in his attempt to relieve the siege of

Figure 10.1. East gate of the fortress of Pelusium (late Byzantine period), built on the site of earlier forts.

Jerusalem and subsequently watched helplessly as Judah, Amon, and Edom fell to Nebu-chadrezzar. For thirty-five years Egypt eschewed military involvement in western Asia.

Then in 569 Apries, who was not noted for his astute planning nor for his tact, made an attempt to invade Cyrene which proved disastrous and thereby provoked an internal rebellion. While Apries and Amasis, the rebel leader, were locked in hostilities, Nebuchadrezzar saw a marvelous opportunity to invade and reduce Egypt at a single stroke. In the summer of 567 B.C., "They came to tell His Majesty: 'the Asiatics in their confidence have rebelled, and are marching along the Way(s)-of-Horus! There are thousands of them there, invading the land, they clog every road! Those on ships are sailing with good despatch, (for) they purpose to destroy our land!'" But Amasis, who had won the civil war and taken the throne, was not to be caught napping. A total mustering of the standing army, territorials, and Greek mercenaries confronted the invaders with a strong defense, and a timely storm wrought havoc among the enemy fleet. Egypt was saved.

For twenty-eight years Egypt basked in the prosperity a strong and intelligent pha-raoh produced before another cloud darkened the horizon: the rise of an expanding world empire. In 539 B.C. Cyrus of Persia entered Babylon without a fight, and at a single stroke the territory of the Neo-Babylonian empire up to the Egyptian frontier passed into

Persian hands. Amasis scrambled to organize his defenses: he seized Cyprus, supported Lydia against Cyrus, and signed treaties with Samos and Cyrene. With a resourceful general-king at the helm Egypt might well have survived, were it not for one unpredictable eventuality: death. In 526 B.C., as the Persian king Cambyses was mustering his forces, Amasis died, leaving the throne to his son, the untried Psamtek III. Beneath the walls of Pelusium, the great fortress at the mouth of the easternmost branch of the Nile, a numerically superior Persian force routed the Egyptians in the spring of 525 B.C. There was no defense in depth: Egypt capitulated at once, and the captive Psamtek III was put to death. For one hundred twenty years Egypt became a backwater, a remote province of the Persian Empire.

Chapter Eleven

Mendes, the Capital of Egypt

··

The end of the Saite regime had come so suddenly that Egypt was taken wholly by surprise. There was little if any resistance; in fact collaboration seems to have been the norm. Udjahoresne, a former admiral under Amasis and an all-around intellectual, took it upon himself to shepherd the conquering Cambyses around the sights of the land and introduce him to the temples. Initially the Persian yoke appears to have been light. Military officers were permitted to keep their rank, and priests were allowed to undertake cultic ritual unhindered. At Mendes the deputy high priest Ny-su-ba-neb-djed, son of Psherbast, apparently made the transition to life under the new regime without mishap, and was duly buried in a tomb east of the temple. If Darius I, Cambyses' successor, showed an interest in Egyptian law, it was solely to familiarize himself with the details of Egypt's fiscal regulations.

Of course the Persians tolerated no king in Memphis, nor princess in Thebes, replacing the former with a governor (and garrison) and terminating the office of the latter. Township administration continued to function, although financial affairs were in the hands of Persian officials. At the upper and intermediate levels Egyptian scribes were gradually phased out in favor of a foreign secretariat employing Aramaic as the language of government business and correspondence.

The benign attitude the Persians showed toward Egypt for the first forty years of their occupation was not to last. Cambyses and Darius proved to be the only kings of Persia sufficiently interested in visiting northeast Africa and viewing their newly won province in person. Thereafter their successors for the most part neglected Egypt, albeit seeing to it that the country was milked by taxation. As time went on rebellions broke out, motivated not so much by politics as by sheer want. An outbreak of armed resistance took place in 486 B.C. only to be brutally suppressed two years later by Darius's successor, Xerxes; even the more ambitious revolt in 463 of Inaros, a scion of the 26th Dynasty, came to naught in spite of Athenian help. The last act of this pitiable attempt to break free came in the spring of 454 B.C. when a small Athenian fleet sailed up the Mendesian branch only to be wiped out by the Persian forces. One wonders what impact the tragedy had upon the citizenry of the city of Mendes itself.

As the fifth century B.C. neared its end disaffection among the Egyptian population

Figure 11.1. Shawabti fragments of the deputy high priest of the Ram, Ny-su-ba-neb-djed, son of Psher-bast, from his as yet undiscovered tomb east of the main temple. Ny-su-ba-neb-djed probably took of-fice under Amasis and survived into the Persian period.

reached a peak. Under the incompetent Darius II the country suffered from increasing neglect and administrative malfeasance, and what we might call food riots began to break out. During 414–413 an uprising of the general populace was quelled with diffi-culty, but rebels continued to riot and destroy Persian property. In 411 the Persian satrap Arsames left Egypt to make report to Darius, and in the following year the Egyptian gar-rison at Elephantine on the southern frontier revolted. This rebellion was soon followed by others, including one at Thebes, and all were accompanied by the destruction of prop-erty and loss of life. The Persian administration, incapable of restoring order, began to melt away.

11.1 An Egyptian General Still Functioning under Darius I (519 B.C.)

General Ahmose . . . he says, while directing this god (the embalmed Apis) in peace to the beautiful West, after he had done everything that is to be done in the embalming chamber, and while he was (still) in his office(?) of battalion commander, in charge of the numerous host, in order to facilitate this god's procession to his seat of the West (i.e., the tomb chamber in the Serapeum): "I am thy servant who acts for thy ku. I passed the night continually awake, without sleeping, seeking anything that might be beneficial to thee! I put the fear of thee in the hearts of every <Egyptian> and the foreigners of every foreign land who were in Egypt, through what I did in your embalming chamber. I despatched messengers hastily to Upper and Lower Egypt alike to summon every nomarch of the towns and townships with their tribute to thine embalming chamber, while the god's-fathers and priests of Memphis were saying: 'O Apis-Osiris! Mayest thou hearken unto the prayer of him that does thee good, general Ahmose . . . !'"
[J. Vercoutter, Textes biographiques du Serapéum de Memphis *(Paris, 1962), Texte H]*

145

Coordination of the rebellion was slow in coming, but by 406 B.C. two cities had taken the lead, Sais and Mendes. In Sais resided Amyrtaeus II, the grandson of a like-named magnate who had participated in the rebellion of Inaros fifty years earlier. By December of 405 he felt sufficiently strong to declare himself king, and his short reign constitutes the Manethonian 28th Dynasty. The timely death of Darius II in the following spring precluded for a time any military retaliation against Egypt; but by 402 B.C. the new Persian king, Artaxerxes II, was beginning to assemble a large army and fleet in Phoenicia in preparation for an attempt to recover the lost province. The revolt of Cyrus, younger brother of Artaxerxes, precluded the attempt for the time being, as the mustered forces were diverted to deal with the rebels. In Mendes, meanwhile, the new spirit of freedom had prompted a local grandee, one Psamtek, to declare a kingship perhaps in emulation of Amyrtaeus; but he seems to have been a disreputable sort. For when an Egyptian freebooter, the admiral Tamos who had been fighting with Cyrus, fled in 400 B.C. from the defeat of the rebels and entered the Mendesian mouth of the Nile, Psamtek seized him, stripped him of his possessions, and put him to death.

Psamtek himself shortly disappeared, and by the spring of 399 a general, Neferites, had taken control of Mendes. Neferites at once set about to consolidate all power in his hands. During the summer he moved against Sais, throwing Amyrtaeus in chains and bringing him to Memphis in late September ostensibly for execution. By the beginning of October Neferites had declared himself king of Egypt.

Figure 11.2. Head of royal statuette, probably a likeness of Neferites I, from his tomb at Mendes. The full face is characteristic of the family of the 29th and 30th Dynasties.

His short reign (399–393 B.C.) inaugurated what the later king-list numbered the 29th Dynasty. Neferites, perhaps as much as Amyrtaeus, was remembered by posterity as the great freedom fighter against the Persians. Although some garrisons, such as the one at Elephantine, continued for a few short months to honor Artaxerxes II, Neferites shortly did away with them; the resident communities that had sided with Persia, such as the Jews and the Arabian tribes on the east side of the Delta, were thrown out. Both Neferites and his second successor, Akoris, became actively and energetically involved in pursuing hostilities with the now much-weakened Persian Empire. Pursuing the age-old policy of securing a Levantine sphere of influence, both kings pushed up the coast, presumably with armed force, and exerted control over Gezer, Accho, Tyre, and Sidon. Alliances were sought with Greek cities, and aid given in the form of money, ships, and grain.

The Peace of Antalcidas concluded by Artaxerxes II with the Greek cities in 386 B.C. freed the hands of the Great King to organize a showdown with rebellious Egypt. For his part Akoris hired a contingent of Greek mercenaries and secured the services of the Athenian general Chabrias. The latter created a defense in depth on the side of the Delta facing Asia, fortifying the city of Pelusium at the mouth of the easternmost Nile branch and building fortified outworks several miles to the east. These measures proved sufficient: several attempts by the Persians over the next two years were abortive, and Egypt gained confidence in the knowledge that her frontiers were inviolate.

Persian failure, scholars have long since concluded, must be put down to military ineptitude rather than Egyptian skill and solidarity, for the political situation inside Egypt was anything but stable. The century following the unsuccessful revolt of Inaros was riddled with coups, murders, and unseatings at the highest levels of power among an extended family of warlords, a veritable "junta." No power-wielder of the day seems to have been safe; none could establish Dynastic legitimacy. Psammuthis, the son and immediate successor of Neferites I who succeeded his father in January 393 B.C., did not succeed in lasting the year; he disappeared mysteriously. The Demotic Chronicle insists

11.2 Shawabti of King Neferites (from His Tomb at Mendes)

The Illuminated One, the Osiris King Neferites, he says: "O ye shawabtis! *If the Osiris King Neferites is (ever) conscripted to perform any work which is (normally) done there, in the necropolis—where grueling tasks may arise!—as a man to his duties, 'here I am!' ye shall say, when ye are detailed at any time to do what is (normally) done there, viz. to plant the fields, to irrigate riparian land, to transport sand from west to east and vice versa, 'here I am!' ye shall <say>."*

[*G. Janes*, Shabtis, a Private View: Ancient Egyptian Funerary Statuettes in European Private Collections *(Paris, 2003), nos. 95a–c*]

that he was removed because he had violated divine law; a more likely reason is that he had preempted his brother Akoris, who considered himself the rightful heir. Akoris in turn was succeeded in late spring 380 B.C. by his son Neferites II, but he was unseated in the late summer by a certain Muthis (or perhaps more correctly Ahmose, the king whose stela we uncovered in 1992). Within weeks Muthis was gone, again in a coup d'état, and another grandson of Neferites I, Nektanebo, seized power.

In spite of this jockeying for the crown, antics which the Greeks termed "mindless," Egypt remained surprisingly strong economically. Persian occupation had not closed the country off from trade: merchant ships continued to arrive from Phoenicia, Cyprus, mainland Greece, and the Greek islands. Wood, iron, silver, opium, and luxury manufactures were traded for Egyptian wheat and natron, a commerce that maintained untold wealth in temple and state coffers. Native quarries and mines continued to be worked, and high Niles brought abundant crops.

Nowhere is the prosperity of the period more evident than in the city of Mendes, which all but stamped its name on an epoch. It was during the 29th Dynasty that the city achieved its maximum extent, stretching north-south approximately 3.5 kilometers. The Temple of the Ram had always provided a focus for the community, and from at least as early as New Kingdom times had always been oriented toward the north. This northern approach was now enlarged by pylons and a dromos.

Figure 11.3. Fragment of a stela found in the debris of Neferites' tomb, showing a kneeling king worshiping the Ram. The prenomen reads *Neb-maa-khnum setepen Khnum*, reminiscent of Akoris's prenomen. The nomen is difficult to read but may be *Mose*. Whether this is the "Mendesian pretender" or the short-lived Muthis remains moot.

11.3 Nektanebo's Self-Laudation

The perfect god, very strong, who crushes the foreign countries, effective in councils of war on Egypt's behalf, protector of the townships, trampling the foreigners (even) the Asiatics, destroying the seat thereof(?), annihilating(?) them; stout-hearted, one who goes forth and does not instantly turn back, (all)-consuming when he shoots with the bow straight ahead; supplying the temples with the greatness of his largesse; what he speaks comes immediately to fruition, as it emerged from (his) mouth, the King of Upper and Lower Egypt, Kheperkare, Son of Re, Nektanebo.

[*E. Naville,* The Shrine of Saft el-Henneh and the Land of Goshen *(London, 1888), pl. 3*]

Figure 11.4. Plan of the city of Mendes at its greatest extent (fourth century B.C.).

A. Butic Canal. The best point of junction with the site is on the north side, though a connecting canal could easily have skirted the city on the west side, making for the southern suburb of Thmuis.   B. The Mendesian branch of the Nile.   C. The northwest harbor, with access from the Butic canal.   D. The great eastern harbor, connecting directly with the Nile.   E. The inner harbor, land-locked in the 30th Dynasty.   F. Unidentified temple (unexcavated).   G. The enclosure of Kom el-adhem ("the hill of bones"), ancient name unknown.   H. Tomb of Neferites I (to the west lies the "Hat-mahyet" fish cemetery).   I. The "palace" of the Great Chiefs of the Me, constructed at the end of the 20th Dynasty.   J. The main temple of Ba-neb-djed.   K. "The Mansion of the Rams,"

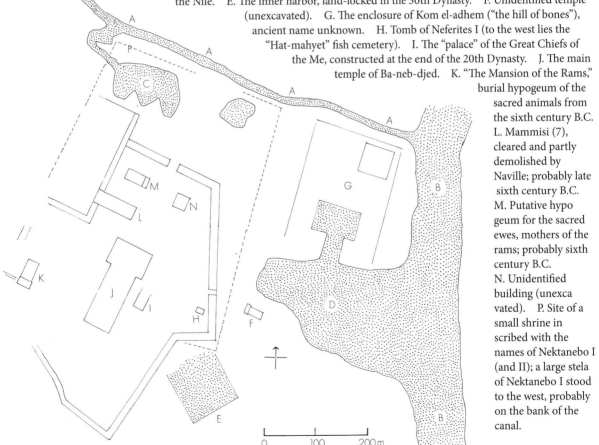

burial hypogeum of the sacred animals from the sixth century B.C. L. Mammisi (7), cleared and partly demolished by Naville; probably late sixth century B.C. M. Putative hypogeum for the sacred ewes, mothers of the rams; probably sixth century B.C. N. Unidentified building (unexcavated).   P. Site of a small shrine inscribed with the names of Nektanebo I (and II); a large stela of Nektanebo I stood to the west, probably on the bank of the canal.

149

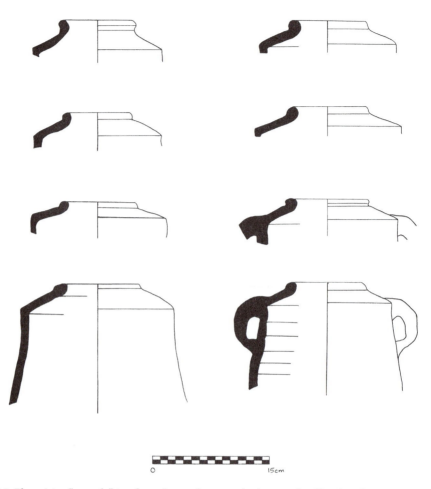

Figure 11.5. Phoenician "torpedo" jars from the northwestern harbor. Made of hard, well-levigated, and well-fired marl clay, these vessels were used to transport oil.

The site admitted access through two points of entry. Travelers from the west would have sailed along a canal, possibly of Saite date, which ran from Buto laterally across the Delta to Mendes. Their first sight of the city, rising modestly from marshes and farmland, would have been of the northwest corner, where a shrine and stela of Nektanebo I welcomed them. Immediately to the south of the shrine (perhaps dedicated to Isis) lay a small harbor approximately 40 × 100 meters in extent, now dried up but still known locally as the "Lake of Crocodiles." Our 2006 excavations revealed that warehouses ran along the southern shore and contained a wealth of storage jars. A preponderance of wine-jars from the Greek islands and oil jars from Phoenicia suggests that perhaps this harbor was the entry point for ships arriving with these cargoes.

Disembarking at a point on the north of the city, they would have passed up a long dromos possibly by way of a pylon in the temenos wall of Nektanebo I. Excavation has not yet been undertaken here, and it remains unclear whether the long approach (some 350 meters) was ever adorned with sphinxes or other decorative pieces in pre-Ptolemaic times. But within one hundred meters of the Ramesside pylon a special *mammisi*, or birth-house, had, as we have seen, been erected on the west side of the dromos to celebrate rites associated with the mythological birth of the god. Travelers from the north or south would undoubtedly have traveled along the Mendesian branch of the Nile which, from the seventh century onward, enjoyed strong discharge, thus easing navigation. Their point of entry lay through a harbor on the east side of the town. As the ship sailed west through this shallow, wedge-shaped tract of water impressive buildings rose on all sides: to the north a cultic installation of unknown use with its own small harbor, dubbed ominously by modern locals *kom el-adhem*, "the hill of bones"; to the west a temple(?) as yet unexcavated; to the south storage rooms and perhaps official residences and offices. Straight ahead at a point where the boat would be beached, beyond additional storage facilities, lay a small temple and then the eastern gate into the temenos of the Ram-god.

The temenos had doubled in size since Ramesside times, expanding hundreds of meters to the north. The old enclosure wall of the New Kingdom had long since fallen into disrepair, and in the Libyan period it had been pitted with poor burials. Nektanebo I replaced it with a new one oriented true north-south. This was hastily erected (as we shall see, in anticipation of a new Persian attack), composed of standard-size mud-bricks forty centimeters long with laterally placed logs for cohesion and occasional seep holes. In the sector opposite Neferites' tomb where our excavations first encountered the wall, we found it over thirteen meters in width and still standing to a height of over 3.5 meters. Between the bricks at the corner of an inset a tiny amulet of Shu with uplifted arms was found inserted, providing the support he had once contributed to the world order when he uplifted the sky!

The Temple of the Ram still stood on its original site, fronted by the Ramesside pylon and forecourt, but beyond the second pylon of Merenptah the central and rear apartments of the temple had been completely renovated. (The initiative was undoubtedly Saite in origin, but the plans continued to be pursued by the 29th and 30th Dynasties.) In this sector the Middle Kingdom structure and those parts dating from the 18th and 22nd Dynasties were razed below ground level, and a large foundation "trough" approximately 60 × 40 meters was excavated down to the Old Kingdom level. On the floor of this foundation trench and penetrating slightly into the earlier levels a drain of interlocking pottery funnels had been laid extending from the center of the court outward toward the east. The external walls were lined with an inner "skin" of quartzite (with some internal features of limestone), on which the relief scenes and inscriptions were carved, and an outer skin of mud-brick. This outer mud-brick skin was in fact a longitu-

Figure 11.6. Eastern face of the Nektanebo temenos wall in the vicinity of Neferites' tomb. The regularly placed holes mark the position of wooden beams, laid laterally in the brickwork to provide cohesion. To the right of the top of the meter pole is a seep hole.

a

b

Figures 11.7a–11.7b. Views of the Nektanebo wall at the point of an inset. The concave "pan-bedding" of the courses of brick is common in all temenos walls, the purpose probably being functional rather than a reflection of religious symbolism.

Figure 11.8. Figurine of the god Shu with arms raised to hold up the sky, found between courses of brick at the corner of the inset.

dinal "coating" to the earlier wall of the Middle Kingdom, which had suffered erosion on its inner face over time. This new inner facing comprised large black bricks, 42 centimeters long, coated with mud plaster on their inner face. Between mud-brick and quartzite, to judge by examples from Buto, a column of sand would have been inserted for purposes of protection against the possible deleterious affects of the Inundation. Into the trough now lined with this refurbished wall of dark mud-brick, fine foundational sand was poured from the eastern and northern sides to a depth of two meters, and on this substantial *soubassement* a floor of stone, approximately 50 centimeters thick, and walls and columns of stone were erected. To judge by surviving drums, the columns were diorite, but the walls that provided the inner "lining" of the mud-brick were quartzite for the most part, with limestone reserved for walls in the southern part of the structure.

Beyond the type of stone involved, it is very difficult to say anything about the internal ground plan of this Late Period temple. The structure was systematically torn asunder in the Middle Ages, a demolition that extended to removing most of the stone and uprooting the foundations of walls. What the Mamluks missed fell to the depredations of treasure-hunters like Edouard Naville in the nineteenth century. Only foundation trenches helped us detect the presence of two pylons, but in the central temple the debris has been churned up to the point that foundation trenches do not easily appear, either in plan or profile.

Figure 11.9. Pottery drain at the bottom of the foundation sand in the court of the temple; Saite period.

Figure 11.10. Fine sand as foundations for the renovated temple of the Saite period.

When we first began systematic excavation of the foundation sand in 1998 we were surprised to encounter lenses of shattered stone penetrating through the sand. Careful scrutiny of these "slots," as we originally called them, both in plan and section, strongly suggested that they followed a rectilinear pattern. On the line along which a slot occurs something had been dug out of the foundation sand, and destruction-shatter had been allowed to pour back into the cavities. By carefully plotting the slots it was clear that we here had the foundation trenches of the walls of the temple interior! It is on the basis of this evidence that the following reconstruction is attempted. Immediately behind the second pylon in all probability lay a hypostyle hall giving onto a centrally placed barque-shrine. Around the latter would have run an ambulatory, off which opened side chambers, some for the preparation of offerings, some for guest cults. These rooms were adorned with columns of diorite holding up a roof of limestone between three and four meters above the floor. The rear wall of this central part of the temple was also of limestone. Around the bottom of the walls of the ambulatory, barque-shrine and side chambers ran a dado of quartzite that Hakoris had decorated with a repeating sequence of upright cartouches bearing his name and prenomen. Some of the walls, also of quartzite, bore relief scenes showing the standard presentation of offerings to the god. There is evidence that an outer walkway ran completely around the temple, and here, on the quartzite surface, ran a long band of text, probably giving the "building history" of the renovations. A surviving block at the southeast corner records a dated event (lost, but probably the resumption of building activities) on the sixth day of the eleventh month of the first year of Nektanebo I (early July 379 B.C.). A similar block at the northwest corner records "His Majesty [. . .] filling the house of his father [Ba-neb-djed with . . .]."

a

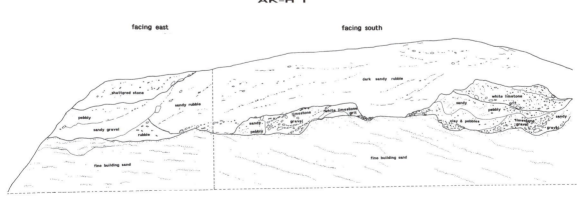

b

Figures 11.11a–11.11b. Section through the Saite foundation sand, showing the "slots."

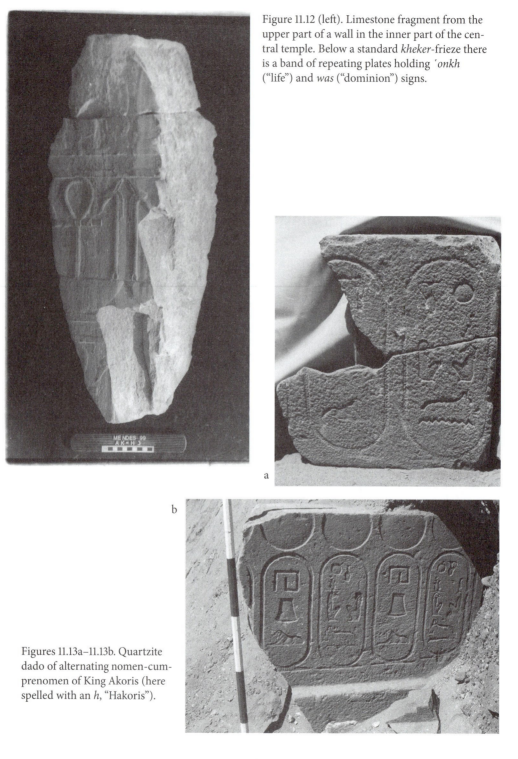

Figure 11.12 (left). Limestone fragment from the upper part of a wall in the inner part of the central temple. Below a standard *kheker*-frieze there is a band of repeating plates holding *'onkh* ("life") and *was* ("dominion") signs.

a

b

Figures 11.13a–11.13b. Quartzite dado of alternating nomen-cum-prenomen of King Akoris (here spelled with an *h*, "Hakoris").

But the greatest feat of building in the temple's history, the results of which even today have left an indelible mark on the site, was the construction of the naos-court. It was Amasis of the 26th Dynasty who conceived and carried through the design of terminating the temple on the south side by a large court, 34 × 28 meters, containing four colossal granite naoi, each hewn from a single block of Aswan granite. These would contain images of the four avatars of the Ram, namely, Re, Shu, Geb, and Osiris. To effect this ambitious construction the Saite architects removed the Middle Kingdom structure (of unknown extent and purpose) that had stood as a southward extension to the temple described above, and dug a very deep foundation of the above dimensions. A sloping ramp somewhat in excess of three meters wide was then cut down from the east through the massive (Old Kingdom?) wall which had once bordered the area on the eastern side; down this ramp were introduced enough limestone blocks, each roughly one meter tall, to provide six courses of foundation. Then the ramp and the southeast corner of the excavation were filled with a packing of coarse, black bricks, and a postern gate was built providing entry to the court from the east. Next the four naoi were floated up a canal, probably extending from the harbor, and dragged into position within the court, one pair facing the other in a square pattern. Mud-brick walls arose on all four sides of the court, but the expanse was too great to be roofed and thus stood open to the sky. Access from the main temple was provided by two side doors, abutting the east and west walls, respectively, and connecting to the outer ambulatory around the temple (see figs. 11.14a–11.14b). Our excavations in 2001 proved that a fourth means of entry had been created on the south side, where a gate approximately 3.8 meters wide and probably founded on a granite threshold had been set athwart the main axis of the temple.

It might have appeared appropriate that this monumental temple was designed to stand amid a maze of storage magazines, houses, and tombs as in the Old Kingdom, but such was no longer the case. Only to the south, within a high, triangular sector of land, approximately 150 meters in length north to south, were houses (for priests?) and storage units still to be found. Elsewhere the house of Ba-neb-djed stood in splendid isolation.

On the far flanks of the temple other structures took shape. Over two hundred meters to the west stood what Ptolemy II was later to call the "Mansion of the Rams," the ceremonial mausoleum for the sacred rams. Probably constructed under Apries by the Nes-Hor mentioned earlier, the Mansion of the Rams opened toward a canal on the west and comprised two distinct parts. On the south stood a columned hall walled with limestone and standing on a sand foundation. Abutting the hall on the north and connected to it by a door and long, lateral passageway lay a series of vaulted, mud-brick cubicles, rising up a low mound. The foundations of this complex of chambers were extremely deep, as there appears to have been in some cases a second tier of cubicles envisaged by the builders. Each of these small chambers originally housed a ram sarcophagus of granite or diorite, fitted with a lid of the same material, and in some cases carved with internal

a

b

Figures 11.14a–11.14b. Views of the single surviving naos of an original four that stood in the southernmost court (the "naos-court") of the Saite temple. The granite "cushion" on which the naos sits represents the original floor level, the six underlying courses of limestone constituting the foundation. None of the walls of the court is still extant, and the eastern postern gate (left of center, above) has been robbed far below the ground level.

a

b

Figures 11.15a–11.15b. View of the south side of the cut where the southeastern postern gate of the naos-court once stood. The sloping ramp built to enable the limestone blocks to be introduced for the foundations is coated with packed limestone chips.

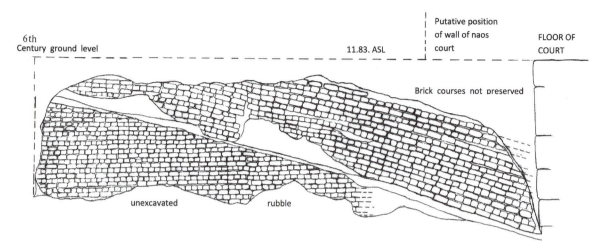

Figure 11.16. The section shows, below the ramp, the earlier (Old or Middle Kingdom) wall of small bricks through which the Saite engineers cut. Once the limestone courses were in place, the ramp was filled over by a packing of large, dark bricks that conformed to the slope of the ramp. The wall of the naos-court, built on this packing, is now gone.

Figure 11.17. Mud-brick foundation of the southern gate of the naos-court, originally providing a base for stone flooring and a granite threshold (the depression against the Middle Kingdom mud-brick on the right).

slots to accommodate the animal's horns. Although the sarcophagi were ostensibly of the same shape and dimensions, detailed observation revealed that no two were exactly alike.

How the cubicles were roofed is difficult to say. The presence of a model of the *pr-nw* shrine, the archetypal Lower Egyptian shrine, found in the excavations makes it tempting to reconstruct a roof patterned after this shape. Altogether fourteen or fifteen granite sarcophagi were identified along with an additional three or four limestone coffins of inferior quality. If Nes-Hor built the mausoleum around 575 B.C., and placing the average life span of a well-kept ram at about fifteen years, we arrive at a date shortly after the middle of the fourth century B.C. as the termination of the series. The significance of this datum will be demonstrated below.

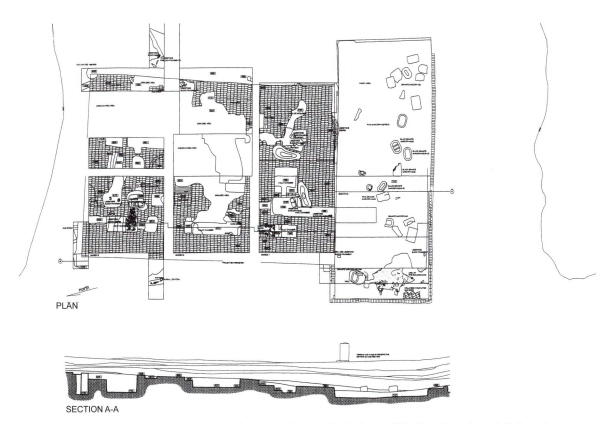

Figure 11.18. Excavation plan of the Mansion of the Rams, showing the (columned?) hall on the right and the burial cubicles encased in mud-brick on the left. In the destruction phase most of the sarcophagi were pulled out of their cubicles and dragged down to the area of the demolished hall. Scale: 1:300.

Figure 11.19. The columned(?) hall at the start of excavations.

Figure 11.20. Mud-brick vaults of two preserved cubicles beginning to appear in excavation.

Figure 11.21. Reconstruction of the Mansion of the Rams, facing east.

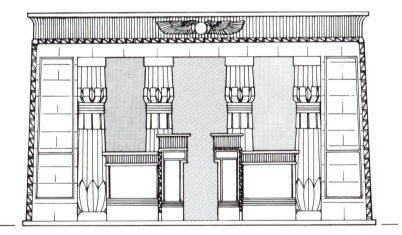

Figure 11.22. Alternate reconstruction of the western approach, with probable intercolumnar screen and winged sun-disc above the door.

Figure 11.24. A sarcophagus still resting in its cubicle.

Figure 11.23 (left). Foundations of the northwest corner of the installation, showing the depth (fourteen courses), which suggests two stories were to be built.

BLACK GRANITE

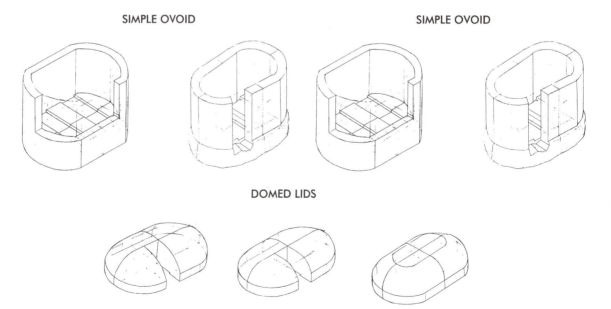

SIMPLE OVOID   SIMPLE OVOID

DOMED LIDS

Figures 11.25 (above, and at right). The variety of shapes and types of stone assumed by the sarcophagi. It seems that those in "black granite" (actually diorite) come first in the series, followed by those in granite. The four limestone sarcophagi come last and date to the early Ptolemaic period.

BLACK GRANITE

BULBOUS INTERIOR

 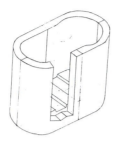

BULBOUS EXTERIOR

 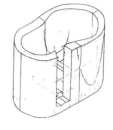

FLANGED INTERIOR

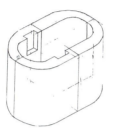 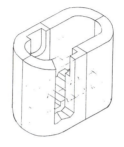

MOTTLED ROSE QUARTZ

BULBOUS EXTERIOR

FLANGED INTERIOR

HIGH DOME LID

 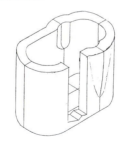 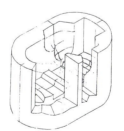 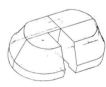

LIMESTONE
FLANGED EXTERIOR

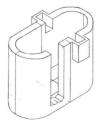 

Figure 11.26. Miniature Lower Egyptian type of shrine.

Figure 11.27. Miniature column capital, of a type known in the 30th Dynasty. This may provide a clue as to the order of column used in the hall.

The Mansion of the Sacred Rams was not the only repository of caprid burials at the site. Approximately 120 meters north of the Temple of the Ram, on the western side of the approach, stood a monumental structure now almost wholly destroyed. This locality appears to be a sort of focal point, a place of origin, for numerous basalt sarcophagi of ovoid shape which today lie scattered in the southwest quadrant of the great northwest enclosure. These have long been known and have been remarked upon by even the earliest travelers. The monumental building has only partly been excavated, but seems from the evidence of satellite imaging to have been fronted by a pylon. The one part of the structure which has been cleared is a sort of hall, approximately 20 × 40 meters, the roof of which was supported by massive granite piers. Into the floor of this hall (now robbed out) pits had been sunk to a depth of one meter, and these conform roughly to the dimensions of the basalt sarcophagi. The latter presumably were let down into the pits, which functioned as below-ground receptacles: their rough sides indicate they never were intended to be seen.

The question arises as to why the cult of the ram enjoyed *two* burying grounds for the beasts. Is the answer to be found in chronology? If Nes-Hor's installation west of the temple lasted until the third quarter of the fourth century B.C., as argued above, then the *second* burying place north of the temple could be understood as the Ptolemaic attempt to revive and promote the Ram-cult through the last three centuries before Christ. One problem, however, should be acknowledged at this point. The basalt sarcophagi are all hollowed out in an oval shape *without* notches to receive the ram's horns; but they could easily receive the mummified body of a ewe! Could it be that in the northern of the two burying places we have a complex devoted to the preparation and burial of the *mothers* of the sacred rams?

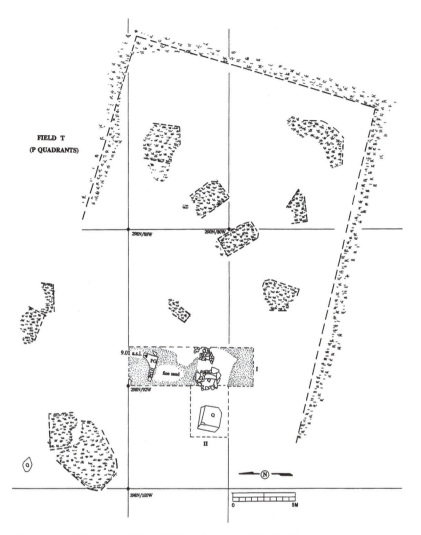

Figure 11.28. Plan of the hall in Field T where, possibly, the diorite sarcophagi were housed. The unexcavated approach lies to the east.

East of the temple, at a distance of only about one hundred meters, lay a Late Period cemetery of uncertain origin. Here was buried the Chamberlain, Scribe of the Treasury, "Separator of the Two Gods," Prophet of Osiris in ʿAnepat, prophet of the ram Ny-su-ba-neb-djed, as well as the Chamberlain and Separator of the Two Gods Wahibre. Although his grave has continued to elude our excavations, the sarcophagus (reused from the New Kingdom) and the shawabtis of the deputy high priest of the Ram, Ny-su-ba-neb-djed, have come to light near the surface (see fig. 11.1). As these worthies all date from the late Saite period through 30th Dynasty, it is reasonable to expect other burials of similar date nearby.

Figure 11.29. Reused New Kingdom sarcophagus.

It was this sector of the enclosure that Neferites I chose for the site of his tomb. Just within the line of the now ruined temenos wall of the New Kingdom, overlooking the harbor, the king laid out a modest mastaba burial. A pit approximately 11 × 19 meters and 1.5 meters deep was sunk in the uneven slope of the tell, filled partly with a sand foundation and limestone filler blocks. In the center of the pit a large, rough-sided limestone monolith was laid down, and a black granite sarcophagus let into the top surface. The sides of the pit were lined with a wall of mud-brick to a height of nearly one meter, and topped from that point upward by a wall of limestone constituting the sides of the mastaba. The roof blocks which have come to light suggest the sometime presence of piers or columns. Access to the grave appears to have been from the north down a gently sloping causeway.

The decoration of the tomb shows that Neferites consciously emulated his forebears of 21st, 22nd, and 26th Dynasties who also constructed their final resting places at Tanis and Sais within the confines of the god's temenos. The external walls, done in sunk relief, showed the king before the ram-headed Ba-neb-djed in his four avatars, while decoration of the interior displayed, inter alia, vignettes taken from the Underworld Books, famous from the Valley of the Kings. Architraves, still daubed with masons' marks, bore his epithets "beloved of the gods" and "founder of the Two Lands." To adorn the approaches to his tomb the king transported several statues of private individuals from the temple, and lined up a number of "fish-stelae" of the late New Kingdom which had originally honored Ḥat-meḥyet. While after his death others may have added commemorative pieces to the complex—his grandson a stela, Nektanebo a small statue—nothing could conceal the essential poverty of this "royal" monument. There simply was neither time nor inclination to celebrate a mere warlord in the true fashion of a monarch.

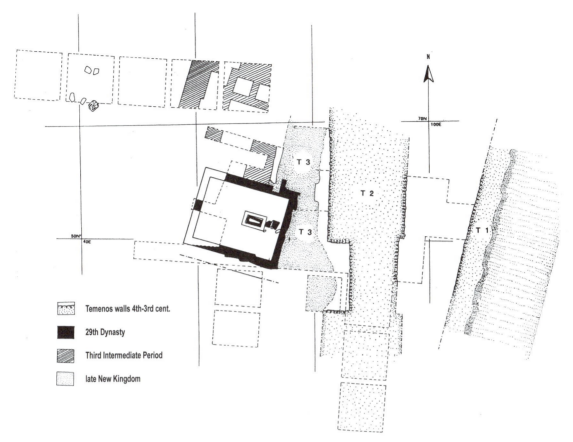

Figure 11.30. Plan of Neferites I's tomb, set into the earlier slope of the fish votives and partly over the demolished wall of the late New Kingdom (T3). T2 represents the line of the wall of Nektanebo I, and T1 the Ptolemaic wall.

Figure 11.31. The sarcophagus of Neferites I before excavation.

Figure 11.32. The burial chamber of Neferites I, viewed from the east.

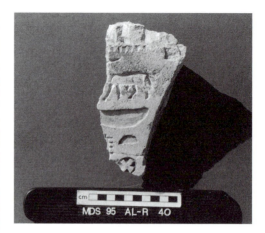

Figure 11.34. "The Ram, the Lord of Djedet."

Figure 11.33. Fragment of limestone relief showing the horn of the avatar of the Ram known as "the living soul of Re."

Figure 11.36. Vulture goddess, with *khu*-fan in her claw, extending her wings above the king.

Figure 11.35. Plumes and sun-disc surmounting the vertical, alternating cartouches of Neferites I.

Figure 11.37. The night-barque of the sun, with names of part of the crew: from the right, *Wep-wawet*, "the Trailblazer"; *Nebt-weya*, "Mistress of the Ship"; *Hor-hekenu*, "Horus the Jubilant"; *Hu*, "(Divine) Utterance."

Figure 11.38. Head of a priest.

Figure 11.39. Architrave with the epithet "Beloved of the Gods," one of the appellatives of Neferites I.

Figure 11.40. Pilaster(?) fragment with the epithet "Founder of the Two Lands," one of the appellatives of Neferites I.

Figure 11.41. So-called Sacred Lake, southeast of the main temple.

South and southeast of the great temenos of the Ram-god described above, little archaeological work has as yet been attempted. Here to the south a rectilinear depression has all the earmarks of a vast water-basin paralleled, again to the south, by a smaller depression. Flanking the basin on the east a prominent ridge tails away in a southeasterly direction and today forms the south side of the harbor. It is tempting to postulate a connection between the harbor and the basin through a low-lying gap between the ridge and the southeast corner of the temenos. Beyond basin and ridge the terrain flattens out until, at the southern tip of the present, northern tell, it rises again into a sizable rectilinear mound. Survey of this mound and a swath of land to its north yielded industrial sherds from the fourth to third centuries B.C.

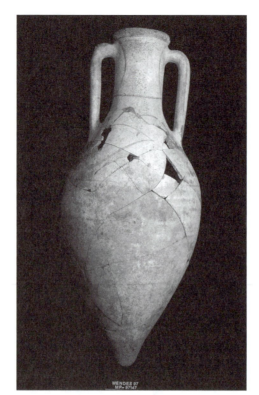

Figure 11.42. Samian amphora, c. 575 B.C.

Preliminary work has made certain conclusions probable. Karen Wilson in her excavations of 1979–80 discovered that the ridge aforesaid was made up of massive artificial fill laid down during the Saite period, possibly dated to the reign of Amasis. Upon this a series of buildings had been constructed, the exact purpose of which remains to be determined. Our excavations in 1997 in the area of the basin (wrongly dubbed the "Sacred Lake") proved that it had been an artificial, square anchorage—perhaps the *'agn* of Ptolemy—97.5 meters on a side, with mud-brick edges capped with limestone. Access to the basin was had originally by means of a narrow gap at its northern corner, communicating with the outer harbor; but this had been filled in about the same time that the ridge was created and covered with a platform of mud-brick on which a building had been erected. This structure, called by us the House of Amulets because of the hundreds of faïence talismans found within its rooms, could be roughly dated by a reused Samian amphora of approximately 575 B.C. let into the floor. Once this massive fill had been laid down by the Saites—we have had occasion to examine similar fills in association with Amasis's naos-court—it is unclear how ships gained access to the basin. Perhaps there is a low-lying gap unexcavated on the west side, where the terrain describes a prominent depression.

Both archaeological and textual evidence concur in support of the thesis that Mendes from the seventh through fourth centuries B.C. enjoyed the status of riverine harbor and international emporium. The strong discharge during this time span of the Mendesian branch of the Nile made the city easily accessible from the Mediterranean, as well as from Upper Egypt. Everywhere in the units under excavation vast quantities of "East Greek" pottery have been unearthed, signaling a lively trade with the islands of Samos, Thasos, and Cnidos, while equal quantities of the small amphorae from Phoenicia, "Phoenician crisp torpedo jars," bear witness to commercial connections with the Levantine coast (see fig. 11.5). Interestingly enough, a recently identified customs officer's logbook which has survived from the year 475 B.C. specifies ships entering an unnamed Egyptian port (Memphis?) as coming from Greece and Phoenicia. While the commodities traded in this case appear to be wood and natron, our ceramic evidence suggests that at times oils and unguents topped the list of trade items.

In this regard mention must be made of a large and distinctive type of amphora that is ubiquitous in the great eastern harbor at Mendes. This is the "basket-handle" jar, a sturdy, thick-walled vessel of marl, standing approximately 1.5 meters tall. It derives its name from the large loop handles that rise on both sides of the neck several centimeters above the level of the rim, undoubtedly to enable the porters to carry the heavy object by means of a pole thrust through the loops. Basket-handle jars were manufactured at several places throughout the Levant during the seventh to fourth centuries B.C., but, in spite of the frequency with which they appear in the Mendes archaeological record (especially in the harbor), element analysis has proven that they were not made there. Cyrenaica along the North African coast seems to have been the point of manufacture for the Mendesian vessels, whence they were shipped to the Delta full of a needed commodity. The latter can only have been oil, probably from the *balanos*-tree prevalent in ancient times in Upper Egypt and the oases.

The reason for the need of such quantities of oil was the perfume industry in Mendes. The city was justly famous as the manufacturing center for the most expensive and most fragrant scent known in Egypt and the Mediterranean world at large to which it was exported down into Roman times in lead-lined containers. Pliny and Dioscorides both describe in some detail the formula and the ingredients involved. To date, however, the "factory" site at Tel er-Rub'a has not been identified, although unguent vessels are common. Presumably, because of the weight of the oil needed the site cannot have been too far removed from the eastern harbor.

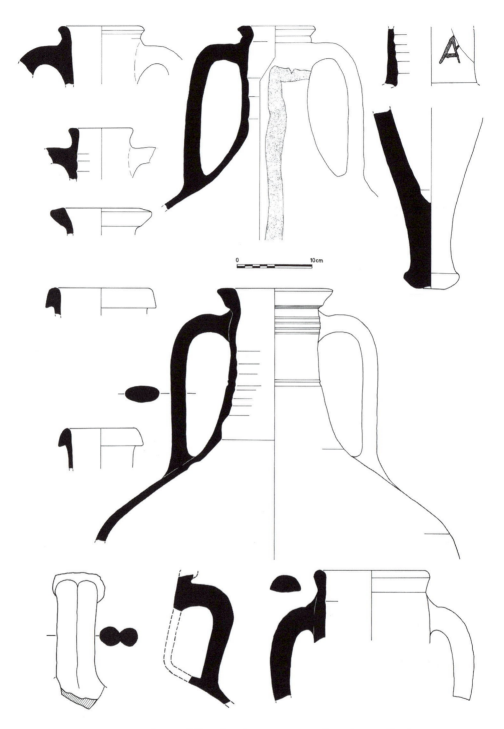

Figure 11.43. East Greek ware, fifth to fourth centuries B.C., from the great harbor.

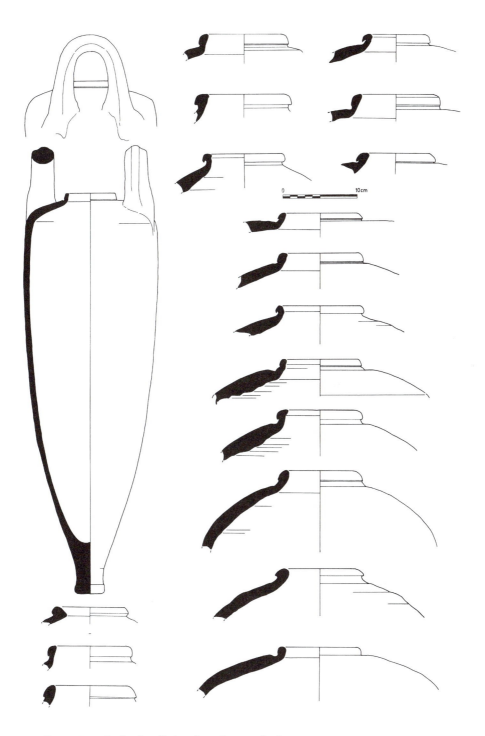

Figure 11.44. Basket-handle jars from the great harbor.

11.4 Mendesian Perfume

Certain places produce the best perfumes . . . of henna the Egyptian is judged the best, next to it being the Cyprian and the Phoenician. . . . [T]he metopion *and the Mendesian are made best in Egypt, and are made from the oil obtained from bitter almonds.*

[*Athenaeus vii.15.688*]

Another local product bearing the denomination "Mendesian" was wine. This may have been close to what Pliny calls "Sebennys"-wine, clearly taking its appellation from the neighboring town of Sebennytos. Pliny describes it as a sweet wine with laxative qualities made from grapes originally imported from Thasos.

The distribution of these industries over the site is partly illumined by the placement of harbors. Recent excavations have brought three harbors to light. Besides the great eastern harbor mentioned above, the smaller northwestern harbor, apparently opening off the Butic canal, revealed warehouses well stocked with Phoenician and Egyptian storage jars but lacking basket-handle jars. A similar absence of such large amphorae was detected in the so-called Sacred Lake, the inner, rectilinear body of water described above, lined with warehouses containing Phoenician and East Greek wares. To date, however, no "factory" installations have been unearthed in any of these areas.

Mendes was now one of the largest cities in the Delta—indeed, in all Egypt. Sometime in the first half of the first millennium B.C. a faubourg had grown up at the southern end of the site, reclaimed from the inundation as "new land" (Egyptian *Tʒ-mʒwt*) and therefore called "Thmuis." Although linked to the main site by proximity and political dependence, Thmuis was separated from it by the river and developed over time as a separate municipal entity. Nonetheless, when linked with its older parent, the suburb gave to the city an overall length in excess of three kilometers and contributed to the glory of Egypt's capital.

At the turn of the twentieth century a tomb was uncovered at Tel er-Rub'a under what appear to be some ancient houses (exact location unfortunately unknown, but probably east of the temple). Stone orthostats and roofing blocks adorned the spacious subterranean installation, and the intact interments were accompanied by hundreds of shawabtis and sundry gold objects. The name of the principal occupant appeared on the shawabtis as Ny-su-ba-neb-djed (Greek "Smendes") with the titles of "Chamberlain, He-Who-Separates-the-Two-Gods, Priest of Osiris in *Anepat*, Scribe of the God's Book,

11.5 Ny-su-ba-neb-djed

[. . . an offering-which-the-king-gives(?) to(?)] Ba-neb-djed, the great living god of Re, the fornicating "bull" who mounts the beauties! May he allow thy name to be for ever in his temple, and a good memory of thee in the "Palace" with the priests, after [. . .] , for the ku *of the Chamberlain-in-Chief, He-Who-Separates-the-Two-Gods, Priest of Osiris in Djedet, Overseer of the We'eb-Priests of Sakhmet in the Mendesian township, Scribe of the God's-Book of the Ram, Count-Archbishop in the Mendesian township, Priest of the Ram and, Ḥȝt-mḥyt and of the Greater and Lesser Ennead who are in Djed[et, (Personal Name) son of . . .]*

[Overseer of the We'eb-Priests of Sa]khmet in the Mendesian township, Scribe of the God's-Book of the Ram, Ny-su-ba-neb-djed, offspring of the Sistrum-Player of the Ram, Tshentoohe, justified. He says: "O priests, divine fathers and functioning(?) we'eb-priests who may enter the temple of Ba-neb-djed, the great living god of Re, the bai *of Re, your resplendent(?) master (Osiris?) shall love and favor you, he in whose presence offering is made(?) . . . your son(s) shall abide upon your seats, your name shall last for ever and not pass into oblivion for aye! as ye recount my name and (my) goodness before the Ram of Re at his offering-(?) and resting-place(?) . . . I was a useful servant for my lord.*

[one who . . .] . . . , a cauldron(?), . . . an offering table(?) and cups; who placed portable libation vessels in the holy place; who knows all the mysteries in the House of the Ram, privy to the secrets of his visible(?) form(?); one who never comes out and tells what he has seen; who has access to the harim-chambers, who knows the holy essences of the Mansion of the Rams, and all the hidden accoutrements in Djedet. I am schooled in the "Horizon" of the Ram, alert when it comes to installing the great ram, door-opener in his great shrine, who sees the Great Sun-Disc in his sktt-*barque, counsellor of the Ram of Re.*

[Mendes 5 M 30; unpublished statue inscription, early fourth century B.C.]

Overseer of the *We'eb*-Priests of Sakhmet in the Mendesian Township, and Priest of the Ram." Thus was brought to light the burial(s) of a priestly family that was to dominate the clergy of Mendes during the 29th and 30th Dynasties.

Further light was shed in 1977 by the discovery of four statues (one anepigraphic) in the destruction debris of the tomb of Neferites I by the New York University expedition. Two belonged to Saite worthies (Ahmose [see above] and Wahibre-em-akhet), but the third, a naophorous statue, was the likeness of the father of Ny-su-ba-neb-djed, owner of the tomb alluded to above. The latter commemorates himself, "his eldest(?) son, whom he loves," on a text below the small naos the statue is proffering, while three col-

11.6 A Saite Worthy Honors the Ram

Revered before Ba-neb-djed, the "Chamberlain-Priest," He-Who-Separates-the-Two-Gods, Prophet of the Ram, Hat-mehyet and the Greater and Lesser Enneads, the Chief We'eb-Priest [who kn]ows his duty . . . Nes-usert, called Wahibre. . . . He says: "O Ram of [Re], Ram of the Great One, Ram of Shu, Ram of Earth! Four faces on a single neck! O entombed rams within the Mansion of the Rams! (Ye for whom) the Nile emerges from the cavern of Elephantine that the fields may sparkle with 'clothing' (of herbage), that beasts may foal in timely season, their sustenance being on the earth, and that Re rises and Atum sets, so as not to impair their offerings day and night! Remember ye my name specifically when offering is made to your kus! Grant ye me an offering at the moment of requital, given at your volition, (and also) a good burial after old age. May I go about as I wish without being blocked at the gates. . . . O ye that go upstream and downstream to see the great rams, thank god for this (my) statue."
[M. Burchardt, "Ein saitischer Statuensockel in Stockholm," ZÄS 47 (1910), 111–15]

umns of text on the back-pillar are given over to the father. The statue was probably once set up in the ambulatory of the main temple, whence it was dragged by the Persians and cast into the destroyed royal tomb. The contents (see sidebar 11.5) illustrate the passage of sacerdotal power into the hands of a fourth-century clergy, divorced from the associated temporal authority the Saite dignitaries of the sixth century had enjoyed in the city. As such it reflects the confidence in religious office, pride in family, and social aspirations within a clerical context of a class that truly interceded between god and man. And what a god it was, embodiment of primordial power and soteriological strength!

With the "Ram of Rams, Ruler of Rulers, King of the Gods, Ba-neb-djed" as resident patron, how could the city ever again suffer adversity?

Chapter Twelve

The Great Disaster

....

Although worsted and driven out in 404 B.C. and again in 385 B.C., the Persians had never given up their resolve to bring recalcitrant Egypt to heel. Theirs was the power of moral suasion. The Saites had contravened international accords, and Cambyses had lawfully terminated their regime. Amyrtaeus and Neferites had rebelled against legally constituted authority and had ipso facto placed themselves outside the law. The Great King had every right to effect their punishment by all means available. The trouble was that he found himself unable to carry through his punitive purpose. The fiascoes into which the attempted invasions during the reigns of Neferites I and Akoris had degenerated not only discouraged the Persian administration but also lent an aspect of ineptness to the once mighty war machine of the Persian Empire in foreign eyes.

Nor could the Great King even capitalize on the occasional moments of weakness among his enemies. The family of Mendesian warlords which passes for the 29th Dynasty suffered a crisis in the summer of 380 B.C. when the death of Akoris threw up two ephemeral successors who passed from the scene quickly, in all probability through family coups. It was now the turn of another branch of the family, and by the early winter of that year Nektanebo (I), a cousin of Akoris, had seized the throne and ensconced himself in the neighboring city of Sebennytos, although he still honored Mendes his native town by adding to the Temple of the Ram. Slow to act, the likable but ineffective Artaxerxes II who had for six years failed to act when the Peace of Antalcidas with the Greeks (386 B.C.) had freed his hands dithered for another six years, giving the impression perhaps of a renunciation of the Persian claim to northeast Africa. The hiatus gave Egypt a breathing space and a chance to restore itself.

The tense international situation from 400 to 380 B.C. coupled with the unstable nature of the 29th Dynasty had blocked internal improvement, but under Nektanebo I the block was removed and energies released toward socioeconomic strengthening. The commercial policies set on foot by the Saite kings of the 26th Dynasty had continued to exert an influence on the Egyptian economy over a century after the last Saite had left the scene; not even the brief attempt of Cambyses and Darius I to tap Egypt's riches could cause a significant downturn. Although as in earlier times the king of Egypt held discretionary powers over the disposal of Egypt's wealth, in fact the current monarchy, little

Figure 12.1. Nektanebo I in red crown of Lower Egypt, east temple, Karnak.

more than a military junta, lacked the legitimacy and authority to ride roughshod over other interest groups. It is to Nektanebo's credit that he realized this and resorted to the age-old process of "equalization payments." The great corporate group which held the most power, the priesthood, benefited most. Endowments were increased and custom dues, exacted at the trade ports of Naukratis and Sais, channeled to temple coffers. In particular Nektanebo inaugurated a program of temple rebuilding throughout the land, adding to and restoring a number of shrines, but also razing and building afresh in many cases. Did anyone realize that this was to be the last comprehensive construction project of native initiative?

As part of the building program Nektanebo included a thorough program of temenos wall construction. Probably every major city in Egypt benefited in this, although such walls survive in whole or in part in only a handful of Egyptian cities, such as Elkab, Thebes, and (now) Mendes. Nektanebo, clearly mindful of the potential of renewed Persian attacks, intended these circumvallations to provide protection for the central areas of the cities in which the major shrines were located. At Thebes the wall was built of crude mud-bricks which included myriad potsherds as keying material, and surrounded the temples of Amun and Ptah, the Osirian temples, and the Khonsu temple, as well as priests' houses. At Mendes we uncovered the only surviving section of Nektanebo's wall due east of the tomb of Neferites. At this point it was thirteen meters thick and rose to a height of approximately 3.5 meters. Wooden beams had been driven into the brickwork to provide strength, and an occasional seep hole filled with limestone chips helped provide runoff in occasional rainstorms (see figs. 11.6–11.8).

In spite of the growing strength manifest in the country, Egypt was not to be spared further Persian attacks. In the mid-370s Artaxerxes commissioned the satrap Pharnabazos to undertake an invasion, and to that end a force of approximately two hundred thousand along with a fleet of six hundred ships began assembling on the Phoenician coast. With the addition of a Greek mercenary force under the command of the Athenian general Iphicrates, Pharnabazos started moving his forces down the coast in May 373 B.C. Nektanebo, anticipating the invasion, however, had so strongly fortified Pelusium and the Pelusiac mouth of the Nile that Pharnabazos was completely deterred and did not risk a frontal attack. After some hesitation he embarked and made for the mouth of the Mendesian branch where he overwhelmed the garrison of the small fortress guarding the entry. Now he hesitated again. Iphicrates urged a rapid assault upriver on the capital Memphis which, intelligence had it, was undefended. But now the annual inundation was rising, and any movement was difficult. Moreover the Egyptian forces had regrouped and were attacking the beachhead with redoubled efforts. By August the situation was desperate and there was nothing for it but to evacuate the troops. Thoroughly beaten by a combination of nature and Egyptian determination, Pharnabazos retreated into Asia, quarreling all the while with the disaffected Iphicrates. One year later a half-hearted attempt was made to remount the attack, but logistics and the plague made this impossible.

In a real sense Nektanebo had beaten the odds. He had proven a successful tactician on the battlefield, and the Egyptian troops had displayed a true élan vital. On the monuments he erected after his victory he is robustly proclaimed as the "defender of Egypt," an appellative that no one could deny.

For the last decade of his life Nektanebo enjoyed the peace brought by total victory. He could now continue the building program and arrange for the succession. He associated his eldest son, Tachos, with him as regent, and made a second son, Tja-hap-emmaw, a general. His nephew Ny-su-ba-neb-djed was also created a general and given the office of mayor of Sebennytos. Also present in the entourage was his grandson, offspring of Tja-hap-emmaw, called Nakht-hor-kheb and later to be crowned as Nektanebo II.

In spite of Artaxerxes II's profession in the aftermath of the fiasco of 373 that he would continue to prepare for hostilities with Egypt, no one, least of all the Persians themselves, was deceived. By 363 B.C. several Persian satraps in Asia Minor were in revolt, and the Greek cities were considering aid. Small wonder that Egypt too should consider entering the fray, now that it appeared that the Persian Empire was on the brink of collapse.

In 362 B.C. Nektanebo I died and his son Tachos assumed full control of the government. Tachos appears to have been a headstrong and volatile individual, lacking his father's perspicacity and strategic sense. Not only did he send money to the rebels (which, in the event, never arrived), but he also set about to carry the war on to Asian soil. To the great dismay of the Egyptians at large, Tachos increased taxes, suspended temple revenues, and with the money thus realized raised a force of eighty thousand men and two hundred ships. Athens and Sparta lent the generals Chabrias and Agesilaus along with ten thousand mercenaries. Ignoring the sage advice of old Chabrias, Tachos remained determined to lead the expeditionary force himself and, in spring of 360 B.C., crossed the frontier into Asia. Unopposed, the Egyptians soon found themselves in Phoenicia from which Tachos dispatched his nephew Nakht-hor-hebef with troops to reduce inner Syria. But morale was low, and unrest spread rapidly through the army. At home, too, people took an unsympathetic view of this attempt by Tachos to revive the glories of an imperial past, and soon Tja-hap-emmaw, Tachos's younger brother who had been left in charge of Egypt, wrote to his son Nakht-hor-hebef urging him to revolt. Betrayed also by Agesilaus and deserted by his troops, Tachos took to flight and threw himself on the mercy of the Persians. Nakht-hor-hebef, now acknowledged as king at least by the army, returned to Egypt accompanied by Agesilaus and the Greek mercenaries (359 B.C.).

The spate of backstabbing and treachery to which Tachos's actions had given rise could have proved a godsend to the Persians, but the empire had been weakened to the point that the Great King could not take advantage of it. Moreover, in the winter of

359–358 B.C. Artaxerxes II finally died, thus rendering the future course of Persian policy uncertain. His successor, Ochus or Artaxerxes III, continued at least initially to cast his anxious gaze toward Asia Minor where rebellion continued.

Tja-hap-emmaw's betrayal of his brother had opened a Pandora's box among the extended family of Neferites I. Upon his arrival in Egypt Nakht-hor-hebef, or Nektanebo II as we shall now call him, met armed resistance from someone else who claimed the kingship. We know this pretender only through the appellation "the Mendesian" (hardly surprising, in that as the eventual loser his name was undoubtedly expunged from all monuments), but it is beyond question that he was a member of the ruling house, perhaps a disaffected son or nephew of Nektanebo I or Tachos. His status in the community and his power and determination are shown by his ability to raise a force of several thousand men and send Nektanebo and Agesilaus fleeing into an unnamed fortified city. It would be interesting to learn the name and location of this fortification. One might presume that a returning member of the 30th Dynasty would make for Sebennytos, where his cousin, general Ny-su-ba-neb-djed, was in charge. But Plutarch's account suggests desperation, if not panic, attended the discovery of an armed pretender; under these conditions Nektanebo may have made for the closest haven. There are several forts, mentioned in inscriptions and papyri, within the Mendesian township, and it may have been into one of these that the Greeks were bottled up. That two waterways lying close to one another should have been a feature of the landscape proves nothing beyond a Delta setting.

What happened next is open to question. The siege with the digging of a fosse, the panic of Nektanebo in contrast to the level-headedness of Agesilaus, the outrage of the Greeks at being faced with a ragtag Egyptian army of tradesmen, the skillful tactics and surprise sally of the Greeks—all this smacks of didactic tropes designed to point up the superiority of Greeks vis-à-vis barbarians. That Nektanebo worsted the pretender with the help of Agesilaus is beyond doubt, but the exact circumstances may never be known.

The character of Nektanebo II crystallizes in the Greek accounts of the period. He was immature, but this could be put down to his youth. Less easy to condone was his arrogance and bluffness when things were going well; his cravenness in the face of adversity. A man who panicked easily was capable only of "mindless" acts, as the Greeks who knew him opined. Because of this, Nektanebo was, of all his family, the least suited to lead Egypt in the crisis that would eventually come.

At first Egypt continued to prosper under the new monarch. The program of temple building continued unabated, and the treasury continued to amass wealth. In his second year the obsequies for the Apis occasioned the epithet "beloved of the living Apis, Ptah redivivus"; and in his fifth year quarries were opened at Abydos and in the Wady Hammamat. Especially favored by the king was the town of Per-hebyet, just north of Sebennytos, where Nektanebo may have been born—he is at least named after the local god Horus who was worshiped there. He planned and began the construction of a beautiful temple to Isis in the town, undoubtedly replacing an earlier building, and this was still in the process of construction when his reign came to its tragic end. By contrast, Mendes received no new buildings nor embellishments to old. Perhaps the memory of the "Mendesian pretender" still weighed heavily upon him.

The new Great King of Persia, from spring 358 B.C., Artaxerxes III, provides both a comparison and a contrast to his contemporary Nektanebo II. He was not a trained warrior and had only a rudimentary grasp of what to do on the battlefield; and, like Nektanebo, he could be arrogant and cruel. But where Nektanebo was quixotic, superficial, and volatile, Artaxerxes III looked far afield to ultimate goals; where Nektanebo panicked easily, the Great King was not easily frightened but showed dogged determination to win through. To boot, he seems to have been a better judge of character than the Egyptian.

To begin with, things did not go well for Persia. In spite of their total ineffectiveness in carrying war to the Nile, the Persian administration continued to insist, as it had done since the days of Neferites I, that it was still preparing for the final showdown. Artaxerxes must have fallen in with longstanding plans and authorized a renewed attack upon the Delta. In 351 B.C. a force of unknown size set off across the desert heading for Pelusium, but again the Egyptians were prepared. One Nektanebo, a young general of promise, had been assigned to the eastern frontier. As a member of the Dynastic family junta—he was the great-grandson of the sister of Nektanebo I—General Nektanebo might have been expected to fare no better than any other of the mediocrities of his clan. But his titles suggest otherwise. He was appointed "Generalissimo of His Majesty's army, Leader of Leaders, Mayor in Sile, Yamet and Sebennytos, supervising Asiatics in the 'Front-of-the-East.'" In other words, he was commander-in-chief posted to the eastern frontier of the Delta, in anticipation of the Persian attack. Once again things went dreadfully wrong for the Persians. No classical author provides any details, but Nektanebo in his autobiography boasts that he was "one who fights for Egypt . . . champion of the Nile-land . . . who repulsed the foreign countries for the Lord of the Two Lands!"

Worse was to follow. As the Persian forces retreated back into Asia, Tennes, the king of Sidon, led a revolt against Persia that eventually engulfed all of Phoenicia and Cyprus. Showing for once an uncharacteristic astuteness, Nektanebo II lent aid to the rebels and even sent four thousand Greek mercenaries. For the time being it appeared that Persia was about to collapse. Such a judgment, however, would not have reckoned with the resilience of Artaxerxes. Capitalizing on the surprising defection of Tennes himself, who promised to betray his own city, the Persians marched against Sidon in the spring of 345 B.C. and overwhelmed it in the summer. All Phoenicia surrendered forthwith, and a follow-up move on Egypt seemed imminent. Through a combination of blandishments and professions of friendship, Artaxerxes won over several Greek cities that promptly dispatched mercenaries to the Great King's host. Almost overnight the tide had turned. The Arabs and the Idumaeans were won over, and the Negeb and perhaps Judaea occupied by garrisons. While the expeditionary forces Artaxerxes commanded are wholly inflated in classical sources, it cannot be doubted that they were far larger than those the Egyptians had called up. In spite of the fact that part of the Persian army was lost in the quicksand bordering Lake Bardawil, the number of troops which hove into view in early July 343 B.C. completely dismayed the defenders on the walls of Pelusium.

And now things began to go wrong for the Egyptian side. Unlike his grandfather, who had been circumspect enough to take advice from his Greek mentors, the head-strong Nektanebo II decided to assume command of all his forces, Greeks as well as Libyans and Egyptians. Part of the mercenary force serving Artaxerxes III entered surreptitiously into a canal west of Pelusium and made camp in a sheltered spot. In spite of the presence of Greek mercenaries in the local Egyptian garrison, the latter was routed in a hard-fought encounter. Instead of standing firm and consolidating his forces, Nektanebo immediately panicked and, contemned by his troops, beat a hasty retreat with a few followers to Memphis. Deserted by their commander, the garrison of Pelusium after a short siege capitulated, and the Persian host began to move down the eastern fringe of the Delta. When the great city of Bubastis fell, Nektanebo panicked a second time and fled south into the Sudan, never to be seen again. Yielding to a promise of leniency promulgated by Artaxerxes, the cities of the Delta began to open their gates.

And so the Persians came back to Mendes. One can only imagine the terror of the inhabitants as the will to resist collapsed. The harbor was occupied, the northern pylon gates opened, and the barbarian horde with strange bulbous headdresses, trousers, and boots began to swarm into the northwestern enclosure.

Our excavations have now given the lie to the canard that the second Persian occupation was benign and devoid of reprisals. The small limestone shrine of Nektanebo I and II which stood in the extreme northwest corner of the city was fired then smashed to pieces, and the destruction pushed into the canal. The large stela of Nektanebo I in the same area suffered a like fate. The warehouses around the inner harbor were destroyed, along with the House of Amulets in the gap, and the storage areas in the outer harbor leveled. The cemetery of the Saite period due east of the temple was uprooted, and sar-

a

Figures 12.2a–12.2b. Six "falls" of fragments from the destruction of Neferites I's tomb, thrown eastward by the Persians over the Nektanebo wall (view looking south). The intervening stria of gritty earth contained a wealth of fifth- to fourth-century pottery (view looking south).

b

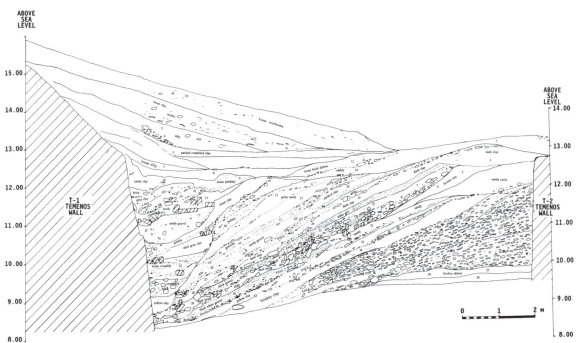

Figure 12.3. Section drawing through the destruction debris of Neferites' tomb. The wall labeled T1 on the left is the later Ptolemaic wall; that on the right (T2) is the wall of Nektanebo I.

cophagi ripped out and their contents destroyed. The Mansion of the Rams and the temple proper undoubtedly were ravaged, but signs of vandalism are difficult to detect, as both were repaired within the succeeding decades.

The "Libyan Palace" did not escape the destruction. The original structure had been partly fired and then abandoned around the time of the Assyrian invasion; and in early Saite times—a sealing of Necho I (died 664 B.C.) seems to clinch the date—the site was rebuilt on a much smaller scale. A small block of rooms with partly curvilinear walls on the exterior arose in the center of the old palace, perhaps partly in the form of a fortified tower. At the time of the Persian invasion someone had piled masses of pottery, over eight hundred kilograms to be precise, into a narrow, plastered corridor at the summit of the building. The *favissa* shows all the earmarks of the kitchen and dining ware of an establishment of some size (the temple perhaps?): long-necked jars, hundreds of conical drinking cups, everting bowls, hole-mouth store-jars, platters for bread making, pilgrim flasks, carinated footed offering cups, and cauldrons. Could some priest in the throes of panic brought on by the sight of the enemy have packed the area with temple paraphernalia for safekeeping? If this had been the motive, it was to be frustrated. The Persians broke into the structure, added combustible material to the pile, and fired the whole in a great conflagration.

The most spectacular act of vandalism was reserved for the tomb of Neferites I, that hated freedom fighter—the Persians would undoubtedly have called him a terrorist—who sixty years before had helped rid Egypt of all trace of the Persians. The roofing blocks were removed, smashed to small pieces, and hurled eastward over the adjacent Nektanebo temenos wall, where they cascaded in three superimposed "falls," each separated from the other by thin lenses of earth. The walls were next dismantled, the reliefs smashed, and the pieces sent to follow the roofing fragments. Superimposed upon the three earlier falls we found three additional ones containing over nine hundred fragments of relief. The burial chamber was then entered, the sarcophagus lid ripped off and left to lie in two pieces at the foot end, and the coffin and mummy destroyed. Even the mud-brick walls of the subterranean foundation were disturbed, and the limestone fill-blocks they had circumscribed were taken away. Then the entire temenos wall Nektanebo had erected around the tomb and temple was leveled to the ground, except in the area due east of the royal tomb where the destruction debris had been thrown and now constituted a mound reaching to the summit of the wall. The final resting place of Neferites was now a pit in the earth that filled with water and became a pool every inundation.

Chapter Thirteen

Dusk and Darkness

THE END OF MENDES

· ·

For about twenty summers the pit marking Neferites' resting place filled and drained, as the Nile flood took its toll. (Our excavations discovered approximately that number of stria in the pit, consisting of alternating bands of fine silt and fine gravel.) The settlement had clearly suffered a traumatic shock and town life was at a low ebb. What was the extent of the damage?

Apart from the tomb of Neferites I, where the destruction was dramatic, it is difficult to assess the scope of Persian reprisals. It is inconceivable that the temple should have escaped unscathed, but it must be admitted that the reliefs and inscriptions show no signs whatever of having been vandalized. Perhaps the scarcity of royal statuary of the 29th and 30th Dynasties finds an explanation in Persian vindictive acts; but beyond removing and destroying these memorials the invaders do not appear to have gone to extremes. A similar uncertainty surrounds the treatment meted out to the Mansion of the Rams to the west of the temple. The presence of late Roman pottery here and the reuse of the hypogeum by Christians undoubtedly accounts for the extensive destruction one sees today. But it is not beyond the realm of possibility that the Persians, by religious inclination predisposed to despise animal worship, hauled at least some of the ram mummies out of their sarcophagi and destroyed them. This animus against polytheism accounts for an act of unbridled meanness that Mendes, along with all the other cities of Egypt, undoubtedly suffered: the confiscation of cult paraphernalia. Bagoas, eunuch and right-hand lackey of Artaxerxes, collected all the sacred books from the temple libraries and all implements necessary for worship and carted them away into Asia. When the priests requested their return, he obliged them to buy them back; but vast quantities of this material still remained in Asia as late as Ptolemy's arrival on the scene at the end of the century.

In spite of the paucity of the evidence, there was sufficient depredation perpetrated against the city that fifty years later a witness could still speak of the "destruction the rebellious foreigners had wrought" which was still visible. The great families had been decimated; there was no one around to underwrite reconstruction. The extended family of

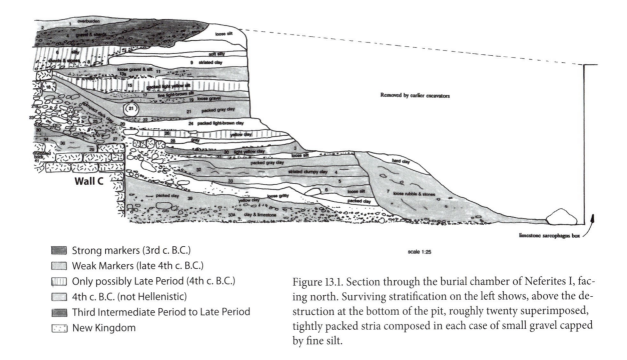

Strong markers (3rd c. B.C.)
Weak Markers (late 4th c. B.C.)
Only possibly Late Period (4th c. B.C.)
4th c. B.C. (not Hellenistic)
Third Intermediate Period to Late Period
New Kingdom

Figure 13.1. Section through the burial chamber of Neferites I, facing north. Surviving stratification on the left shows, above the destruction at the bottom of the pit, roughly twenty superimposed, tightly packed stria composed in each case of small gravel capped by fine silt.

Neferites I, in both its Mendesian and Sebennytic branches, had been dispersed: the last king had fled, his heir taken captive to Persia and many of his relatives murdered.

But now there was genuine and widespread unrest. In spite of the return of a satrap and his Persian administration to Memphis, the civil administration was fast losing control of the country. A chief priest, one Petosiris of Hermopolis, tells what it was like to live in those troublous times.

> I passed seven years as *lesonis*-priest (temple manager) of this god (Thoth) administering his income, and no indiscretion (of mine) was ever found therein; when all the while a foreign ruler was the *Dominus* over Egypt and nothing was in its former place. For war had broken out in Egypt: the south raged and the north was in uproar and people went about bewildered. No temple had its staff (for) the priests were dispersed(?); there was no telling what might happen (in Egypt) in the future!

The satrap's power was so diminished that by 335 B.C. an Egyptian of foreign extraction (Libyan?), one Khababash, was able to set himself up as king somewhere in the Delta and dole out land to interest groups. Two years later, when a Macedonian rebel fled to Egypt, he was hailed in the streets by crowds of Egyptians in a display of overt anti-Persian feeling.

And now events on an international stage overtook the Persians. In 334 B.C. the king of Macedon, a young stripling still in his teens, having united the Greeks, crossed the Hellespont in an effort to bring to fruition the hope of two and one half centuries: the punishment of the Persians for the destruction they had wrought in Greece in 480 B.C. The young king's name was Alexander, and he was on a crusade. An advance force of Persians was swept away at the Granicus River in western Asia Minor, and within two years all of Anatolia was in his hands. The grand Persian army, a slow-moving juggernaut at the best of times, finally opposed the invader at Issus in November 333 B.C. and was routed in one of the great turning points of history. By the late autumn of 332 B.C. Tyre and Gaza, loyal to Darius III, had been reduced, and Alexander moved on Egypt. The Persian satrap, deprived of his forces in the call-up for the battle of Issus, realized that resistance was pointless and simply surrendered the country to the Macedonians.

All Egypt was jubilant! Alexander was hailed as a deliverer, and immediately fitted into the pharaonic mold. His transliterated name was placed in a cartouche, a fivefold titulary was fashioned for him, and his figure in Egyptian style began to appear on temple walls. The honor he showed to Memphis and Heliopolis and their gods, as well as the trip to the Siwa oasis to commune with Amun, did much to raise his prestige in Egyptian eyes. When, however, he departed from Egypt with his army in the spring of 332 B.C., leaving a Greek garrison and Greek administrators, there could be no question of a return of sovereignty to the Egyptians: the country was now firmly in Greek hands, and a new city was under construction in the Delta which would be wholly Greek in constitution, population, and ethos.

The events of the next twelve years found Egypt an historic backwater. The country played no role in the crushing defeat of the Persian host at Gaugamela and the disintegration of the Persian Empire. The spotlight next focuses on the marching of the Macedonians into central Asia to the borders of the Punjab and the incipient consolidation of Alexander's empire. Only with the conqueror's sudden and untimely death at Babylon in 323 B.C. did Egypt spring once again into prominence, not of its own volition but through the decisions of Alexander's successors. In the hasty and ad hoc arrangements made by Alexander's generals for the running of the empire, general Ptolemy Lagus received Egypt as a satrapy and took up residence in Memphis. Two years later by a skillful ruse he hijacked Alexander's funeral cortege as it made its way to Macedonia and brought it to Egypt where eventually it occupied a magnificent tomb in Alexandria.

During the wars of the successors Egypt remained quiescent and the native population refused to take sides. Taking their lead from governor Ptolemy, the Egyptians continued to honor Alexander's half-brother and nominal successor, Philip (III) Arrhidaeos. The Persian destruction of Mendes had not completely terminated temple service, and sometime between 321 and 317 B.C. the priests set up a life-size statue of Philip in the naos-court of Amasis. (Much later it was thrown out of the south door of the court and ended up in the gate area where we unearthed it in 2001.) The form is traditionally phara-onic: the king is represented in a *shendiyet* kilt, kneeling and about to offer a libation from two globular containers he holds in his hand. An inscription on the back-pillar an-nounces this to be a likeness of "[the King of Upper and Lower Egypt], the Perfect God, Lord of the Two Lands, beloved of Re and chosen by Amun, the Son of Re, Lord of Dia-dems Philipos, beloved of Ba-neb-Djed, living [forever]." The honor was short-lived: in 317 Philip was murdered. By 314 Egypt had a new capital, Alexandria, and in 305 B.C. a new king, Ptolemy I.

Greek occupation soon proved a mixed blessing for the Egyptians. Greeks now poured into Egypt as settlers, their immigration actively encouraged by the Ptolemaic kings. Twenty years after Ptolemy declared himself monarch Greeks were to be found every-where in Egypt, as far south as the Thebaid and Elephantine, living cheek by jowl with the native inhabitants. Properties were bought or confiscated, and friends of the king soon got rich. Alexandria developed as a purely Greek city with Greek institutions and through emulation provided other Greek settlements throughout Egypt with an Hellenic model. Throughout most of the third century B.C. there was little meaningful interaction

Figure 13.2. Statue of Philip Arrhidaeus as it appeared in excavation.

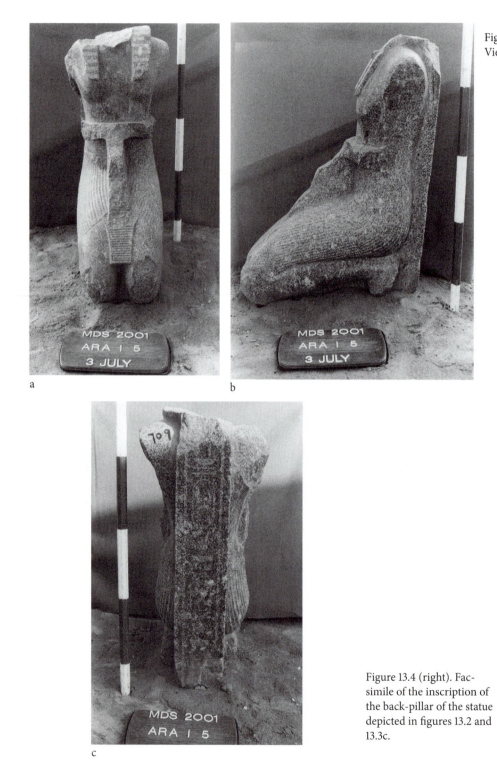

a

b

c

Figures 13.3a–13.3c.
Views of the kneeling statue.

Figure 13.4 (right). Fac-
simile of the inscription of
the back-pillar of the statue
depicted in figures 13.2 and
13.3c.

between Greek and Egyptian. Greeks lived the dolce vita on the backs of the native underclass. The Egyptians could enjoy their own culture and use their own script and language among themselves; but as soon as a Greek became involved in the context of commerce or law, the legal instruments had to be written up in Greek. While a few of the Egyptian military remained in control of isolated townships, the spotlight until 205 B.C. is squarely upon the Hellenic element in the personnel constituting the governing class.

On the other hand, the first three Ptolemies, Soter (I), Philadelphos (II), and Euergetes (III), showed themselves remarkably discreet in their dealings with the native Egyptians. Before he became king, while yet still a satrap, Ptolemy Lagos had taken steps to ensure the return of temple paraphernalia confiscated by Bagoas and taken to Persia in 342 B.C.; and his son and grandson continued his efforts. In Memphis, arguably the premier "royal" city of the pharaohs, Ptolemy I treated the high priest of Ptah as a sort of "ethnarch," and he and his synod of priests became point-men in the government's dealings with the native peoples. Upon occasion a new king would repair to Memphis to undergo a traditional pharaonic coronation. To soothe sensibilities, but also to learn about the land they occupied, the Ptolemies commissioned the Egyptian intelligentsia to compose treatises in Greek on the history and religion of the country for their own instruction. To some extent the new regime subsidized temple construction, although many of the largest shrines dated their foundation and structural completion to the preceding 30th Dynasty. In any event, the temples and their priesthoods clearly continued to form the nuclei of the native community, and it was expedient and enlightened not to disturb them appreciably.

13.1 The Gods Return!

He (Ptolemy Lagos) brought the images of the gods which were found in Asia, together with all the cult implements and all the sacred texts of the temples of Upper and Lower Egypt, and he returned them to their places.
[*Satrap stela: Urk. II, 14*]

The king (Ptolemy II) crossed the Asiatic frontier and reached Persia, and found the gods of Egypt there—all of them! He brought them to Egypt in (his) company . . . and the magnates of Egypt hastened in joy [to meet(?)] these gods.
[*Pithom stela: Urk. II, 91*]

as for the divine implements which the vile ones of Persia had stolen . . . His Majesty (Ptolemy III) journeyed to the land of Asia, seized them, brought them to Egypt and put them (back) in their places in the temples whence they had formerly been removed.
[*Kanopus decree: Urk. II, 128–29*]

Ptolemy II Philadelphos, son and successor of Ptolemy Lagus (Soter), in his dealings with Mendes, exemplifies the welcome discretion the early Ptolemaic monarchs displayed in their approach to the autochthonous community. According to a large stela which Ptolemy ordered to be set up in the Temple of the Ram, the king had decided early in his reign to pay a visit to Mendes. In late August probably in or about the year 280 B.C.,

> His Majesty visited the living ram on the first occasion that he visited any of them (the gods) since [he] acceded to the throne [of his father] . . . as [was done for]merly b[y] the kings who had inaugurated (the practice of) visitation. His Majesty took the prow of this god's barque, rowing him north on the "Great Canal," and south on the "Water of the Anchorage," as the kings who were before him had done, performing all the ritual of Visitation for him in accordance with what is in writing, until he arrived at Djedet-'Anepat. And so His Majesty made his (the ram's) festal appearance upon his barque-dais, while he was in this god's train. . . . [His Majesty] ferried the god over to Wep-nutray, his seat of Visitation of the "First Occasion." Then His Majesty made the circuit of the Mansion-of-the-Rams and he found the House of the Ram still under reconstruction, as His Majesty had ordered, to remove the destruction the rebellious foreigners had wrought in it. His Majesty ordered to have it finished in eternal workmanship, when His Majesty saw the Ram's residence beautified and renovated; and he gave a charge to his . . . to [in]stall the Ram in Anpet on his throne there.
>
> Then His Majesty put his instructions in the temple of this city and did benefactions for the sacred rams, in accordance with what is found in the script of Thoth. And afterwards His Majesty journeyed to his residence, his heart happy through what he had done for his fathers, the very great living rams, pre-eminent in 'Anepat, since they had given him a great kingship in happiness of heart.

This text is of great importance for us on two counts. First it reflects the deference Ptolemy displayed toward native tradition. It is not without significance that Mendes is represented as the first of the native cities and temples that the king visited: the 30th Dynasty was of Mendesian origin, and the memory of the last independence remained strong. Ptolemy inserts himself into this tradition by acknowledging the intervention of the Ram in elevating him to the kingship. He further suffers himself to be cast in the role of the pharaonic celebrant of the cult, performing all the ceremonial in conformity with the hieroglyphic ritual texts, perhaps in fact some of those he had been instrumental in having returned to Egypt. Like any good pharaoh, he sees to it that his "instructions" (regulatory texts, or simply ritual formulae) are inscribed on the walls of the refurbished temple. One can sense the pride and gratitude of the priests for the signal honor Ptolemy has accorded them in the way in which they laud him in thoroughly Egyptian verbiage. Ptolemy is "victorious king with overpowering might, dextrous one who seizes in his power, fighting in the breach, courageous in the melee, with strong arm smiting his en-

13.2 Ptolemy II, Son of the Ram

The Perfect God, likeness of the Ram, living image of "Him-That-Is Pre-eminent-in-the-Horizon," divine seed of the Bull-Ram, true son of the (Ram)-Ejaculatory, . . . whom he engendered to found the temples and to refurbish the divine townships; eldest son of the Ram, the "Child-Maker," who sits on the throne of him that sits over the gods, exact replica of the "Child of the Townships," engendered to be the Lord; ruler, son of a ruler, born of Her-That-Rules, to whom was bequeathed the office of Ruler of the Two Lands when he was (still) in the womb, before he was born; he took (his inheritance) while still in diapers, he began to rule while still being suckled. Charming one, attractive and beloved, respected like the Ram in the Fish-nome, victorious king with overpowering might, dexterous one who seizes by his power, fighting in the breach, courageous in the melee, with a strong arm, smiting his enemies; effective planner with a successful record, a winner to be boasted of, lord of ma'at *with lenient laws—his heart is conversant with "God's-Way"—watching over Egypt, prospering the temples, a wall of bronze around their tenants!* [*Mendes stela, lines 2–5*]

emies, effective planner with a successful record, a winner to be boasted of, lord of justice with lenient laws—his heart is conversant with 'God's-way'—watching over Egypt, prospering the temples, a wall of bronze; everyone dances at sight of him, inasmuch as he has saved them! . . . All the temples are flooded with his largess!" If Ptolemy ever had these phrases in the stela translated for him, it must have been gratifying to realize that his actions had neutralized potential dissent and that even the natives were now "on side." Wisely he was to ingratiate himself even more with the towns' inhabitants by rescinding transit dues and lessening the tax burden in the Fish-township.

A second important aspect of the stela, and one which appeals more to the modern excavator, lies in the information it contains regarding the topography of Mendes in the early third century B.C. In fact Ptolemy's perambulations constitute a sort of gazetteer for the site, and we have already made some use of its contents. His approach to Mendes brings him north on the Great Canal then south on the Water of the Anchorage. We had earlier concluded that the former was the outer harbor and the latter the square, inner basin; but this is now seen to be impossible, as the gap between the two has been proven by excavation to have been filled in since Saite times. Perhaps the Anchorage is the outer harbor, in which case the Great Canal would have to be a term for the Mendesian branch. The latter equation, however, seems unlikely, in that Ptolemy, coming from Alexandria, would undoubtedly have approached Mendes along the Butic canal, which seems to have touched the site at the northern end of the northern mound. Perhaps its final course lay in a roughly northerly direction. His activity after landing involved ritual at the barque-dais, that is to say within the main temple, an appropriate first stop in the visit. He then led the god's flotilla across some body of water to a place whose name, Wep-nutray, means "He-Who-Separates-the-Two-Gods." A similar epithet attaches itself to the site of Hermopolis Parva, capital of the adjacent township to the west, in the form *Pi-Tehuty-wep-rehwy*, "The-House-of-Thoth-Who-Separates-the-Two-Contestants." In both cases the reference is to the role of Thoth in the Osiris myth in judging equitably between Horus and Seth. But are we to assume that Ptolemy's itinerary now takes him away from the city, to backtrack ten kilometers west to Hermopolis Parva? Since priestly functions within Mendes, as attested by numerous titles, also includes this epithet, should we not look for an identification within the environs of the city itself? Kom el-Adhem, flanking the harbor on the north, has as yet no firm identification, and it is tempting to assign the epithet to this mysterious structure which certainly had to be approached by water.

Beyond Wep-nutray Ptolemy's movements become intelligible. He now makes the circuit (an appropriate term if he is coming from Kom el-Adhem) to the Mansion of the Rams, the great burial hypogeum due west of the main temple. This is in ruin, but reconstruction has already begun; and Ptolemy purposes to restore it to the standard of the main temple. Having issued the order to inscribe parts of the renovated temple with his "instructions," he retires, perhaps never to see the city again.

Archaeological traces of Ptolemy's renovations are not as numerous as we had hoped. A small, battered sphinx came to light in the northwest entry into the naos-court, and with difficulty Ptolemy II's prenomen could be made out on its chest. Blocks with Ptolemaic inscriptions appear occasionally, but it is uncertain whether they date to the time of Philadelphos. If he restored the hypogeum of the sacred rams, as he implies he did, it is tempting to see the transition to the third century B.C. in the change in the material of preference for the manufacture of the sarcophagi from granite to limestone. There are three or four coffins made out of limestone, each with the slots required to receive the horns, a number which would adequately fill out most of the third century.

A thornier problem as to date is posed by the *second* hypogeum for sacred animals, located north of the temple and apparently connected with the *mammisi*. We have suggested that it was intended to house the burials of ewes, the "mothers of the rams." This sector of the northwest enclosure is signalized by the presence of the diorite sarcophagi, described above, scattered at random over the terrain. They have long lain in their present position—all early travelers remark on them—a mute witness to Christian anathema. The foundation trench of the walls showed ceramics with a consistent horizon of the sixth through fourth centuries B.C., but whatever *native* form of worship had been carried on in this "House of the Ewes" certainly lapsed shortly after the time of Christ. By the late first century C.E. the area had become a sometime bivouac for troops (see below); from the second through sixth centuries masses of late Roman pottery were dumped here. Whether the building was actually occupied by Christian prelates, or used simply as a refuse pit, we cannot tell.

13.3 The Cult "Gazetteer" of Mendes

[The king . . .] comes to thee O Horus the Behdedite, the Great God, Lord of Heaven] that he might bring thee the Hat-mehyet township and Pi-Ba-neb-djed, with the "Phallos" and with the four-faced one, and the living bais in ʾAnepat, the living bai *of Re, united with his two fledglings in the Mansion of the Rams; he-who-separates-the two gods (even) he whose decay is hidden, makes offering to his* ku, *while she-who-makes-hale-his-soul plays the sistrum before him; Ḥpr-ḥȝt (the sacred barque) moors in the "Anchorage"; the sacred tree, the zisyphos, (grows) in the "Mound-of-the-Souls." He celebrates his great and fair festival in the fourth month of Inundation, day 4 (and) the fourth month of Planting, day 18; its abomination: to touch(?) the* itn-*fish; he provides sustenance for the "Awful One" (the serpent); it floods the "front-of-the-lagoons" (Ḥȝt-mḥyt) (to) the district of Tjaru, it directs her cool water to the *Laḥaḥta-backwaters.* [Edfu I, 334]

One major construction project which now admits of no doubt as to date is the present temenos wall of the northwest enclosure. This irregular circumvallation today encloses an area measuring approximately 600 × 350 meters, containing the temple, the *mammisi,* the two ram hypogea, the royal necropolis, and (on the south) a restricted domestic quarter. A major axial approach led from the north through two pylons to the Ramesside pylon of the temple proper, while a substantial gateway connected the temenos with the harbor. On the west side two or perhaps three apertures allowed communication with houses and waterways flanking the city. Apparently no gate pierced the wall on the south, and thus the temenos was cut off from direct access to the city proper. Our excavations east of the tomb of Neferites laid bare the foundation trench of the temenos wall over a stretch approaching fifteen meters in length; and the diagnostic pottery recovered included Saite, fourth century, *and* a little Ptolemaic. The same picture emerged from the excavations of the northwest harbor, where the foundation trench of the adjacent stretch of temenos wall showed a fourth-century horizon in terms of pottery, with a slight admixture of early Ptolemaic. There can be no doubt, therefore, that when the foundations of the present temenos were dug, Ptolemaic ceramics were in use. But who actually built the wall is in doubt. Although he does not claim it among the construction projects listed on the stela, Ptolemy II might be the likely candidate. On the other hand, the amount of Hellenistic ware in the foundation trenches is rather sparse, arguing for a date around 300 B.C. or a little before. Could it be that Ptolemy I, while satrap, had already authorized the construction?

One curious feature of the wall at the southeast corner of the temenos may presage future discoveries. For nearly 100 meters west of that corner and approximately 75 meters

Figure 13.5. Inner, western face of the Ptolemaic temenos wall, in Field AL, adjacent to the tomb of Neferites.

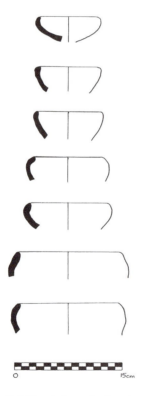

Figure 13.6. Vessels from the foundation trench of the present temenos wall.

Figure 13.7. Outer glacis of the Ptolemaic temenos (T1), facing south, and bordering the inner harbor on the north.

north of it the wall ceases to show two vertical faces. Only the inner face is vertical; the outer slopes down at approximately 45 degrees in the form of a glacis. The only possible reason for the immense thickening of the circumvallation at this point must be the weight of debris within the angle, and the likelihood is that the Persian demolition here had left substantial ruins that were not cleared away. To sustain the wall and contain the rubble, therefore, the reinforcement of a glacis was necessary.

During the third century B.C. Mendes and Thmuis enjoyed a brief return to the thriving economy and lifestyle they had known in the immediate past. Coins from the harbor show intensive activity from Alexander the Great to Ptolemy IV (died 204 B.C.), and surface surveys on widely scattered transects over the mound reveal enormous quantities of early Ptolemaic ware. In the wake of Ptolemy II famous Greeks began to visit Mendes, and Greeks now resided in the city, some leaving their mark internationally. There was an Asclepiades and a Ptolemy of Mendes, both of whom wrote histories of Egypt; a Harpokration who wrote on cooking; and a Thrasyllus who wrote on natural history. Bolos of Mendes, although Egyptian, made his mark as a sacred scribe and wiseman, and achieved a certain status as the Pseudo-Democritus. Greek and Egyptian mingled at a commercial level: both Greek and Egyptian foremen signed off on shipments in the harbor, and Greek bankers guaranteed deliveries abroad of native manufactures of perfume and papyrus. A local worthy, Ankh-hor, named his son by the Greek name Philolaus, and the son transcribed it into hieroglyphs on his statue. Some Egyptians, at the outset of the Ptolemaic period at least, caught the eye of the Greek regime and were given political responsibility. One Payom who incredibly arrogated the title "King's-Brother" unto himself, was given military command in the township, and another whose statue does not preserve his name was trusted by the new administration with the governance of the district. A deputy high priest of the god, one [. . .]-Amun son of Pa-miu, boasted of having extended the arable land in the township, making possible increased population. The temple thrived once more and priests could contemplate longevity and a Dynastic hold on office: "[I] gained a reputation . . . in the shrine of the Ram, Lord of Mendes, rejuvenating the Ram incessantly. I witnessed my son in the shrine . . . placing the collar upon the Ram and burning incense. I witnessed my son's son elevating food offerings."

By the beginning of the second century B.C., however, the end was in sight for the Mendes of old. Coins from the harbor facilities come abruptly to an end with the death of Ptolemy IV (who, incidentally, is the last Ptolemy to contribute to the temple's decoration), and some of the storage buildings were abandoned at about the same time. It is a fair guess that Mendes became caught up in the unrest which ravaged the Delta from the

Figures 13.8a–13.8b Early Ptolemaic coinage from the harbor showing head of king (obverse, left) and the Ptolemaic eagle (reverse, right).

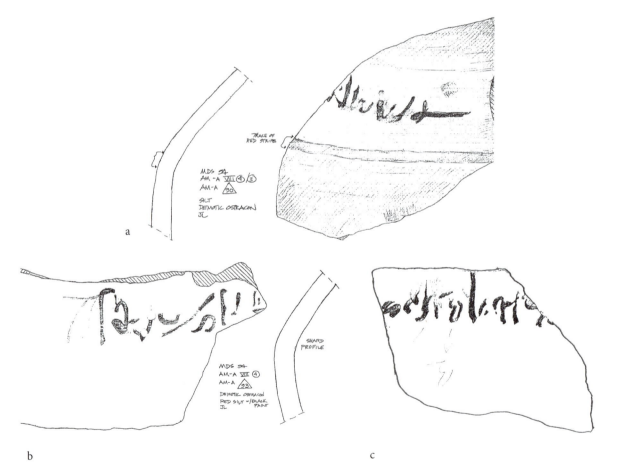

a

b

c

Figures 13.9a–13.9c. Demotic ostraca from the harbor: (a) *Klwd(?)*; (b) *Ḥr-tḥwty*; (c) *Ḥr-ʿȝ* son of *Pȝ-di-Wsir(?)*.

13.4 A Greek Banker and the Perfume of Mendes

Promethion to Zenon, greeting: I previously gave your agent Herakleides 150 drachmae in silver from your account, as you wrote to me to do, and he is bringing you now ten hin *(about five liters) of perfume in twenty-one vases which have been sealed with my finger ring. Although Apollonius wrote to me to buy and send him 300 wild pomegranate wreaths, I did not manage to give him these at the same time, as they were not ready, but Pa [. . .] will bring them to him at Naukratis, for they will be finished before the 30th. I paid the price both of these and of the perfume from your account, as Apollonius wrote. I have also paid a charge of ten drachmae in copper for the boat in which he is sailing up. And 400 drachmae in silver have been paid to Iatrocles for the papyrus rolls which are being manufactured in Tanis for Apollonius. Take note that these affairs have been settled thus. And please write yourself if ever you need anything here. Goodbye.*

[*A. S. Hunt and C. C. Edgar,* Select Papyri I *(Cambridge, MA, 1970), 271 (no. 89)*]

last decade of the third century B.C., although it certainly was not the center of the rebellion. While the uprising in Upper Egypt was essentially political in nature, resulting in an independent Thebaid which survived for twenty years, the Lower Egyptian uprising combined aspirations of independence with social grievances. In 196 B.C. the Ptolemaic forces captured a main rebel stronghold in the neighboring township of Busiris, but the rebellion continued for another ten years before it was finally put down by Polycrates, the general of Ptolemy V. As if to compound Mendes' woes, that branch of the Nile, the Mendesian, on which the very existence of the city depended, began to lose the strength of its discharge as its course meandered away to the east. By the end of the first century B.C. the great harbor had completely dried up, threatening the commerce of the community; domestic occupation moved south toward Thmuis, which continued to prosper.

13.5 An Egyptian Boy Makes Good under the Ptolemies

Hereditary Prince, Count, Unique Friend, King's-Brother, Great Commander of Troops in the township of Djedet, whom the [. . .] of the Lord of the Two Lands consulted and whom they petitioned, contented as they were with the statements he spoke, one with a happy character and good disposition . . . overseer of ch[ariotry(?)] combat officer, commander(?) of the "Troops-of-the-Lord," who keeps them under control for him, who understands whatever his heart conceives, who does whatever he says without demur, who proceeds loyally without plotting . . . (Amun-payom). [Mendes II, pl. 24, no. 61]

Attempts were made at the same time to build new retaining walls around the dwindling inner harbor, but it silted up faster than the outer harbor. On the western edge of the inner harbor we unearthed hundreds of terra cotta figurines of women on beds, Bes-figures and musicians, tossed into the receding waters from the bank. Was this a desperate, eleventh-hour, votive act, an attempt to stop the fructifying waters from disappearing altogether? By the time Antony and Cleopatra VII lost the battle of Actium (September 2, 31 B.C.) and Rome annexed Egypt as a province, one year later, both harbors were flat ground, the outer devoid of any foliage, the inner supporting a cover of bushes exactly coextensive with its rectangular shape.

The final act in the history of the outer harbor introduces a mysterious and perhaps sinister note. Around the time of Christ, at the northwestern corner of the former body of water, a substantial building was erected in fired brick. Its exact plan remains to be uncovered, as only a single corner was exposed, but a pottery cache found outside the wall indicated a rather special function. The ceramic types included decanters for wine, bifurcated lamps with the head of Isis on the finials, "cornets" for the affixing of torches, oil or unguent vessels, and a large rectangular form made in imitation of basketry with the heads of comedy and tragedy on opposing rims.

That we may be dealing with a cultic structure, perhaps a Roman "burial society" (*collegium funeraticium*), increases in likelihood in the light of the mortuary use to which the silted harbor was now put. In the same general area a number of burials came to light, most lacking in grave goods. One, however, yielded gold finials and appliqués of Roman eagles, perhaps originally sewn onto fabric. Immediately adjacent to the fired brick structure the badly preserved remains of eleven individuals were uncovered, of which three were sub-adults and two had been cremated.

At the time the fired brick building was erected and the corpses interred, that is, approximately 50 B.C. to 50 C.E., the Temple of the Ram continued to function as a place of worship. Statues of local worthies, now in Roman style, were still erected in the ambulatory of the shrine. A priest of the time of Augustus lists all the time-honored titles—"Prophet, Chamberlain-Priest, He-Who-Separates-the-Two-Gods, Prophet of the Ram, Priest of Harpokrates, Prophet of Ḥat-meḥyet"—and business papyri of the same reign show by the theophoric personal names they list that the worship of the old gods was thriving.

But in the succeeding century the formal worship of the Ram and the sanctity of the northwest temenos suffered a continuous decline. In 68 C.E. Titus, son of Vespasian and future emperor, transferred a legion of troops from Alexandria to Jerusalem to reinforce his father's siege of the Judaean city, made famous by Flavius Josephus. Eschewing maritime transport, Titus had the legionaries sail east along the Butic canal to Mendes, where they disembarked and marched overland via Tanis and the Sinai transit corridor to Jerusalem. On the return the same legion must have retraced its steps and encamped at

Figure 13.10. Terra cotta figurines from the inner harbor (fourth or early third century B.C.).

Figure 13.11. Corner of "Roman" building constructed of field brick (first century C.E.).

Figure 13.12. Cache of Roman pottery.

Figure 13.13. Amphorae in the *depinto* style, of sixth to seventh century date; from the area of the Mansion of the Rams.

Mendes on an overnight stop. In the ruins of the *mammisi* in 1995 we unearthed a coin of "year 2 of the liberation of Zion," a known issue struck in 67 C.E. Are we to conclude that in the last third of the first century C.E. the temple service at Mendes had been reduced to the point that devotees lacked the numbers and the authority to prevent Roman soldiers from bivouacking within the sacred precincts?

About seventy years after the passage of the Roman legion Mendes and its township became caught up once again in serious civil disturbances. In the second half of the second century plague, economic decline, and crop failures brought on perhaps by ecological factors combined to render the agricultural life of the Delta intolerable. Bands of brigands abounded in the marshes, and people fled thither to escape onerous taxation and the burden of liturgies. The latter, public tasks discharging one's obligations to the state, hit the wealthy very hard indeed and induced many to flight. As such liturgies included dyke repair, canal digging, and crop maintenance, failure to perform resulted in a decline in food production. Villages, instead of "retaining their former populous condition, have now been reduced to few residents because some have become impoverished and left, and others have died without kin. For this reason we (the tax-collectors) run the risk of deserting the office of tax-gathering through lack of resources." The chance find by Naville over one hundred years ago, of a room in Thmuis filled with charred papyri, has cast further light on these hopeless conditions. "The village secretary reported that the citizens registered (in a certain village) had for the most part disappeared. For when the assessment for the poll tax was established some time ago, there were fifty-four subject to the tax, but now there were only four who were impoverished, and these also had fled; nor could the collection of taxes be made."

The Roman authorities tried to rectify the situation by repressive measures, but these only worsened the economic and social chaos. The edict of Liberalis (154 C.E.) recognized the situation: "some have left their homes because of the recent disturbances and are providing the necessities of life from other sources," while "others in escaping from certain liturgies because of the poverty of the time, still live abroad in fear of the proscriptions which were immediately declared." Yet Liberalis's solution was draconian in the extreme: "If anyone is found roaming away from his home after this great manifestation of my clemency (he had granted amnesty to runaways if they returned within three months), he shall be arrested as an acknowledged, no longer as a suspected, criminal, and sent to me." The result could have been predicted. Fugitives joined bandit gangs of *bukoloi*, also known as the "impious Nikochites," and raided villages at will, murdering those farmers who had chosen to remain. Retaliation by the authorities often finished off the villagers suspected of being sympathetic to the outlaws. The papyri from Thmuis show us a local administration in 170–171 C.E. trying to set things straight by ascertaining who had fled, who had been killed, and what the outstanding taxes should be.

Clearly this time of troubles proved detrimental to Mendes, its citizenry, and especially the cult of the Ram-god. While the township to a certain extent revived economically at the beginning of the third century C.E., the personal names show an almost total absence of theophoric names honoring the old gods of pharaonic times. If, in Byzantine times, devout Christians could still complain about celebrations in favor of the Ram of Mendes, they were either for polemical reasons assuming the continuance of practices already moribund or referring to unofficial rites performed by the laity.

The papyri from Thmuis give us the last clear picture of the layout, demography, and administration of the city of Mendes-Thmuis. The former was now considerably smaller than the latter, as many families had abandoned the northern half of the site for the land adjacent to Thmuis; but it still bore the name of "metropolis" and shared with the larger town a single municipal secretary, as well as a common rate for the poll tax of eight drachmas. The 3,560 houses of Thmuis were apportioned among quarters divided into numbered blocks of domiciles, the latter also identified by number. Mendes was organized along the same lines, but the number of houses is unknown.

It must have been during the third century that Christianity began to make significant inroads in the township of Ḥat-meḥyet. By the end of the century the size of the city of Thmuis, and of the Christian community within it, had elevated its status to that of a bishopric of outstanding merit; under Diocletian it suffered its mede of persecution. The local bishop at the time, one Phileas, was a very wealthy man, quite able, as his judge remarked, to sustain the entire town. He was also renowned for his scholarship in classical literature and philosophy; but, being arrested and taken to Alexandria, he remained steadfast and wrote to his parishioners in Thmuis that they should do the same, and he was duly martyred in 305. Forty years later another "scholar" and erstwhile abbot, Serapion, whose name indicates a recent pagan ancestry, was appointed bishop of Thmuis and for his oratory became known as the "angel of the church of the Thmuitae." That he was supplanted by an Arian bishop, Ptolemaeus, indicates that as a major Christian center, Thmuis/Mendes was caught up in the great theological upheavals of the period.

Archaeological evidence for Christianity at Mendes is circumstantial and has to do largely with earlier cultic and mortuary installations. It must have been at this time that the presence of tombs and parts of the temple constructed of limestone excited the interest of builders avid of lime for the cement favored in Roman construction. Lime kilns began to sprout east and south of the temple as tombs were dismantled and their component blocks committed to the flames. The distribution of the kilns suggests that they were so located to prevent smoke from blowing into the temple area—the prevailing winds are, of course, from the north—a fact suggesting that the temple was still used by someone. The ceramic record confirms such a supposition: well over 65 percent of the pottery recovered from the destruction level at surface within the temple dates from the Late Roman period (third through seventh centuries C.E.). For reasons given earlier, this could scarcely have been deposited by devotees of the Ram-god: it is much more likely that, as was the practice elsewhere in Egypt, the temple was given over to a garrison of soldiers from the time of Diocletian. In fact the report of a medieval writer who saw the site singles out a brick-built guard hut still standing above the pylon, a feature that would suggest the type of maximum security a barracks would require. Reuse required architectural adjustment. The southern access to the naos-court seems to have been blocked up. The gate blocks were removed, the flagstones taken away, and statues from inside the court (including that of Philip Arrhidaeus) thrown into the abandoned sand foundations.

Elsewhere signs of Christian habitation appear sporadically. The Mansion of the Rams to the west of the temple was subjected in Christian times to desecration, as the ram mummies were torn from their sarcophagi and perhaps used in the industrial process of manufacturing glass. The great transverse hall was dismantled, the columns dispersed, and some of the limestone blocks from its walls dumped in a well at the west end. The sarcophagi themselves were dragged from their cubicles and deposited on the sand *soubassement* of the hall whence the flooring blocks had been removed.

The small temple north of the main temple that we have identified as the *Mansion

Figure 13.14. Fragments of a limestone sarcophagus used to block up the entry in Christian times.

of the Ewes, the mothers of the rams, was likewise desecrated. Floors and walls were ripped out or smashed, and piers and architraves allowed to tumble. The sarcophagi for the animals were taken from their emplacements and scattered over the terrain to the southwest. Late Period pottery, some painted with the ⳨ monogram, leave no doubt as to the perpetrators.

Although primarily intended thoroughly to desecrate the cult, sacred space, and memory of the anathematized Ram-god, these acts of destruction were also designed to pave the way for some sort of renewal. Some cubicles were cleaned out, their walls replastered, and new partition walls constructed of pieces of old limestone sarcophagi. These new "cells" were to be used as habitations for Christian monks and anchorites, a practice of reuse paralleled elsewhere throughout Egypt.

The date of this Christian transformation is unknown—it presumably follows the Edict of Theodotian in 391 C.E.—but Christian occupation lasted as the pottery tells us into the seventh century C.E. And then came the end. With the Islamic conquest of 641 C.E. all occupation of the great northern mound of Tel er-Rub'a, the ancient Mendes, ceased. Thmuis, under the vocalization Tumay, survived the Arab occupation as a bishopric and an administrative district, and some of its land was confiscated for the use of a contingent in the conquering army. But attempted revolts (725 and 810–832) in which Muslim intestine feuding sought support among overtaxed Christian peasantry utterly devastated the city and its surrounding villages.

The date of the final destruction of the temple of Ba-neb-djed is not certainly known, although descriptions indicate that as late as the early Middle Ages it continued to stand largely intact. Those who finally dismantled the long derelict structure primarily sought the limestone masonry in abundance in the temple and surrounding tombs. The roofs, columns, and flooring of basalt were torn down or uprooted, and the quartzite walls attacked. Fires were lit in all the naoi and cold liquid poured over the hot stone in order to crack and remove the granite and gain access more easily to the underlying limestone. Three naoi came crashing down, and a large number of granite fragments continue to litter the area; but the naos of Shu defied the vandals and continues to stand.

13.6 The Mendesian Branch

[the canal/river] empty of detritus, lest it not receive silt in compensation. It flowed into it in the vicinity of "Amun [. . .]" of Sile, having fertilized the township and the arable land in front of it, beginning with the "Bank of Sf" and their lagoons, from the township of Mendes as far as the "Field-of-Tanis", watered each [year].
[L. Borchardt, Statuen *(Cairo, Catalogue generale III), no. 687*]

In order to dislodge the quartzite lining of the outer walls, the mud-brick "skin" was taken down, and as the courses of quartzite were removed one by one, the denuded, unsupported mud-brick collapsed into the temple court. In subsequent centuries sculpture and relief were carted off to grace European collections, leaving a denuded ruin devoid of architectural or art historical interest.

The fabric of urban living disintegrated along with the temple in the early Middle Ages. By the eleventh century there was no longer a bishop in Thmuis, no longer habitation in either city; small hamlets skirted the ruins of both mounds, much as they do today. Naught remained but garbled names, Tumay (*Tȝ-mȝwy*), Tata (*Djedet*), and Mondid (*pr-Bȝ-nb-ḏd*), and dim memories of a holy ram, and his devilish, lascivious ritual.

Notes to Chapters and Further Readings

CHAPTER ONE

Egypt is ill served by histories. Those that have been written over the past thirty-five years are few in number and traditional in their approach. Some that have multiple authors suffer from the inevitable unevenness and superficiality that results from "history by committee." Others tend at times to degenerate into a mere catalogue of monuments, texts, and objets d'art. Nevertheless there are several outstanding historical works of high merit, including (in English) the following:

B. G. Trigger, B. J. Kemp, D. O'Connor, and A. B. Lloyd, *Ancient Egypt, a Social History* (Cambridge, 1983)

B. J. Kemp, *Ancient Egypt: Anatomy of a Civilization* (London, 1989)

S. Quirke and J. Spencer, *The British Museum Book of Ancient Egypt* (London, 1992)

N. Grimal, *A History of Ancient Egypt* (Oxford, 1992)

D. P. Silverman, ed., *Ancient Egypt* (London, 1997)

E. Hornung, *History of Ancient Egypt: An Introduction* (Ithaca, NY, 1999)

J. Assmann, *The Mind of Egypt: History and Meaning in the Time of the Pharaohs* (New York, 1996)

For reports on archaeological work done at the site of Mendes, one should consult in particular the following:

E. Naville, "Mendes," in *Ahnas el-Medina (Heracleopolis Magna)* (London, 1894)

D. P. Hansen, "Mendes 1965 and 1966," *JARCE* 6 (1967), 5–51

H. De Meulenaere and P. Mackay, *Mendes II* (Warminster 1976)

K. L. Wilson, *Mendes: Preliminary Report on the 1979 and 1980 Seasons* (Malibu, CA, 1982)

D. B. Redford et al., "Three Seasons in Egypt, 3: The First Season of Excavations at Mendes (1991)," *JSSEA* 18 (1988 [pub. 1992]), 49–79.

D. B. Redford, "Mendes," in J. Yoyotte, ed., *L'Égypte du Delta: Les capitales du nord, dossiers d'archéologie* (Dijon, 1996)

S. Redford and D. B. Redford, "The Sacred Animal Necropolis at Mendes," in S. Ikram, ed., *Ancient Egyptian Animal Mummies* (Cairo, 2004)

D. B. Redford, *The Excavations at Mendes*, vol. 1: *The Royal Necropolis* (Leiden, 2004)

On the West Semitic root of the earliest stratum of toponymy in the eastern Nile Delta, see D. B. Redford, "Some Observations on the Northern and North-eastern Delta in the Late Predynastic Period," in B. M. Bryan and D. Lorton, eds., *Essays in Egyptology in Honor of Hans Goedicke* (San Antonio, 1994), 201–10.

The coring program of the late Larry Pawlish demonstrated that the present site of Mendes sits upon four ancient levees of the Mendesian branch of the Nile. All of these are angled southwest to northeast. The greatest depth of human occupation was found in a nine-hundred-square-meter tract between the depression of the "Sacred Lake" on the south and the low land bounding the temple mound on the north, the second and third stream beds counting from the north. On this high ground Excavation Units AJ-A and U probed through five meters of Old Kingdom deposition to reach 1st Dynasty floor surfaces (see below). Coring proved that a further 3.5 to 4 meters of human occupation lay beneath these floors upon the basal sand.

On the archaeological evidence regarding contact between Palestine and the Delta during the Predynastic and Archaic periods the literature is now extensive. See, among others, J. Hennessy, *The Foreign Relations of Palestine during the Early Bronze Age* (London, 1967); E. Oren, "The Overland Route between Egypt and Canaan in the Early Bronze Age: A Preliminary Report," *IEJ* 23 (1973), 198–205; R. Gophna, "Egyptian Trading Posts in Southern Canaan at the Dawn of the Archaic Period," in A. Rainey, ed., *Egypt, Israel, Sinai: Archaeological and Historical Relationship in the Biblical Period* (Tel Aviv, 1987), 13–21; K. Kroeper, "Palestinian Ceramic Imports in Pre- and Protohistoric Egypt," in P. Miroschedji, ed., *L'Urbanization de Palestine* (British Archaeological Reports, 1989), 407–21; M. Wright, "Contacts between Egypt and Syro-Palestine during the Protodynastic Period," *BA* 48 (1985), 240–52; B. Andelkowic, *The Relations between Early Bronze Age I Canaanites and Upper Egyptians* (Belgrade, 1995); E.C.M. van den Brink and T. E. Levy, eds., *Egypt and the Levant: Interrelations from the 4th through the Early 3rd Millennium B.C.E.* (London, 2002).

On the geomorphology of the Nile Delta in early times, see E.C.M. van den Brink, *The Archaeology of the Nile Delta: Problems and Priorities* (Amsterdam, 1988); idem, *The Nile Delta in Transition: 4th–3rd Millennium B.C.E.* (Tel Aviv, 1992); L. Krzyzaniak et al., eds., *Environmental Change and Human Culture in the Nile Basin and Northern Africa until the Second Millennium B.C.* (Poznań, 1993). On the Nile Branches in prehistoric times, see E. Gamili, "Defunct Nile Branches Inferred from a Geo-electric Resistivity Survey of Sammanoud Area, Nile Delta, Egypt," *Journal of Archaeological Science* 28 (2001), 1339–48.

The reconstruction promoted in this chapter relies on the significant demographic shift uniting the Levantine coast with the northeast Delta in Predynastic times, a shift that lies at the root of the toponymy of the region. The earliest levels reached on a broad scale by our excavations at Mendes are those of the beginning of the 1st Dynasty, but our coring program has demonstrated that prehistoric occupation at the site extends downward for another four meters and certainly features the Buto-Ma'adi culture. See, most recently, M. J. Adams, "Mendes in the Old Kingdom" (Ph.D. thesis, Pennsylvania State University, 2007).

The phrase *Tȝ-mḥw* certainly involves the root *mḥi*, "to flood, drown," and is sometimes translated "the drowned land." We have opted for a bound construction rather than a participle.

On the plant cover and the fauna of the environs of Mendes in ancient times, see A. C. d'Andrea, "Nile Delta Palaeoethnobotanical Project: Preliminary Report" (unpublished, 1993); A. S. Krywinski, "Archaeo-palaeological Thought on *Vicia Faba*-Type Pollen from Ancient Mendes," in D. Moe et al., eds., *Garden History: Garden Plant Species from Pompei to 1800* (Rixensart, 1984), 25–36; M. A. Murray, "Fruits, Vegetables, Pulses and Condiments," in P. T. Nicholson and I. Shaw, eds., *Ancient Egyptian Materials and Technologies* (Cambridge, 2000), 642; D. J. Brewer, *Domestic Plants and Animals: The Egyptian Origins* (Warminster, 1995).

On the Big Man phenomenon, see L. R. Binford, *In Pursuit of the Past: Decoding the Archaeological Record* (New York, 1983); A. W. Johnson and T. Earle, *The Evolution of Human Societies* (Stanford, 1987); P. Jay, *The Wealth of Man* (London, 2000); A. Gat, "Rural Petty-state and Overlordship: Missing Links in the Evolution of the Early State," *Anthropos* 98 (2003), 127–42. Despite an increasing volume of evidence, the putative transition from Big Man system through chiefdom and paramount chiefdom to monarchy is not easy to document or analyze in an Egyptian context. Arguably the transition from Big Man to chieftain with its hereditary overtones took place when communal diagnosis of performance became crucial; and the Big Man's handling of deviance within the community transcended a single generation. Only then would the necessity arise to create new leadership succession processes.

On the material from Buto, see D. B. Redford, "Notes on the History of Ancient Buto," *BES* 5 (1983), 67–102; B. Midant-Reynes, *The Prehistory of Egypt* (Oxford, 2000), 218–19; T. Von der Way, "Buto," in D. B. Redford, ed., *The Oxford Encyclopaedia of Ancient Egypt* (New York, 2001), 1:218–19. The part of the "classical" Osiris Myth that takes Buto as its setting must be seen as a discrete narrative involving the ravening monster, the protective mother, and the defenseless baby, a triad and plot pattern well-known along the Levantine coast from time immemorial: see D. B. Redford, "The Sea and the Goddess," in S. Groll, ed., *Studies in Egyptology Presented to Miriam Lichtheim* (Jerusalem, 1990), 2:824–35.

S(h)erakhu: any derivation from an Egyptian causative of the root *rḫ*, "to know," is impossible for lexical reasons (*srḫ* has a negative, if not pejorative, sense). Rather the noun is a loan word from Akkadian *saraḫu*, "to be splendid, glorious, uplifted" (often used of kingship and the palace itself), and means "the glorious building," that is, the palace. See J. Black et al., *A Concise Dictionary of Akkadian* (Wiesbaden, 2000), 359.

On the "Uruk phenomenon" of Mesopotamia, involving commercial expansion and the quest for resources, see P. B. Adamson, "The Possibility of Sea Trade between Mesopotamia and Egypt," *Aula Orientalis* 10 (1992), 175–79; J. Oats, "Trade and Power in the Fifth and Fourth Millennia B.C.," *World Archaeology* 24, no. 3 (1993), 403–22; M. S. Rothman, ed., *Uruk Mesopotamia and Its Neighbours* (Oxford, 2001); on contact between Egypt and Mesopotamia in Naqada II/III, see S. Mark, *From Egypt to Mesopotamia: A Study of Predynastic Trade Routes* (London, 1997); G. Algaze, *The Uruk World System* (Chicago 2005).

Chapter Two

For Buto, see the summary articles D. B. Redford, "Notes on the History of Ancient Buto," *BES* 5 (1983), 67–102; Von der Way, "Buto"; on Hierakonpolis, see R. F. Friedman, "Hierakonpolis," in Redford, *Oxford Encyclopedia of Ancient Egypt*, 2:98–100.

The *shma*-plant is sometimes identified with the *scirpus*-reed or sedge in flower (Gardiner Sign-list M26). At a very early date it became emblematic of Upper Egypt, the Nile Valley.

On the "Gerzean" boats and their female occupant, see F. El-Yahky, "Remarks on the Armless Figurines Represented on Gerzean Boats," *JSSEA* 12 (1981), 77–84; idem, "Clarifications on the Gerzean Boat Scenes," *BIFAO* 85 (1985), 187–96. On the "Great Mother," see F. Hassan, "Primeval Goddess to Divine King: The Mythogenesis of Power in the Early Egyptian State," in R. F. Friedman and B. Adams, eds., *The Followers of Horus* (Oxford, 1992), 307–21.

The symbols of power begin to proliferate at the close of the fourth millennium in all registers of art, betraying a hegemonic discourse of violent control. Since the signs seek to portray multifaceted strength in a variety of avatars, there is no guarantee that a plurality of symbols could not be applied to one man. Thus it may be unwise to conjure up individual kings: "Scorpion," "Crocodile, "Bull," and so forth. Only when limiting convention hit upon the *falcon* on a *serekh* did a single definition, a *name*, enter the picture: see W. Barta, "'Falke des Palastes' als ältester Königstitel," *MDAIK* 24 (1969), 51ff; M. A. Berger, "Predynastic Animal-Headed Boats from Hierakonpolis and Southern Egypt," in Friedman and Adams, *The Followers of Horus*, 107–20; W. Davis, "The Origins of Image Making," *Current Anthropology* 27 (1986), 193–202; idem, "Representation, Legitimation and the Emergence of the Early Egyptian State," in J. Gledhill et al., eds., *State and Society: The Emergence and Development of Social Hierarchy and Political Centralization* (London, 1988); L. D. Morenz et al., eds., *Herrscherpräsentation und Kulturkontakte* (Münster, 2003).

The problems of the advent of complex society and state formation have called forth the most vibrant and innovative debate in current Egyptology. The salutary result has been, partly through the introduction of new data, to eliminate some old theories that held the field up to forty years ago. New anthropological models have been introduced (in particular those based on the work of Richard Carneiro) that work admirably in an Egyptian setting. Of the welter of books and articles one could cite, in addition to works already referred to, the reader is advised especially to consult the following: K. W. Butzer, *Early Hydraulic Civilization in Egypt* (Chicago, 1976); G. Dreyer, "The Royal Tombs at Abydos," *Near East in Antiquity* 3 (1992), 55–67; all the articles in Friedman and Adams, *The Followers of Horus* and in Gledhill, *State and Society*; W. Helck, "Gedanken zur Entstehung des altägyptischen Staates," *FS Von Beckerath* (1990), 97–118; W. Kaiser, "Zur Entstehung des gesamtaegyptischen Staates," *MDAIK* 46 (1990), 287–300; J. Seeher, "Gedanken zur Rolle Unterägyptens bei der Herausbildung des Pharaonenreiches," *MDAIK* 47 (1991), 313–18; A. J. Spencer, *Early Egypt: The Rise of Civilization in the Nile Valley* (London, 1993); idem, *Aspects of Early Egypt* (London, 1996); T. Von der Way, *Untersuchungen zur Spätvor- und Frühgeschichtliche Unterägyptens* (Heidelberg, 1993); R. J. Wenke, "Egypt: Origins of Complex Societies," *Annual Revue of Anthropology* 18 (1989), 129–55; idem, "The Evolution of Early Egyptian Civilization: Issues and Evidence," *Journal of World Prehistory* 5 (1991), 279–329; T. Wilkinson, *State Formation in Egypt: Chronology and Society* (Oxford, 1996); idem, *Genesis of the Pharaohs* (London, 2003).

On the nascent Egyptian script, see, among others, W. Fairservice, *Hierakonpolis: The Graffiti and the Origins of Egyptian Hieroglyphic Writing* (Poughkeepsie, NY, 1983); H. G. Fischer, "The Origins of Egyptian Hieroglyphs," in W. M. Senner, ed., *The Origins of Writing* (Lincoln, NE, 1990), 59–76; O. Goldwasser, *From Icon to Metaphor: Studies in the Semiotics of the Hieroglyphs* (Fribourg, 1995); C. C. Lamerge-Karlovsky, "The Emergence of Writing in Mesopotamia, Egypt and the Indus Civilizations," in E. W. Andrews, ed., *Research and Reflections in Archaeology and History: Essays in Honor of Doris Stone* (Middle America Research Institute Publication 57, 1986), 149–58; L. D. Morenz, "Die Phonetisierung des Bildes und ihre Folgen: Ein Modell fur die Entstehung der ägyptischen Schrift," *Saeculum* 53 (2002), 175–92.

CHAPTER THREE

For preliminary notices on the excavations of the Delta sites in question, the reader is referred to J. Leclant et al., "Fouilles et travaux en Egypte et au Soudan" published annually in *Orientalia*. On Tell Ibrahim Awad, see W. Van Haarlem, "Les Fouilles de Tell Ibrahim Awad," *BSFE* 141 (1998), 8–19; on the Old Kingdom excavations at Mendes, see the preliminary reports in the *Akhenaten Temple Project Newsletter* (*ATPN*): "The Eighth Campaign of Excavations at Mendes," *ATPN* (October 1998); "The Ninth Campaign at Mendes (Summer 1999)," *ATPN* (October 1999); "Report on the Mendes Excavations 2000 (10th season)," *ATPN* (September 2000); "Report on the 11th Season of Excavations at Tel er-Rub'a (Mendes)," *ATPN* (September 2001). The final report will appear in the ongoing *Excavations at Mendes* (Leiden), as volume 2: *The Temple of Ba-neb-djed*.

It is tempting to link the interruption suggested by the debris between levels V and IV with the activity of Khasekhemwy. On the latter, see G. Dreyer, "Khasekhemwy," in Redford, *Oxford Encyclopaedia of Ancient Egypt*, 1:231 (who takes the number 47,209 as a [misplaced?] census figure). The podium and temple, the foundation trench of which has now been probed, shows no Archaic Period pottery but an assemblage of high Old Kingdom ceramics pointing to the 3rd or 4th Dynasty as the date of construction.

The basic meaning of *dd* is "to remain, to be firm, stable; to be continuous, without interruption"; the root lends itself to the idea of a necropolis, and as an appellative to the ancestral dead who reside there. It may enjoy a remote cognative association with Protosemitic *SD(D)*, "side, mountain," but this is doubtful.

The original name of Busiris was *'nd*, and its god *'nd.ty*. The root is not Egyptian but West Semitic: *'nz*, "to wander," from which derived nouns are "goat" and "goatherd, shepherd." The most appropriate meaning of the original place-name is thus "Pasturage," and the god (whose accoutrements point to shepherding), the "Shepherd, Herdsman."

The administration of the Egyptian "provinces" (better "townships," i.e., metropolis + territorium) by the "Center" has been increasingly subject to investigation. See in particular E. Martin-Pardey, *Untersuchungen zur ägyptischen Provinzialverwaltung bis zum Ende des Alten Reiches* (Hildesheim, 1976); idem, "Provincial Administration," in Redford, *Oxford Encyclopaedia of Ancient Egypt*, 1:16–20; N. Kanawati, *The Egyptian Administration in the Old Kingdom* (Warminster, 1977); idem, *Governmental Reforms in Old Kingdom Egypt* (Warminster, 1980); J. C. Morena Garcia, Ḥwt *et le milieu rural égyptien du IIIe millénaire* (Paris, 1999).

The best entrée into the enormous topic of "Osiris" and his origins is had by perusal of the works of J. G. Griffiths and the sources cited therein: see in particular his *Plutarch's De Iside et Osiride* (Cardiff, 1970); idem, *The Origins of Osiris and His Cult* (Leiden, 1980); idem, "Osiris," in *Lexikon der Ägyptologie* (Wiesbaden, 1982), 4:623–33; idem, "Osiris," in Redford, *Oxford Encyclopaedia of Ancient Egypt*, 2:615–19.

Personal names compounded with the "Ram" occur as early as the late 2nd Dynasty: Kaplony *IÄF* III, 98:406. The town ˀAnepat and its god seem already to be attested in the 1st Dynasty (W.M.F. Petrie, *The Royal Tombs at Abydos II* [London, 1901], pl. V, 1), and the cult of the Mendesian ram turns up in Manetho in a 2nd Dynasty entry (Waddell, *Manetho*, 36). The cult of the "Ram of ˀAnepat /Djedet" is attested at the capital in the 3rd and 4th Dynasties: W.M.F. Petrie, *Meidum and Memphis III* (London, 1910), pl. XXI; B. L. Begelsbacher-Fischer, *Untersuchungen zur Götterwelt des Alten Reiches* (Gottingen, 1981), 223. The "Pooh-bah"-like mandarin Metjen was sometime plantation manager, irrigation-overseer, and superintendent of messengers in the 16th township of Lower Egypt (D. Jones, *An Index of Egyptian Titles, Phrases and Epithets of the Old Kingdom* [Oxford, 2000], 1:357 [1325]); and the region was deemed important enough to contribute towns and estates to the mortuary endowment of prince Nekaure, son of Khafre (*LD* II, Bl. 15). For the mortuary estates in general, see H. Jacquet-Gordon, *Les noms des domaines funéraires sous l'Ancien Empire égyptien* (Cairo, 1962).

Chapter Four

Like most of his Old Kingdom predecessors, little is known of Pepy II. On his funerary complex, see G. Jecquier, *Le monument funéraire de Pepy II* (Cairo, 1936); on the story of Sisine, see G. Posener, "Le Conte de Néferkare et du général Sisiné (Recherches litteraire VI)," *RdE* 11 (1957), 119ff.

The collapse of the Old Kingdom is slowly becoming a battleground among scholars. Even the term "collapse" is being questioned! Debunkers have begun to try to turn conventional views on their heads: the subsequent First Intermediate Period (c. 2200–2000 B.C.) was not the time of poverty and downsizing many have claimed; the economy was sound, and considerable wealth was still to be found (S. Seidelmayr, *Gräberfelder aus dem Übergang vom Alten zum Mittleren Reich: Studien zur Archaeologie der Ersten Zwischenzeit* [Heidelberg, 1990]). Needless to say, the evidence from Mendes does not support this contention. A much more nuanced view is necessary, as parochial situations may not be applicable to the country as a whole. See, among others, S. Grunert, "Die aegyptische Revolution im 3. Jahrtausend v.u.Z.," *Das Altertum* 23, no. 4 (1977), 213ff; R. Müller-Wollermann, *Krisenfaktoren im ägyptischen Staat des ausgehenden Alten Reiches* (Tübingen, 1986). It should be noted that recent research, especially that of Fikri Hassan, tends to highlight the role played by climate change in the last quarter of the third millennium, a view first mooted by Barbara Bell nearly thirty-five years ago: B. Bell, "The Dark Ages in Ancient History, I: The First Dark Age in Egypt," *AJA* 75 (1971), 1–26; F. Hassan and G. Tassie, "Modelling Environmental and Settlement Change in the Fayum," *Egyptian Archaeology* 29 (2006), 37–40. On the comparable effect of volcanic eruption, see L. Oman et al., "High-Latitude Eruptions Cast Shadow over the African Monsoon and the Flow of the Nile," *Geophysical Research Letters* 33 (2006). I am indebted to Matthew Adams for this last reference. See also K. Butzer, "Delta," *LdÄ* 1 (1973), 1043–52; J. D. Stanley et al., "Short Contribution: Nile Flow Failure at the End of the

Old Kingdom, Egypt: Strontium Isotope and Petrologic Evidence," *Geoarchaeology* 18, no. 3 (2003), 395–402.

On the examination of dental enamel, see N. C. Lovell and I. Whyte, "Patterns of Dental Enamel Defects at Ancient Mendes, Egypt," *American Journal of Physical Anthropology* 110 (1999), 69–80. On the famine texts, see W. Schenkel, *Memphis, Herakleopolis, Theben: Die epigraphischen Zeugnisse der 7.–11., Dynastie Aegyptens* (Wiesbaden, 1965), 29–66; M. Lichtheim, *Ancient Egyptian Literature*, vol. 1: *The Old and Middle Kingdoms* (Berkeley, 1973), 85–90. On the "Admonitions" of Ipuwer, see Lichtheim, *The Old and Middle Kingdoms*, 1:149–62; W. Helck, *Die "Admonitions" Pap. Leiden I 344 recto* (Wiesbaden, 1995); R. Enmarch, *The Dialogue of Ipuwer and the Lord of All* (Oxford, 2005). Though in part generic, there is no doubt that Ipuwer, which can be shown to date before the 12th Dynasty, correctly reflects the society and its woes of the First Intermediate Period: D. B. Redford, *Pharaonic King-lists, Annals and Day-books* (Mississauga, 1986), 144n69.

Chapter Five

On the Coffin Texts, see R. O. Faulkner, *The Ancient Egyptian Coffin Texts*, 3 vols. (Warminster, 1978); M. Heerma von Voss, "Sargtexten," *Lexikon der Ägyptologie* (Wiesbaden, 1984), 5:468–71; L. H. Lesko, "Coffin Texts," in Redford, *Oxford Encyclopaedia of Ancient Egypt*, 1:287–88; H. Willems, ed., *Social Aspects of Funerary Culture in the Egyptian Old and Middle Kingdoms* (Louvain, 2001); for Coffin Texts from Mendes, see D. P. Silverman, "Coffin Texts from Bersheh, Kom el-Hisn and Mendes," in H. Willems, ed., *The World of the Coffin Texts* (Leiden, 1996), 129–41.

For the instruction of Akhtoy III(?) for his son and future king Merikare, both of Herakleopolis, see the translations of J. A. Wilson, in *ANET*, 414–18; Lichtheim, *Ancient Egyptian Literature*, 1:97–112; W. Helck, *Die Lehre für König Merikare* (Wiesbaden, 1977); J. Quack, *Studien zur Lehre für Merikare* (Wiesbaden, 1992). For Ipuwer, see R. Ennarch, *The Dialogue of Ipuwer and the Lord of All* (Oxford, 2005).

It is difficult, from both archaeological and textual sources, to assess the impact on Mendes of the reunification of the country through the agency of Montuhotpe the Great, scion of the upstart 11th Dynasty of Thebes. At this stage in our understanding it is quite gratuitous to postulate a siege and destruction of the city, or of any other Delta town. In all probability, and in the light of the indifferent reputation suffered by the kings of Herakleopolis, the sacking of this capital city would have brought with it the quick surrender of the mayors of the Delta towns. The problem will be taken up in the author's article, "The End of the Old Kingdom and the First Intermediate Period at Mendes," *Delta Reports*, vol. 2 (London, forthcoming).

On the Middle Kingdom in general, see, among others, the works of E. Blumenthal, *Untersuchungen zur ägyptischen Königtum des Mittleren Reiches* (Berlin, 1970); D. Franke, "The Middle Kingdom in Egypt," in J. M. Sasson, ed., *Civilizations of the Ancient Near East* (New York, 1995), 2:735–48; idem, "The Middle Kingdom," in Redford, *Oxford Encyclopaedia of Ancient Egypt*, 2:393–400; C. Obsomer, *Sesostris Ier: Étude chronologique et historique du règne* (Paris, 1995); S. Quirke, ed., *Middle Kingdom Studies* (New Malden, 1991); W. Grajetzki, *The Middle Kingdom of Ancient Egypt* (London, 2006).

In the Middle Kingdom, according to the précis of the land cadaster on the White Chapel, the Mendesian township (LE 16) was reckoned as 129 kilometers from north to south, that is, from just north of Tel Moqdam to the Mediterranean coast: W. Helck, *Die altaegyptischen Gaue* (Wiesbaden, 1974), 194.

On the mayor Iy-pu-wer, see *Mendes II*, p. 172, no. 39; also no. 162. On the controller, see G. T. Martin, *Egyptian Administrative and Private-Name Seals* (Oxford, 1971), no. 440; W. A. Ward, *Index of Egyptian Administrative and Religious Titles of the Middle Kingdom* (Beirut, 1982), no. 849. For the steward of the divine income of Sobek of *Djedet*, see Martin, *Seals*, no. 1565; Ward, *Index*, no. 173; D. Franke, *Personendaten aus dem Mittleren Reich* (Wiesbaden, 1984), no. 645.

The bibliography on the Hyksos is enormous and continues to expand. Perhaps the most up-to-date treatments are M. Bietak, ed., *Trade, Power and Cultural Exchange: Hyksos Egypt and the Eastern Mediterranean World, 1800–1500 B.C.* (Vienna, 1995); E. Oren, ed., *The Hyksos: New Historical and Archaeological Perspectives* (Philadelphia, 1997); see also K.S.B. Ryholt, *The Political Situation in Egypt during the Second Intermediate Period* (Copenhagen, 1997); A. Caubet, ed., *L'acrobate au taureau: Les découvertes de Tell el-Dab'a et l'archéologie de la Méditerranéen orientale* (Paris, 1999).

On the Thera eruption, see D. Davidson, "Aegean Soils during the 2nd Millennium B.C. with Reference to Thera," in *Thera and the Aegean World* (London, 1978), 1:725ff; H. Goedicke, "The Chronology of the Thera/Santorin Explosion," *Aegypten und Levante* 3 (1992), 57–62; M. Bietak, "Le début de la XVIIIe Dynastie et les Minoens à Avaris," *BSFE* 135 (1996), 5–29; C. F. MacDonald, "Chronologies of the Thera Eruption," *AJA* 105 (2001), 527–32.

CHAPTER SIX

For an overview of the creation of the Egyptian empire, one might profitably consult the following: P.J. Frandsen, "Egyptian Imperialism," in M. T. Larsen, ed., *Power and Propaganda* (Copenhagen, 1979), 167–90; J. M. Galan, *Victory and Border: Terminology Related to Egyptian Imperialism in the XVIIIth Dynasty* (Hildesheim, 1995); M. G. Hasel, *Domination and Resistance: Egyptian Military Activity in the Southern Levant, 1300–1185 BC* (Leiden, 1998); S. C. Heinz, *Die Feldzugdarstellungen des Neuen Reiches: Eine Bildanalyse* (Vienna, 2001); M. Liverani, *Prestige and Interest: International Relations in the Near East ca. 1600–1100 B.C.* (Padova, 1990); P. Lundh, *Actor and Event: Military Activity in Ancient Egyptian Narrative Texts from Tuthmosis II to Merenptah* (Uppsala, 2002); E. F. Morris, *The Architecture of Imperialism: An Investigation into the Role of Fortresses and Administrative Headquarters in New Kingdom Foreign Policy* (Leiden, 2005); D. B. Redford, *The Wars in Syria and Palestine of Thutmose III* (Leiden, 2003); D. Warburton, *Egypt and the Near East: Politics in the Bronze Age* (Paris, 2001); D. Polz, *Der Beginn des Neuen Reiches* (Berlin, 2007).

For Mendes in place-name lists, see P. Lacau and H. Chevrier, *Une Chapelle d'Hatshepsout à Karnak* (Cairo, 1979), vol. 2, pl. 5, block 97 (a kneeling personification of the Mendesian township followed by that of Baqlieh). The Ram-god, however, does not figure prominently in birth- or coronation texts of Hatshepsut (once "beloved of the Ram": Sethe, *Urk.* IV, 224).

For the list of Thutmose III's refurbished temples, see W. Helck, *Urk.* IV, 1443.

On the putative foundation deposit of Thutmose III, see Hansen, "Mendes, 1965 and 1966," pl. IX, fig. 9.

On Amenophis III, see D. O'Connor and E. Cline, *Amenhotep III: Perspectives on His Reign* (Ann Arbor, MI, 1998); Mendes and its gods are conspicuous by their absence from the inscriptions of this king: see M. Schade-Busch, *Zur Königsideologie Amenophis' III* (Hildesheim, 1992).

For the statue inscription of Ibaba, see J. Vandier, "La statue d'un grand prêtre de Mendes," *JEA* 54 (1968), 89–94.

On the Egypto-Hittite war, see W. J. Murnane, *The Road to Kadesh* (Chicago, 1985); idem, "Kadesh," in Redford, *Oxford Encyclopaedia of Ancient Egypt*, 1:219–21; J. Sturm, *La guerre de Ramses II contre les Hittites* (Paris, 1996).

On Per-Ramesses, see the papers now published in *Aegypten und Levante* vol. IX (Vienna, 1999).

On Horemheb at Mendes, see *Mendes II*, p. 193, no. 17; for Sety I, see P. Brand, *The Monuments of Seti*

I: Epigraphic, Historical and Art Historical Analysis (Leiden, 2000). On Merenptah and his monuments throughout Egypt, see H. Sourouzian, *Les monuments du roi Merenptah* (Mainz, 1989).

For the statue of Paser, see *Mendes II*, pl. 17(41).

For Hery, see W. Helck, *Materialien zur Wirtschaftsgeschichte des Neuen Reiches*, vol. 2, fasc. 1 (Wiesbaden, 1961), 970.

Ḥȝt-mḥyt was formerly thought to be a dolphin. The correct identification is due to the work of Professor Douglas Brewer: see his article "Fish," in Redford, *Oxford Encyclopaedia of Ancient Egypt*, vol. 1, especially 535; in general, see D. J. Brewer and R. F. Friedman, *Fish and Fishing in Ancient Egypt* (Warminster, 1989). For a study of *Ḥȝt-mḥyt*, see R. Mittelmann, "Hat-mehyt: An Investigation of Her Fish Cult at Mendes" (M.A. thesis, Pennsylvania State University, 2006).

For the devotion accorded by the 20th Dynasty to Ba-neb-djed, see P-M II (2nd ed.), 503 (Ramesses III offers to the Ram, Medinet Habu); P-M II (2nd ed.), 174 (519-3); *LD* III, Bl. 15 (Ramesses III offers to Amun, Khonsu, and the Ram; Karnak, 8th pylon); P. Berlin 14230 (Ramesses VI honoring the Ram of Mendes); P-M I (2nd ed.; pt. 2), 756 (queen Ese, mother of Ramesses VI, offers incense to the Ram of Mendes); P-M I (2nd ed., pt. 2), 546; Jean-François Champollion, *Notices descriptives*, 1:464 (Ramesses-hik-hopshef, son of Ramesses IX, adores and libates to Ptah, Thoth, and the Ram of Mendes).

CHAPTER SEVEN

The problems that attach themselves to the "Sea Peoples" have long since given rise to an acrimonious debate that shows no signs of abating. No two scholars seem to agree on anything, and the brief thumbnail description offered in this chapter will undoubtedly provoke dissent in detail. While archaeological evidence continues to come in, the body of textual evidence has not appreciably expanded in four decades. The main corpus of direct inscriptional evidence, that of the temple of Ramesses III at Medinet Habu, is couched in persuasion rhetoric, in which high-flown imagery takes precedence over factual records.

This era of short returns not withstanding, a number of profitable, in-depth discussions are available for perusal. The most recent of these include: H. G. Buchholtz, *Ugarit, Zypern, und Agäis: Kulturbeziehungen im zweiten Jahrtausend v. Chr.* (Münster, 1999); W. V. Davies and L. Schofield, eds., *Egypt, the Levant and the Aegean: Interconnections in the Second Millennium B.C.* (London, 1995); T. Dothan and M. Dothan, *People of the Sea: The Search for the Philistines* (New York, 1992); Y. Duhoux, *Des Minoens en Égypte? "Keftiou" et "les îles au milieu du Grand Vert"* (Louvain, 2003); P. W. Haider, *Griechenland—Nordafrika: Ihre Beziehungen zwischen 1500 und 600 v. Chr.* (Darmstadt, 1988); C. Manassa, *The Great Karnak Inscription of Merenptah: Grand Strategy in the 13th Century BC* (New Haven, 2003); E. Noort, *Die Seevölker in Palästina* (Kampen, 1994); O. Margolith, *The Sea Peoples in the Bible* (Wiesbaden, 1994); E. Oren, ed., *The Sea Peoples and Their World: A Reassessment* (Philadelphia, 2000); S. Wachsmann, *Seagoing Ships and Seamanship in the Bronze Age Levant* (London, 1998). Forthcoming is a major collection of studies edited by Ann Killebrew on this topic.

Less study has been devoted to the Libyans in their homeland; see, among others, M. H. Fantar, "Sur les traces des Libous, ancêtres des Berbères," *Atti della Accademia nazionale dei Lincei: Rendiconti*, vol. 11, fasc. 1 (2000), 141–56; N. Grimal, "Les oasis du desert libyque: L'eau, la terre, et le sable," *CRAIBL* (2000), 909–38; A. Leahy, "The Libyan Period in Egypt: An Essay in Interpretation," *Libyan Studies* 16 (1985), 51–65; idem, ed., *Libya and Egypt, c 1300–750 BC* (London, 1987); M. Liverani, "The Libyan Caravan Road in Herodotos iv, 181–185," *JESHO* 43 (2000), 496–520.

On the founding of the 20th Dynasty and the reign of Ramesses III, see P. Grandet, *Ramses III: Histoire d'un règne* (Paris, 1993); F. Fèvre, *Le dernier Pharaon: Ramses III ou le crepuscule d'une civilisation* (Paris, 1992).

On the social, economic, and political decline of Egypt during the 20th Dynasty, see J. Černý, "Prices and Wages in Egypt in the Ramesside Period," *JWH* 1 (1953–54), 903ff; H. Goedicke, "The Waning of the Ramessides," *JSSEA* 8 (1978), 74–80; J. J. Janssen, *Commodity Prices from the Ramessid Period* (Leiden, 1975); K. A. Kitchen, "The Twentieth Dynasty Revisited," *JEA* 68 (1982), 116ff; A. G. McDowell, *Jurisdiction in the Workmen's Community of Deir el-Medina* (Leiden, 1990).

On the failing Nile, see K. W. Butzer, "Nile," in Redford, *Oxford Encyclopaedia of Ancient Egypt*, 2:550.

On the vizier's letter regarding Libyans around Pi-hboye, see G. Maspero, *Memoire sur quelques Papyrus du Louvre* (Paris, 1875), 110.

On Tanis, see P. Brissaud, "Tanis, enigmes et histoires," *BSFE* 138 (1997), 18–35; G. Graham, "Tanis," in Redford, *Oxford Encyclopaedia of Ancient Egypt*, 3:348; P. Montet, *Les enigmes de Tanis* (Paris, 1952); and this author's three volumes in the series *La nécropole royale de Tanis* (Paris, 1947–60); idem, *Le lac sacré de Tanis* (Paris, 1966); M. Romer, "Tanis," *LdÄ* 6 (1986), 6:194–209.

On Un-djeb-en-djede, see P. Montet, *Les constructions et le tombeau de Psousennès I à Tanis* (Paris, 1951), p. 54, fig. 17, p. 84, fig. 31 (see sidebar 7.4), pl. 41.

On the army settlements near the Fayum, see S. Katary, *Land Tenure in the Ramesside Period* (London, 1989).

The 21st, Tanite, Dynasty suffers from a lack of source material when compared with the relative wealth of documentation for the 19th and 20th Dynasties. What has survived has been subjected to an exhaustive analysis by K. A. Kitchen in his *The Third Intermediate Period in Egypt (1100–650 B.C.)* (Warminster, 1986); see also J. Černý, "Egypt from the Death of Ramesses III to the End of the Twenty-first Dynasty," *CAH*, vol. 2, pt. 2 (1975).

The study of the period of Libyan domination in Egypt, from c. 930 to 711 B.C., continues to be bedeviled by spotty and uneven sources, which make the political history and chronology of the country a matter of controversy. Apart from Kitchen's basic *Third Intermediate Period* referred to above, see in particular F. Gomaà, *Die libyschen Furstentümer des Deltas vom Tod Osorkons II: Bis zur Wiedervereinigung Aegyptens durch Psametik I* (Wiesbaden, 1974); K. Jansen-Winckeln, *Ägyptische Biographien der 22. Und 23. Dynastie* (Wiesbaden, 1985); J.-M. Kruchten, *Les Annales des prêtres de Karnak (XXI–XXIIImes Dynasties) et autre textes contemporains rélatifs a l'initiation des prêtres d'Amon* (Louvain, 1989); K. Mysliwieć, *First Millennium B.C.E.: The Twilight of Ancient Egypt* (Ithaca, NY, 2000); J. Yoyotte, "Les Principautés du Delta au temps de l'anarchie libyenne," in *Mélanges Maspero* (Cairo, 1961), 1:121–79. For the Theban rebellion, see R. A. Caminos, *The Chronicle of Prince Osorkon* (Rome, 1958); R. K. Ritner, *The Libyan Anarchy: Inscriptions from Egypt's Third Intermediate Period,* Atlanta, 2009.

For the monuments at Hermopolis Parva, modern-day Baqlieh, see A. Zivie, *Hermopolis et le nome de l'ibis: Recherches sur la province du dieu Thot en Basse Égypte* (Cairo, 1975); for the family of the Great Chiefs of the Me at Mendes, see Gomaà, *Die libyschen Fürstentümer des Deltas vom Tod Osorkons II*, 74–89. On the decoration Sheshonq III added to the temple, see *Mendes II*, pl. 9, no. 4.

Excursus: The Family of the Great Chiefs of the Me(shwesh) at Mendes

The descent of the Libyan chiefs of Mendes adopted here is based on all available records and could be deemed a "maximalist" reconstruction (see table).

Problematic is the position (and even the title!) Of "the great and chief heir(?) of the priests of Ba-neb-djed Ny-su-ba-neb-djed," whose statue was retrieved in Syria, whither one might imagine it to have been taken off by the Assyrians as booty from Mendes: W. Spiegelberg, "Eine aegyptische Göttergruppe aus Syrien," *OLZ* 32 (1929), 14–16. Could he be an early member of the family who lived at a time prior to the taking of the title "Great Chief"?

The Family of the Great Chiefs of the Me(shwesh) at Mendes

B.C.	Name	Great Chief of Me	Dux	High-Priest	Bishop
840	Sheshonk	X	—	—	—
820	Eskheby	X	—	—	—
800	Hornakht (I)	X	X	—	—
780	Ny-su-ba-neb-djeb (I)	X	X	X	—
760	Hornakht (II)	X	X	X	—
740	Ny-su-ba-neb-djeb (II)	X	X	X(?)	—
720	Djed-Amun-efonkh	X	—	—	—
700	Onkh-hor (I)	?	?	?	?
680	Djed-hor (I)	X	—	—	X
660	Onkh-hor (II)	—	—	—	—
640	Djed-hor (II)	—	—	—	—

The king under whom Hornakht (II) carved his inscription is not honored in the inscription, his cartouches being left blank (G. Daressy, "Inscriptions historiques mendésiennes," *RT* 35 [1909], 126); but on the basis of the genealogical sequence imposed by the evidence, it can be neither Sheshonq III nor Pamay. It is tempting to identify him with the Sheshonq who goes under the prenomen *'ȝ-ḫpr-Rʿ*, who elsewhere suffered the same indignity: cf. Yoyotte, "Principautés," pl. 1, no. 1 (Buto stela of Tefnakhte).

Ny-su-ba-neb-djed II was in office in or sometime subsequent to year 21 of a King Awepet. There was probably more than one king named Awepet in this period, but it is impossible to date *this* bearer of the name earlier than year 11 of Sheshonq IV. It is most likely that the Awepet here is to be identified with the king of Tantremu (Tel Muqdam?) of line 114 of the Piankhy stela. In that case Djed-Amun-efonkh, who is variously called in the stela either "Great Chief of the Me" or "mayor (of Mendes)" (lines 18, 114–15), must have succeeded Ny-su-ba-neb-djed shortly before Tefnakhte's invasion. He was at the time already a mature man with a grown son responsible for the neighboring town of Hermopolis Parva. This, coupled with the new onomasticon in the family, militates in favor of a change in family. Was Djed-Amun-efonkh a protégé, perhaps, of Tefnakhte?

The last three generations are known from a funerary cone from Thebes (M. F. Laming MacAdam, *A Corpus of Funerary Cones* [Oxford, 1956], no. 378). This belongs to Djedhor II, who was clearly buried in the south; but this fact holds no implications for his grandfather, who had obviously been a Mendesian functionary. It is tempting to envisage the family fleeing to Thebes at the time of Taharqa's rout in 666, leaving a lesser scion, Payom, in charge of the patrimony.

Chapter Eight

The troubles afflicting Egypt between the Kushite thrust north (c. 730 B.C.) and the withdrawal of the Assyrians (663 B.C.) had a great influence on the collective psyche of the nation and its willingness to celebrate or lament the events in narrative form, didactic or admonitory. By the end of the sixth century B.C. the plot pattern of dire prediction (and fulfillment) of an invasion from the north had created a popular genre of national solace and encouragement (Redford, *Pharaonic King-lists, Annals and Day-books*, 276–96); while a series of chastening tales had begun to take shape involving the priests of Heliopolis and their women (K. Ryholt, "An Elusive Narrative Belonging to the Cycle of Stories about the Priesthood at Heliopolis," in K.

Ryholt, ed., *Acts of the Seventh International Conference of Demotic Studies* [Copenhagen, 2002], 361–66). More distant in time of composition (Ptolemaic period) but rooted in the events of the seventh century B.C. is a cycle of tales identified by the name of Petubastis, "king" of Tanis at the time of the Assyrian invasions. One of these stories deals with a contest among the Delta Dynasts over possession of the armor of the fallen hero Inaros, a motif clearly inspired by the Iliad (F. Hoffmann, *Der Kampfe um den Panzer des Inaros* [Vienna, 1996]).

Among the cities and their leaders mentioned in this narrative, Mendes figures prominently. The armor in dispute is at one time said to be stored in "the Island of Mendes," most probably Thmuis, already in existence in the seventh century. "The militia of the Township of Mendes" is described as "very large," and often goes forth to battle in consort with the militias of Tanis, Natho, and Sebennytos. Significantly the tradition remembers specific individuals: "Djed-hor (Tachos) son of Onkh-hor, the commander of the militia of the Township of Mendes," and "the family of Hor-nakht the son of Ny-su-ba-neb-djed," which is "hostile to the son of Inaros." The former can only be Djed-hor I, son of Onkh-hor I, the *Ṣiḫurru* mentioned in Assyrian texts. The Hor-nakht, son of Ny-su-ba-neb-djed, by whom the family is identified is obviously Hor-nakht II, the contemporary of Sheshonq IV. As the Mendes clan appears to be the villains of the piece, the author must reflect an external viewpoint, but whether this is justified is unknown.

On the Divine Worshiper of Amun, see J. Leclant, *Enquêtes sur les sacerdoces et les sanctuaires égyptiens a l'époque dite "éthiopiènne"* (Cairo, 1954); J. Yoyotte, "Les adoratrices de la troisième période intermédiaire," *BSFE* 64 (1972), 31ff; E. Graefe, *Untersuchungen zur Verwaltung und Geschichte der Institution der Göttesgemahlin des Amun vom Beginn des neuen Reiches bis zur Spatzeit* (Wiesbaden, 1981); G. Robins, *Women in Ancient Egypt* (Cambridge, 1993), 149–56; R. K. Ritner, "Fictive Adoptions or Celibate Priestesses?" *GM* 164 (1998), 85–90.

On the Piankhy stela, so central to the history of the period, see N.-C. Grimal, *La stèle triomphale de Pi(ankh)y au musée du Caire* (Cairo, 1981).

On Kush and its relations with Egypt prior to and during the 25th Dynasty, see in particular P. L. Shinnie, *Ancient Nubia* (London, 1996); L. Török, *The Kingdom of Kush: Handbook of the Napatan-Meroitic Civilization* (Leiden, 1997); D. A. Welsby, *The Kingdom of Kush: The Napatan and Meroitic Empires* (London, 1996); D. B. Redford, *From Slave to Pharaoh: The Black Experience of Ancient Egypt* (Baltimore, 2004). The chronology of the period has been complicated by the discovery that already in 705 B.C. Shebitku occupied a position of power (as co-regent?): G. Frame, "The Inscription of Sargon II at Tang-I Var," *Orientalia* 68 (1999), 31–57; D. B. Redford, "A Note on the Chronology of Dynasty 25 and the Inscription of Sargon II at Tang-I Var," *Orientalia* 68 (1999), 58–60.

For a general introduction to Assyria and its relations with Egypt, one might consult the chapters by A. K. Grayson in *CAH*, vol. 3, part 2 (Cambridge, 1991), 71–161; G. Roux, *Ancient Iraq* (Harmondsworth, 1976), 272–305; for specific topics, see, among others, J. Von Beckerath, "Aegypten und der Feldzug Sanheribs im Jahre 701 v. Chr.," *UF* 24 (1992), 3–8; M. Elat, "The Economic Relations of the Neo-Assyrian Empire with Egypt," *JAOS* 98 (1978), 20ff; G. Fecht, "Zu den Namen aegyptischer Fürsten und Städte in den Annalen des Assurbanipal und der Chronik des Asarhaddon," *MDAIK* 16 (1958), 112ff; A. K. Grayson, "Assyria's Foreign Policy in Relation to Egypt in the 8th and 7th Centuries B.C.," *JSSEA* 11 (1981), 85–88; M. Hutter, "Überlegungen zu Sanheribs Palaestinafeldzug im Jahr 701 v. Chr.," *BN* 19 (1982), 24–30; K. A. Kitchen, "Egypt, the Levant and Assyria in 701 B.C.," in *Fontes atque Pontes* (Wiesbaden, 1983), 243–53; N. Na'aman, "The Brook of Egypt and Assyrian Policy on the Border of Egypt," *Tel Aviv* 6 (1979), 68–90; H.-U. Onasch, *Die assyrischen Eroberungen Aegyptens* (Wiesbaden, 1994); E. D. Oren, "Ethnicity and Regional Archaeology: The Western Negev under Assyrian Rule," in *Biblical Archaeology To-day 1990* (Jerusalem, 1993), 102–5; R. Reich, "The Identification of the 'Sealed *karu* of Egypt,'" *IEJ* 34 (1984), 132–8; A. J. Spalinger, "Esarhaddon and Egypt: An

Analysis of the First Invasion of Egypt," *Orientalia* 43 (1974), 295–326; idem, "The Foreign Policy of Egypt Preceding the Assyrian Conquest," *CdE* 53 (1978), 22–47; H. Verreth, "The Egyptian Eastern Border Region in Assyrian Sources," *JAOS* 119 (1999), 234–47.

On Mendes in the saga *The Fight for the Armour of Inaros*, see Hoffmann, *Der Kampfe um den Panzer des Inaros*. Mendes was drawn upon for other characters in the fiction of the times: cf. K. Ryholt, *The Petēse Stories* II (Copenhagen 2006), frag. D7, pp. 120–21 (priest of the Ram).

CHAPTER NINE

For the name *Pr-bꜣ-nb-ḏd*, whence "Mendes," see Sir A. H. Gardiner, *Ancient Egyptian Onomastica* (Oxford, 1947), vol. 2, no. 404.

For the main temple, see D. B. Redford, "An Interim Report on the Temple of the Ram god at Mendes," *Delta Reports*, vol. 1 (London, 2009). Several naos fragments (all but one anepigraphic) have been retrieved from the debris, presumably housing for "guest gods." Many parts of the temple and ancillary buildings are identified in the Mendes stela of Ptolemy II (on which see below).

On the *mammisi* in Late Period worship, see F. Daumas, *Les mammisis des temples égyptiens* (Paris, 1958).

On the color of the Mendesian animal (white), see J. Vandier, *Le Papyrus Jumilhac* (Paris, 1953) n. 900 (iv.20); cf. R. L. Vos, "The Colors of Apis and Other Sacred Animals," in W. Clarysse, ed., *Egyptian Religion: The Last Thousand Years* (Louvain, 1998), 1:715.

The "Mound of the Shearing" is a provisional translation. On the priest of the god's-book of this place, see *Mendes II*, pl. 25, no. 63.

On the description by classical authors of the devotion to sacred animals, see Herodotus ii.65–76; Diodorus I.84.4–8; Clement Alexandrinus *Paed.* ii.4.2ff; also D. Kessler, *Die heiligen Tieren und der König*, vol. 1 (Wiesbaden, 1989); on the sacred hypogeum at Mendes, see S. Redford and D. B. Redford, "The Cult and Necropolis of the Sacred Ram at Mendes," in S. Ikram, ed., *Divine Creatures: Animal Mummies in Ancient Egypt* (Cairo, 2005), 164–98.

An incisive treatment of priests and priesthoods, and their function in cult and society during the Late Period, remains to be written. Details of the Mendesian priests and the cult they celebrated may be gleaned from the great Edfu nome-list (for Mendes, see E. Chassinat, *Edfu*, 1:334; cf. *Dendera* X, 24:2), the hieroglyphic papyrus from Tanis (F. Ll. Griffith, *Two Hieroglyphic Papyri from Tanis* [London, 1889], pl. XI), and from statue inscriptions from Mendes, *Mendes II* passim; H. De Meulenaere, "Sculptures mendésiennes de Basse Époque," *JEOL* 35–36 [2001], 33–38), Tanis (P. Montet, "Inscriptions de Basse Époque trouvées a Tanis," *Kêmi* 8 [1946], 29–126; C. Zivie-Coche, *Statues et autobiographies de dignitaires de Tanis à l'époque Ptolémaïque* [Paris, 2004]), and Baqlieh (Zivie, *Hermopolis*). Curiously "priests of Sakhmet," that kind of healing witch doctor found in Egypt, seem to proliferate at Mendes during the Saite period: H. D. Schneider, *Shabtis: An Introduction to the History of Ancient Egyptian Funerary Statuettes* (Leiden, 1977), 2:184–85; G. Janes, *Shabtis, a Private View* (Paris, 2002), no. 96; see also S. Aufrère, *Collections des musées département de Seine maritime* (Paris, 1987), no. 102.

For priests seen against a societal backdrop, and the distinction between parochial (serving) priests and prebend holders, see the Demotic Papyrus Rylands IX (late sixth century B.C.): G. Vittmann, *Die Demotische Papyrus Rylands IX* (Wiesbaden, 1998). Since prebends could be granted in several different temples to the same individual, it is dangerous to take the list of priestly titles in any statue inscription as indicative of the roster of cults at the site where the statue was found.

For ancillary functions at Mendes, see the following: M. Burchardt, "Ein saitischer Statuensockel in

Stockholm," *ZÄS* 47 (1910), 111–12 (chief *we'eb*-priest); *Hieroglyphic Texts . . . in the British Musem* IX (London, 1982), pl. 98, no. 312 (*we'eb*-priest and songstress); *Mendes II*, pl. 13:21 (songstress), pl. 19:47 (sistrum player); K. A. Kitchen, "Two Donation Stelae in the Brooklyn Museum," *JARCE* 8 (1969–70), 59–67 (flautist); catalogue, *Ny Carlsberg Glyptothec: Egypt* (Copenhagen, 1998), vol. 2, no. 121 (draftsman scribe); Zivie, *Hermopolis*, 52 (scribe); F. Von Kaenel, *Les Prêtres-ouâb de Sekhmet* (Paris, 1984), 111, no. 50 (overseer of the Sakhmet priests); Aufrère, *Collections des musées departementaux de Seine Maritime*, no. 102 (scribe of the treasury, overseer of the priests of Sakhmet); P-M III(3), 800, 814 (*sm*-priest, "god's-father")(?); the title of the deputy high priest, "Commander-of-the-host," raises the problem of ambiguity if it is found alone: P. M. Chevereau, *Prosopographie des cadres militaires égyptiens de la Basse Époque* (Paris, 1985), nos. 239, 253, 266, etc. Cf. P. Vernus, *Athribis* (Cairo, 1976), 187 (b).

For the bestiality associated with the Mendesian nome, see the sources and discussion in *Mendes II*, 1–4; A. B. Lloyd, *Herodotus Book II: A Commentary* II (Leiden, 1976), 216. The "fornicating ram . . . who mounts the beauties" is a constant epithet of Ba-neb-djed: cf., e.g., S. Sauneron, *Esna* (Cairo, 1963), 2:46; J. C. Goyon, "Le ceremonial de glorification d'Osiris du papyrus du Louvre I 3079," *BIFAO* 67 (1967), 136n234; A. Moret, *Le rituel du culte divin journalier en Égypte* (Geneva, 1988), 139 (of Amun in his form of the ram); Plutarch *Bruta animalia ratione uti* 989; G. Michailidis, "Moule illustrant un texte d'Herodote relatif au bouc de Mendes," *BIFAO* 63 (1965), 139–60.

For the Ram of Mendes as the progenitor of the royal claimant, see KRI II, 263:5–11; *Urk.* IV, 224:17; H. Kees, *Die Götterglaube im Alten Aegypten* (Berlin, 1956), 439. For the passage in the Contendings another explanation is possible, namely, that the Mendesian ram's longtime association with the epithet "he who separates the two gods" may have suggested his presence at the trial. For the similarity of Ram-cults at Mendes, Herakleopolis, and Elephantine, see Vernus, *Athribis*, 297; P. C. Smither and A. N. Dakin, "Stelae in the Queen's College, Oxford," *JEA* 25 (1939), pl. XX; cf. KRI VII, 95:5; M. G. Mokhtar, *Ihnasya el-Medina (Herakleopolis Magna)* (Cairo, 1983), 167–70; idem, "Similarity between the Ram Gods of Ihnasya and Elephantine," *MDAIK* 47 (1991), 253–54; L. Kakosy, "Beiträge zum Totenkult der heiligen Tiere," *Studia Aegyptiaca* 7 (1981), 207–12; for Atum's association with the ram, see K. Mysliwiec, *Studien zum Gott Atum* (Hildesheim, 1979), 2:200–201; for the "living one of Re" and the "*bai* of Re," see Zivie, *Hermopolis*, 52–53 (b); R. O. Faulkner, *The Papyrus Bremner-Rhind* (Bruxelles, 1933), 25, 23; A. Piankoff, *The Litany of Re* (New York, 1964), 105:13; Kees, *Götterglaube*, 165; *Edfu* 1:334, etc.

The concept of the four-headed ram, the four divine essences united in one, is perhaps the most recondite of the doctrines centering on Ba-neb-djed in the Late Period. It is certainly already present in the late New Kingdom: T. Bacs, "Amun-re-Harakhti in the Late Ramesside Royal Tombs," *Studia Aegyptiaca* 14 (1992), 43–53; J. F. Borghouts, *Ancient Egyptian Magical Texts* (Leiden, 1978), 9 (Ch.B. VIII); E. Hornung, *Das Amduat* (Wiesbaden, 1963) 1:145ff, 2:147ff; idem, *The Ancient Egyptian Books of the Afterlife* (Ithaca, NY, 1999), p. 77, fig. 41, and p. 109, fig. 60. In the Late and Greco-Roman periods the form is ubiquitous.

On the oracular propensities of the ram, see L. Kakosy, "Prophecies of Ram Gods," *Studia Aegyptiaca* 7 (1981), 139–54; L. Koenen, "Die Prophezeiungen des 'Topfers,'" *ZPE* 2 (1968), 178ff; Redford, *Pharaonic King-lists, Annals and Day-books*, 284–87.

CHAPTER 10

The period from the seventh through fourth centuries B.C. stands in need of a good, up-to-date historical treatment. The reader is directed, in general, to the pertinent chapters in the *CAH* (vol. 3), and the entries (by period as well as individual kings) in the *LdÄ* and the *Oxford Encyclopaedia of Ancient Egypt*; as well as to K. Jansen-Winckeln, "Bild und Charakter der aegyptischen 26. Dynastie," *Altorientalische Forschungen* 28

(2001), 165–82. The family tree of the dynasty poses few problems: see G. Vittmann, "Die Familie der säitischen Könige," *Orientalia* 44 (1975), 375ff. Textual sources of royal provenance are being republished: see O. Perdu, "Prologue à un corpus des stèles royales de la XXVIe Dynastie," *BSFE* 105 (1986), 23–38; idem, *Recueil des inscriptions royales saïtes*, vol. 1: *Psammetique Ier* (Paris, 2002). For donations under Apries, see Helck, *Die altaegytische Gaue*, 98–99; M. Römer, *Gottes- und Priesterherrschaft in Aegypten am Ende des Neuen Reiches* (Wiesbaden, 1994), 320.

For the passage about the "Bronze Men," see Herodotus ii.152; for the "Cocks" of Tementhes, see Polyaenus vii.3.

For Psamtek I, see W. Wessetsky, "Die Familiengeschichte des Peteese als historische Quelle fur die Innenpolitik Psametiks I," *ZÄS* 88 (1962), 69ff; A. J. Spalinger, "Psammetichus, King of Egypt, I," *JARCE* 13 (1976), 133ff; for the epithet "the Great," see Rylands IX 5, 14.

On the Greeks in Egypt, see A. B. Lloyd, "Triremes and the Saite Navy," *JEA* 58 (1972), 268–79; T.F.R.G. Braun, "The Greeks in Egypt," *CAH*, vol. 3, pt. 3 (Cambridge, 1982), 32–56; O. Masson and J. Yoyotte, "Une inscription ionienne mentionnant Psammetique Ier," *Epigraphica Anatolica* 11 (1988), 171–79; H. T. Wallinga, "Polycrates and Egypt: The Testimony of the *Samaina*," *Achaemenid History*, vol. 6: *Asia Minor and Egypt: Old Cultures in a New Empire*, ed. Heleen Sancisi-Weerdenburg and Amélie Kuhrt (Leiden, 1991), 179–97; S. Pernigotti, *I Greci nell'Egitto della XXVI Dinastia* (Imola, 1999).

On Saite administration, see D. A. Pressl, *Beamte und Soldaten: Die Verwaltung in der 26. Dynastie in Aegypten (664–525 v. Chr.)* (Frankfurt, 1998).

For the spread of the Ram-cult, see P-M III, pt. 2, 810 (Psamtek II—Apries); P-M VII, 283–84, 299 (Kharga Oasis: Darius); D. Klotz, *Adoration of the Ram: Five Hymns to Amun-re from Hibis Temple* (New Haven, 2006); 305–9 (Bahriya Oasis: Amasis); G. Maspero, *Sarcophages des époques persane et ptolemaïque* (CCG; Cairo, 1914), pl. 9–13; Helck, *Die altaegyptische Gaue*, 98–99; E. Naville, *The Shrine of Saft el-Henneh and the Land of Goshen* (London 1888), pl. 5, register 2; R. Giveon, "A Late Egyptian Statue from the Eastern Delta," *JARCE* 12 (1975), 19–21; D. J. Thompson, *Memphis under the Ptolemies* (Princeton, 1988), 30, 142; H. Beinlich, *Das Buch vom Fayum* (Wiesbaden, 1991), Taf. 4, 16; S. Davies and H. S. Smith, "Sacred Animal Temples at Saqqara," in S. Quirke, ed., *The Temple in Ancient Egypt* (London, 1997), 118; Heinrich Karl Brugsch, *Thesaurus inscriptionum Aegyptiacarum: Altägyptische Inschriften* (Graz, 1968), 751–52 (Esna); I. W. Schumacker, *Der Gott Sopdu, der Herr der Fremdländer* (Freibourg, 1988), 142.

Sources for the texts translated are as follows: Psamtek I's donation: Perdu, *Recueil des inscriptions*, 1:27–29; Harsiese: *Mendes II*, pl. 17b–c; his son(?) Keref-er-Ptah: *Mendes II*, pl. 20, no. 50; Ny-su-baneb-djed: P-M III (3), 648; Basa: H. Wild, "Statue d'un noble Mendésien du règne de Psametik Ier aux Musées de Palerme et du Caire," *BIFAO* 60 (1960), 43–67; Tja-ba-neb-djed-memau: *Mendes II*, pl. 20 (49); H. De Meulenaere, "Un notable mendésien de la 26e Dynastie," in *Mélanges Gamal eddin Mokhtar* (Cairo, 1985), 1:187–98; Ahmose: *Mendes II*, pl. 18(45); D. B. Redford, "New Light on Egypt's Stance Towards Asia, 610–586 BCE," in *Rethinking the Foundations (Van Seters FS)* (Berlin, 2000), 183–95; see also E. Lipinska, "The Egypto-Babylonian War of the Winter 601–600 B.C.," *Annali del istituto orientale di Napoli* 22 (1972), 235ff; Nes-Hor: *Mendes II*, pl. 21 (52); O. Perdu, "Neshor à Mendes sous Apries," *BSFE* 118 (1990), 38–49; Th. F. Christensen, "Comments on the Stela AEIN 1037 (E 872; A 759) Ny Carlsberg Glyptotek Copenhagen," *GM* 65 (1983), 7–24; Amasis stela: E. Edel, "Amasis und Nebukadrezzar II," *GM* 29 (1978), 13–20.

Chapter Eleven

Oddly enough, the first Persian occupation of Egypt has been well treated in the literature. See in particular E. Bresciani, "Egypt, Persian Satrapy," in *The Cambridge History of Judaism* (Cambridge, 1984), 1:358–71; idem,

"The Persian Occupation of Egypt," in *The Cambridge History of Iran* (Cambridge, 1985), 2:502–28; idem, "L'Égypte des satrapes d'après la documentation araméenne et égyptienne," *CRAIBL* (1995), 97–108; S. Donadoni, "L'Egitto achemenide," in *Modes de contacts et processus de transformation dans les sociétés anciennes* (Pisa-Rome, 1983), 27–40; W. Hinz, "Darius und der Suezkanal," *Archaeologische Mitteilungen aus Iran* (Berlin, 1975), 115–21; I. Hofmann, "Kambyses in Aegypten," *SAK* 9 (1981), 179–99; T. Holm-Rasmussen, "Collaboration in Early Achaemenid Egypt," in *Studies in Ancient History and Numismatics Presented to Rudi Thomsen* (Aarhus, 1988), 29–38; J. H. Johnson, "The Persians and the Continuity of Egyptian Culture," in *Achaemenid History*, vol. 8: *Continuity and Change*, ed. Heleen Sancisi-Weerdenburg, Amélie Kuhrt, and Margaret Cool Root (Leiden, 1994), 149–59; A. B. Lloyd, "Herodotus on Cambyses: Some Thoughts on Recent Works," *Achaemenid History*, vol. 3: *Method and Theory*, ed. Amélie Kuhrt and Heleen Sancisi-Weerdenburg (Leiden, 1988), 55–66; J. D. Ray, "Egypt 525–404 B.C.," *CAH* (Cambridge, 1988), 4:254–86; idem, "Egypt: Dependence and Independence (425–343 B.C.)," *Achaemenid History*, vol. 1: *Sources, Structures and Syntheses*, ed. Heleen Sancisi-Weerdenburg (Leiden, 1987), 79–95; D. B. Redford, "The So-called 'Codification' of Egyptian Law under Darius I," in *Persia and Torah: The Theory of Imperial Authorization of the Pentateuch* (Atlanta, 2001), 135–59.

For the end of the first Persian occupation, the Aramaic papyri from Elephantine and elsewhere provide a vivid, and sometimes detailed, description of events: see B. H. Porten and A. Yardeni, *Textbook of Aramaic Documents from Ancient Egypt* (Winona Lake, IN, 1986–99), vols. 1, 4; G. R. Driver, *Aramaic Documents of the Fifth Century B.C.* (Oxford, 1957); H. Sternberg-Hotabi, "Politische und sozio-ökonomische Strukturen im perserzeitlichen Aegypten: Neue Perspektiven," *ZÄS* 127 (2000), 153–67.

The best in-depth study of the 29th Dynasty is still that of C. Traunecker, "Essai sur l'histoire de la XXIXe Dynastie," *BIFAO* 79 (1979), 395–436. It can now be supplemented to a certain extent by our discoveries in the excavations (mainly the prominence of Akoris and the stela of the "new king").

The Late Period temple and (to a lesser extent) the city have been the burden of excavation strategy from 1997 to the present. The temple will be the subject of the third volume in the series *Excavations at Mendes*. For a preliminary report, see D. B. Redford, *Delta Reports*, vol. 1 (London, 2009). On the Butic canal which, arguably, approached the site at its northern tip, see J. Ball, *Egypt in the Classical Geographies* (Cairo, 1942), 128–30; M. Bietak, *Tell el-Dab'a* (Vienna, 1975), 2:27, 52 passim. The stela and shrine of Nektanebo I at the northwest corner of the site were brought to light by the Mansura inspectorate of the Supreme Council of Antiquities within the last fifteen years. They remain unpublished. The *mammisi* was partly uncovered by Naville, who retrieved the fragment of a Hathor pilaster now standing before the Egyptian museum, Cairo (*Mendes II*, p. 113; see fig. 9.2). Trial trenches were excavated in the outer harbor in 1993–94; but considerable follow-up work must be undertaken before final publication. On the Amasis naos-court, see Hansen, "Mendes 1965 and 1966," 5–51; D. Arnold, *Temples of the Last Pharaohs* (New York, 1999), 81–82; idem, *Lexikon der ägyptischen Baukunst* (Dusseldorf, 2000), 158–59; idem, *The Encyclopaedia of Ancient Egyptian Architecture* (Princeton, 2003), 148. For the "Mansion of the Rams," see A. F. Redford and D. B. Redford, "The Sacred Animal Necropolis at Mendes," in Ikram, *Divine Creatures*, 164–98. For the tomb of Neferites, see Redford, *Excavations at Mendes*, vol. 1: *The Royal Necropolis*.

The circumvallation of the sacred temenos in the Late Period remains problematic. The wall, identified with some confidence as that of Nektanebo I (see below), has been uncovered in the vicinity of Neferites' tomb, where it is running due (compass) north. Its eastern, northern, and (in part) its western lines can be conjectured as they appear in fig. 11.4, but whether they followed the same deep angular alignment south of the temple as the Ptolemaic wall was later to do cannot be ascertained at present. If they did, the enclosed area would have taken in the Mansion of the Rams. Puzzling is the absence of evidence as to what the Saite temenos looked like. Did Nektanebo simply rebuild an earlier wall? Were there several earlier and smaller temenoi? Or had the Saites bothered with temenos walls at all?

On foreign trade, see A. Yardeni, "Maritime Trade and Royal Accountancy in an Erased Customs Account from 475 B.C.E. on the Ahiqar Scroll from Elephantine," *BASOR* 293 (1994), 67–78; P. Briant and R. Descat, "Un registre douanier de la satrapie d'Égypte à l'époque achéménide," in N. Grimal and B. Menu, eds., *Le commerce en Égypte ancienne* (Cairo, 1998), 59–104; A. D. De Rodrigo, "On the Origin of Basket Handle Jars from Mendes," in C. J. Eyre, ed., *Proceedings of the Seventh International Congress of Egyptologists, Cambridge 3–9 September, 1995* (Leuven, 1998), 965–74.

For the perfume industry, see A. Lucas and J. R. Harris, *Ancient Egyptian Materials and Industries*, 4th ed. (London, 1988), 87; L. Manniche, *An Ancient Egyptian Herbal* (Austin, 1989), 48.

For the wine produced in the area, see Pliny xiv, 9; H. D. Betz, *The Greek Magical Papyri in Translation* (Chicago, 1986), 5, 53; P. Dils, "Wine for Pouring and Purification in Ancient Egypt," in J. Quaegebeur, ed., *Ritual and Sacrifice in the Ancient Near East* (Louvain, 1993), 120–21 (on the "Mendes maze" tables).

Thmuis may well have come into existence in late New Kingdom times, although it is first mentioned by Herodotus, who mistakenly believes it to have been the center of a township distinct from Mendes: ii.166; A. B. Lloyd, *Herodotus Book II: A Commentary* (Leiden, 1988), 3:193. Ptolemy correctly unites the two, although by his time Thmuis took precedence: *Geog.* Iv.5.22. See J. Yoyotte, "A propos des 'terrains neufs' et de Thmouis (toponymie de l'Egypte pharaonique III)," *Comptes rendus du groupe lingistique d'Etudes Chamito-sémitiques* 9 (1960); J.-Y. Carrez-Maratray, "A propos du Nome Thmouite," *RdE* 54 (2003), 31–46.

CHAPTER TWELVE

On the family tree of the 30th Dynasty, see H. De Meulenaere, "Les monuments des culte des rois Nectanebo," *CdE* 35 (1960), 92–107; idem, "La famille royale de Nectanebo," *ZÄS* 90 (1963), 90–93; idem, "Nektanebo I," *LdÄ* 4 (1982), 450–53; J. Josephson, "Nektanebo," in Redford, *Oxford Encyclopaedia of Ancient Egypt*, 2:517–18; see also the individual entries in Chevereau, *Prosopographie.*

For the details of the history of this period, see P. Briant, *From Cyrus to Alexander: A History of the Persian Empire* (Winona Lake, IN, 2002), 645–90. For Egypt, see F. K. Kienitz, *Die politische Geschichte Aegyptens vom 7. Bis 4. Jhrdt vor u.z.* (Leipzig, 1953); J. H. Johnson, "The Demotic Chronicle as an Historic Source," *Enchoria* 4 (1974), 1–17; A. B. Lloyd, "Egypt 404–332 B.C.," *CAH*, vol. 6, pt. 2 (Cambridge, 1994), 337–60; J. D. Ray, "Nectanebo, the Last Egyptian Pharaoh," *History Today* 42 (February 1992), 38–44; idem, "Thirtieth Dynasty," in Redford, *Oxford Encyclopaedia of Ancient Egypt*, 2:275–76.

For the classical sources on the expedition assigned to Pharnabazos, see Diodorus xv.29.4, 41–43; Plutarch *Artaxerxes* xxiv.1; on the sphinxes along the avenue leading north from the Luxor temple, Nektanebo I inscribed fulsome epithets describing himself as savior of Egypt (unpublished). On Tachos, see Diodorus xv.90–92; Plutarch *Agesilaus* xxxvi.2–4, xxxvii.4–6, xxxviii.1–2; Polyaenus iii.11.5; on the "Mendesian," see Lloyd, *CAH*, 6:341 and the sources in 341n18. His insurrection is to be dated to autumn 360 B.C.: Kienitz, *Die politische Geschichte Aegyptens*, 173–75.

On the donations of Nektanebo II to the temples, see D. Meeks, *Le grand texte des donations au temple d'Edfou* (Cairo, 1972), 76*, 133; idem, "Les donations aux temples," in E. Lipinski, ed., *State and Temple Economy in the Ancient Near East* (Louvain, 1979), 2:605–88; on the temple at Per-hebyet, see C. Favard-Meeks, *Le temple de Behbeit el-Hagara: Essai de reconstitution et d'interpretation* (Hamburg, 1991).

For the attack of Artaxerxes III in 343 B.C., see Diodorus xvi.44.1–46.5; Demosthenes, *Epist. Phillip.* 6; Frontinus *Strat.* Ii.5.6; Aelian *Var. Hist.* Iv.8, vi.8. The Persians created advanced military installations in the Negev, and perhaps a new administrative district in Idumaea: M. Stern, *Material Culture of the Land of the Bible in the Persian Period* (Jerusalem, 1982), 79–82; I. Eph'al, *The Ancient Arabs: Nomads on the Borders of the Fertile Crescent 9th–5th Cent. B.C.* (Leiden, 1982), 199.

Because of tectonic shifts in the terrain of the eastern Delta, the present landscape of desert belies the nature of the area in the fourth century B.C., with a major river branch and numerous lagoons. The sometime mouth of the Pelusiac branch, however, broader than might have been expected, can still be made out, with the mound of Pelusium and its Byzantine fort rising on the western bank.

Classical sources give ludicrously inflated numbers to Artaxerxes' forces: 3,000,000 men, 30,000 cavalry, 300 triremes, and 500 transports: Diodorus xvi.40; Theopompus FgrH II, 1,B (fr. 263). The informing element "3" and multiples thereof betray the origins of the inflation. The pluralization of numbers in Egyptian by writing the numeral three times is the standard mode of generalizing large figures (always in descending order): thus "millions (or myriads), tens of thousands and hundreds." Misunderstanding the scribe's intent, and construing the pattern as indicating a *specific* number, would yield precisely 3,000,000, 30,000, and 300. There can be no doubt, therefore, that the fantastic figures in the classical authors descend via an Egyptian source.

The romance *The Dream of Nektanebo*, which is built around the events of 343 B.C., gives the date July 6 of that year, which may preserve an accurate datum for the invasion: U. Wilcken, *Urkunden der Ptolemaerzeit* (Berlin/Leipzig, 1927), 369–74.

The evidence of Persian destruction in Mendes has been presented in Redford, *Excavations at Mendes*, vol. 1: *The Royal Necropolis*.

CHAPTER THIRTEEN

The short-lived second occupation by the Persians has often been described by modern historians in terms favorable to the Persians (cf., e.g., Bresciani, in *Cambridge History of Iran* [Cambridge, 1985], 2:526; J. D. Ray, *Achaemenid History*, vol. 1: *Sources, Structures and Syntheses*, ed. Heleen Sancisi-Weerdenburg [1987], 84, 90). Stories of atrocities and repression have been dismissed, in spite of the uniformly damning evidence from classical writers (see Plutarch, *De Iside et Osiride*, 355C, 363C; Aelian, *Varia hist.* Vi.8; *Natura animal.* x.28). The evidence from the Mendes excavations may assist in delineating a truer picture. The confiscation of sacred paraphernalia perpetrated by Bagoas is reflected in the inscriptions of the first three Ptolemies: *Urk.* II, 14:9–11, 91–93, 128:11–129:4; see K. Winnicki, "Carrying Off and Bringing Home the Statues of the Gods: On an Aspect of the Religious Policy of the Ptolemies towards the Egyptians," *Journal of Juristic Papyrology* 24 (1994), 149–90.

On the inscription of Petosiris, see G. Lefebvre, *Le tombeau de Petosiris* (Paris, 1924).

For the feat of Alexander and the subsequent Ptolemaic period the bibliography is gargantuan. One might consult the following for general introductions: E. R. Bevan, *The House of Ptolemy: A History of Hellenistic Egypt under the Ptolemaic Dynasty* (Chicago, 1968); A. K. Bowman, *Egypt after the Pharaohs, 332 BC–AD 642* (Berkeley, 1986); P. M. Fraser, *Ptolemaic Alexandria* (Oxford, 1972); P. Green, *Alexander to Actium: The Historical Evolution of the Hellenistic Age* (Berkeley, 1990); G. Holbl, *A History of the Ptolemaic Empire* (London, 2001); C. Jacob and F. De Polignac, eds., *Alexandria, Third Century BC: The Knowledge of the World in a Single City* (Alexandria, 2000); J. Johnson, ed., *Life in a Multicultural Society: Egypt from Cambyses to Constantine and Beyond* (Chicago, 1990); C. A. Lada, *Foreign Ethnics in Hellenistic Egypt* (Louvain, 2002); N. Lewis, *Greeks in Ptolemaic Egypt* (Oakville, 2001); A. E. Samuel, *From Athens to Alexandria: Hellenism and Social Goals in Ptolemaic Egypt* (Louvain, 1983).

For the high priest of Ptah as "ethnarch," see J. Quaegebeur, "The Genealogy of the Memphite High Priest Family in the Hellenistic Period," in D. J. Crawford, ed., *Studies on Ptolemaic Memphis* (Louvain, 1980), 43–82; E.A.E. Reymond, *From the Records of a Priestly Family from Memphis* (Wiesbaden, 1981).

For the Mendes stela of Ptolemy II, see *Mendes II*, 174–77.

For Kom el-Adhem and its excavations, see N. C. Lovell, "The 1992 Excavations at Kom el-Adhem, Mendes," *JSSEA* 21/22 (1994), 20–36.

The second ram hypogeum is yet to be published. For preliminary reports, see D. B. Redford, "The Fifth Season of Excavations at Mendes," in the *Akhenaten Temple Project Newsletter*, December 1995; idem, "Five Years of Excavation at Mendes," in *Akhenaten Temple Project Newsletter*, May 1996.

It is important to note that the great northwest enclosure, fully 40 percent of the northern mound, has very little domestic occupation in the Greco-Roman period. Factoring its area into the whole in order to obtain estimates of population would be misleading.

For Greek visitors and residents, see P. W. Pestman, *A Guide to the Zenon Archive* (Leiden, 1981), 224 (Zenon was a visitor for a week in April 257 B.C.); Athenaeus iii.83c (Asklepiades); Athenaeus xiv.648b (Harpokration); Tatian *Or. Adversus Graecos* 38 (Ptolemy); L. Berkowitz and K. A. Squittier, *Canon of Greek Authors and Works* (Oxford, 1990), p. 390, no. 2428 (Thrasyllus); W. Speyer, *Bücherfunde in der Glaubenswerbung der Antike* (Göttingen, 1970), 26–27, 72–73 (Bolos). For Philolaus, see *Mendes II*, pl. 25, no. 64; see also Erich Lüddeckens, *Demotisches Namenbuch* (Wiesbaden, 1987), 1:473. For Promethion, Mendesian banker to Zenon, see A. S. Hunt and C. C. Edgar, *Select Papyri* (Cambridge, 1970), vol. 1, no. 89; for Amun-payom, see *Mendes II*, pl. 24 no. 61; for [. . .]-Amun son of Pamiu, see *Mendes II*, pl. 25, no. 63. At times Mendes was chosen as a garrison post for Ptolemaic troops: in 102 B.C., for example, contingents from the Fayum were stationed in Mendes and Pelusium during the Egypto-Syrian war: E. Van't Dack, "L'Armée de terre Lagide: Reflet d'un monde multiculturel?" in Johnson, *Life in a Multicultural Society*, 339.

Pomponius Mela (*Chor.* I.9, mid-first century C.E.) mentions the Mendesian as the fifth of his main branches entering the Mediterranean, but Ptolemy (iv.5.5; mid-second century C.E.) fails to include this branch: for these observations I am indebted to Mlle. K. Blouin, who rightly observes that Ptolemy's omission must mean that, in his day, the Mendesian branch was considered minor. See her thesis, "La Gestion du risque fluvial et ses implications socioenvironnementales dans le nome mendésien à l'époque romaine (1er au 6e s.)" (Ph.D. thesis, Université Laval, 2007), 86. The last vestiges of the Mendesian branch may have been transmogrified into the meandering drain that runs by Timai el-Amdid, five kilometers east of the site. In the fourth and third centuries B.C. this branch enjoyed such a powerful discharge that it was still navigable by fleets of ships: Thucydides I.110.4; Diodorus xv.42–43. Plutarch's reference (*De Iside et Osiride* D 10, 43; cf. Griffith, *Plutarch's De Iside et Osiride*, 462) to the height of the inundation at Mendes being seven cubits (in excess of three meters) sounds impressive, whatever the datum point may have been. He certainly did *not* derive the figure from contemporary records; it most likely comes from a Saite or fourth-century B.C. source. Similarly, Ammianus Marcellinus appears to be parroting a much earlier source in his identification of the traditional "seven" Nile branches: xxii.15.10.

For the textual evidence from the time of Augustus, see J.-C. Grenier, "Le prophète et l'autokrator," *RdE* 37 (1986), 81–89; H. Verreth, "A Tax List from the Mendesios of the Time of Augustus," in Clarysse, *Egyptian Religion*, 455–76. For the passage of Titus's Alexandrian troops to Jerusalem via Mendes, see Josephus *Bellum* iv.11.5.

On the disturbances of the second century, and the epidemic and disruption caused by the Boukoloi, see A. C. Johnson, *An Economic Survey of the Roman World* (Baltimore, 1936), 147, 253, 326; J. Yoyotte and P. Chuvin, "Les hors la loi qui ont fait trembler Rom," *L'Histoire* 88 (1986), 4–48; J. M. Bertrand, "Les Boukoloi ou le monde à l'invers," *REA* 90 (1988), 139–49; R. Alston, *Soldier and Society in Roman Egypt* (London, 1995), 83–84.

For the papyri from Mendes, and their bearing on toponymy and demography in the second century, see S. Kambitsis, "Sur la toponymie du nome Mendésien," *BIFAO* 76 (1976), 225–30; idem, *Le Papyrus Thmouis I, colonnes 68–160* (Paris, 1985) (other publications, pp. 1–4); also J. Quaegebeur, "Documents grecs et géographie historique: Le Mendésien," *L'Égyptologie en 1979: Axes prioritaires de recherche*, vol. 1 (Paris, 1982).

For a detailed and up-to-date treatment of Mendes during the Roman period and of the papyri in particular, see Blouin, "La Gestion du risque fluvial." The date of the destruction of the room in which the papyri were found is confined, by the evidence of coins, to the reigns of Aurelian and Probus: C. C. Edgar, "Notes about the Delta I: Clay Sealings from Thmuis," *ASAE* 8 (1907), 154–57.

In spite of the decline of Mendes, Thmuis remained a town of great importance into the fourth and fifth centuries: cf. *Itiner. Antonin* 153.2; Ammianus Marcellinus calls it one of the most important cities in Egypt: xx.16.6. Epiphanius continues to complain about the diabolical worship of the Mendesian ram in the fourth century: D. Frankfurter, *Religion in Roman Egypt: Assimilation and Resistance* (Princeton, 1998), 59–60.

For the importance of Thmuis as a bishopric, see Ball, *Egypt in the Classical Geographies*, 163–76. On bishop Phileas, see Eusebius, *Ecclesiastical History* viii.10.2–10; C. W. Griggs, *Early Egyptian Christianity from Its Origin to 451 CE* (Leiden 1989), 98; on Serapion, see R. P. Casey, ed., *Serapion of Thmuis against the Manichees* (Cambridge, MA, 1931); M. E. Johnson, *The Prayers of Serapion of Thmuis* (Rome, 1995). Sources for the history of the site and environs from the Arab conquest through the Middle Ages are assembled in *Mendes II*, 6–13.

The question of exactly when the temple was dismantled remains moot. No archaeological "signature" has been recovered thus far, and it is difficult to draw reasonable inferences. Lime-burning kilns in the southern parts of the northwest enclosure attest to the dismantling of limestone structures (presumably tombs); but, as these describe an arc extending from the east to the south of the temple, they appear to be sited so as not to discharge their smoke into the sacred area. The temple, therefore, was presumably still in use. During the early Middle Ages the region had turned into such a remote backwater that it is difficult to argue a local need for lime that might have occasioned the thorough destruction of limestone walls. By the early eighteenth century, however, when the first modern eyewitnesses record the place, it is clear that the site of the temple had already suffered the demolition one sees today. Might one dare to focus on the founding of Mansura in the thirteenth century as likely terminus a quo for the use of the site as a quarry?

Index

6th Dynasty, 45, 46, 50

9th–10th Dynasties (House of Akhtoy), 59

12th Dynasty, 60–61, 62

18th Dynasty, 77

19th Dynasty, 76–78; favoring of northern gods, 77; focus on the sun-cult and its cultic satellites, 77; royal residence of (*Per-Ramesses-'aȝ-nakhte* ["The House of Ramesses Great of Victory"]), 77, 100

20th Dynasty, devotion accorded to Ba-neb-djed, 218

21st Dynasty, 102

22nd Dynasty, 105; end of, 111–12

25th Dynasty, 118

28th Dynasty, 146

29th Dynasty, 147, 179

"Abiding Place" (*Djedet*), 28; end of, 45, 50–51, 57

Abydos, 10, 35

Actium, battle of, 202

Adams, B., 214

Adams, Matthew J., 40, 212, 215

Adamson, P. B., 213

administrative texts, 19

Aegean coalition, 97

Aelian, 226, 227

'Agen ("the Anchorage"), 2

Agesilaus, 182, 183

Aha-pu-ba ("The Ram Is a Support"), 28

Ahmose, 140, 141, 148

Akhenaten, 75; anathematization of, 75–76; monotheistic revolution of (the sun cult-worship of "Re-Harakhte, He-Who-Rejoices-in-the-Horizon-in-His-Name-of-Light-Which-Is-in-the-Disc"), 75

Akhenaten Temple Project Newsletter, 214

Akhetaten (modern Amarna), 75

Akhtoy, 59

Akoris, 147, 148, 179

Alexander the Great, 190, 199

Alexandria: as a Greek city, 190, 191; as "the *Iȝt-tȝwy* of the Greeks," 61

Alston, R., 228

"Amarna Period," 75–76

Amasis, 23, 37, 38, 39, 142, 143, 157

Amenemhet I, 60–61, 62; palace of (*'Imn-m-ḥȝt-iṯ-tȝwy*, lit., "Amenemhet-Is-the-Seizer-of-the-Two-Lands"), 60–61; prophecy of the coming of, 61

Amenemhet III, 62

Amenophis III, 71, 74, 95; as the "Dazzling Sun-Disc," 71

Amenophis IV. *See* Akhenaten

Amenophis son of Hapu, 74

Ammianus Marcellinus, 228, 229

Amun-re ("King of the Gods"), 77, 111–12, 134, 136

Amyrtaeus II, 146, 179

Anatolia, 10

Andelkowic, B., 212

'Anepat ("Place of Greenness"). *See* Mendes

'Aneza ("the Pasturage"), 4, 17, 29, 35

Ankh-hor, 199

Antef, 59

Antony, 202

'Anzata ("Shepherd"), 4, 32, 35

Apis, 35, 183–84

Apries, 141, 157

architecture: cement construction, 207; defensive architecture, 46; flag-staves, 78; introduction of the widespread use of stone, 40–41; and limestone construction, 28; mud-brick construction, 6–7; the papyrus-bundle column, 85; temenos wall construction, 181

Arnold, D., 225

Arsames, 145

Arsaphes, 134

Artaxerxes II, 146, 147, 179, 181, 182, 183

Artaxerxes III, 183, 184–85

231

Asclepiades, 199
'Ash, 10
Ashurbanipal, 122, 138
Asshur, 117
Assmann, J., 211
Assyria/Assyrians, 95, 117–20, 122, 138, 140
Athenaeus, 228
Athribis, 74
Aufrère, S., 222, 223
authority, as distinct from ancestry, 15
Avaris ("Plantation of the Desert Tract"), 62, 65–66
Ay, 75

Bacs, T., 223
Bagoas, 188
bai ("ram"), 35
bai ("soul, personality, idiomorph"), 35
Ball, J., 225, 229
Barta, W., 213
Basa, 139–40
"Beatification Spells." *See* Pyramid Texts
Begelsbacher-Fischer, B. L., 215
Beinlich, H., 224
Bell, Barbara, 215
Berger, M. A., 213
Berkowitz, L., 228
Bertrand, J. M., 228
Betz, H. D., 226
Bevan, E. R., 227
Beya, 98
Bietak, M., 217, 225
"Big Man" (*wer* ["great (one)" or "magnate"]), 5–6, 8; the Big Man religious narrative, 6; death of, 5–6; as depicted in heraldic devices on ships, 12–13; dwelling/ building (*s[h]erakhu* ["the elevated, glorious (building)"]) of, 7; function of, 5; the transition from Big Man to chieftain, 212
Binford, L. R., 212
"birthing-house" (*msḫnt*), 126
Black, J., 213
Blouin, K., 228, 229
Blumenthal, E., 216
Bocchoris, 116, 137
Bolos of Mendes, 199; as the Pseudo-Democritus, 199
Borghouts, J. F., 223
Bowman, A. K., 227
Brand, P., 217–18
Braun, T.F.R.G., 224
Bresciani, E., 224, 227

Brewer, D. J., 212, 218
Briant, P., 226
Brissaud, P., 219
Brugsch, Heinrich Karl, 224
Bubastis, 74, 185
Buchholtz, H. G., 218
Burchardt, M., 222–23
Busiris, xix; meaning of the original place-name, 214
Buto, 8, 68, 213; trade occurring in, 8, 10
Butzer, K. W., 214, 215, 219

Cairo Calendar of Lucky and Unlucky Days, 126
Cambyses, 143, 144, 179
Caminos, R. A., 219
Carneiro, Richard, 213
Carrez-Maratray, J.-Y., 226
Casey, R. P., 229
Caubet, A., 217
cemeteries. *See* mortuary practices
Černý, J., 219
Chabrias, 147, 182
Chassinat, E., 222
Chevereau, P. M., 223, 226
Chevrier, H., 217
chief: the ineffable link between the chief and "Life"/"River"/"Young Grain," 32–33, 35; the transition from Big Man to chief, 212
Christensen, Th. F., 224
Christianity, 207–8
Chuvin, P., 228
civic titles/epithets: "beloved of the Ram-Lord-of *Djedet*," 61; "controller," 61; "Great Chief of the Me [Meshwesh]," 103, 105, 106; "Hereditary Prince and Mayor, Great Chief of the Meshwesh, *dux*, and Bishop of the Ram Lord of Djedet," 118; "king's agent," 28; mayor, 61; "Palace Chamberlain, Governor of the Land of the Flood," 61; "Residence men," 28; in the Saite administration, 139; "Steward of the Divine Income of Sobek of *Djedet*," 61
Clement of Alexandria, 222
Cleopatra VII, 202
Cline, E., 217
Coffin Texts, 58–59, 136; as "beatifications" (*sꜣḫw*), 58
"Contendings of Horus and Seth, The," 133–34
council (*djadje*), 5
cultic practices: animal cults, 126, 127–28; dedicatory stelae, 89, 92; the "offering menu," 130; offerings, 80, 89, 92, 130; music, 130–31; piety as the motivation for, 92
Cyprus, 94
Cyrus, 142–43, 146

Dakin, A. N., 223

Damascus, 117

d'Andrea, A. C., 212

Daressy, G., 220

Darius I, 144, 179

Darius II, 145, 146

Daumas, F., 222

Davidson, D., 217

Davies, S., 224

Davies, W. V., 218

Davis, W., 213

dd ("to remain, to be firm, stable, to be continuous, without interruption"), 214

De Meulenaere, H., 211, 222, 224, 226

De Polignac, F., 227

De Rodrigo, A. D., 226

Demosthenes, 226

Den, 19

Dendera, 35

Descat, R., 226

Dils, P., 226

Diocletian, 207

Diodorus, 127, 222, 226, 227, 228

Dioscorides, 173

Djed-Amun-efonkh, 114–15, 118

Djedet. *See* Mendes

Donadoni, S., 225

Dothan, M., 218

Dothan, T., 218

Dream of Nektanebo, The, 227

Dreyer, G., 214

Driver, G. R., 225

Duhoux, Y., 218

Earl, T., 212

Edel, E., 224

Edgar, C. C., 228, 229

Edict of Theodotian (391 C.E.), 208

Edjo ("Green One"), 8; protection of Horus, 14; shrine of ("House-of-the-Flame"), 14

Egypt/Egyptians, 10; during the 19th Dynasty, 76; during the 20th Dynasty, 99–100; during the 21st Dynasty, 103; during the 22nd Dynasty, 111; during the 29th Dynasty, 148; during the "age of Sesostris," 67; historical works on, 211; the "kings of Egypt," 118; shifting of communities by, 95; support of Assyria, 140; third-millennium climate change effects on, 42–43, 45; thirteenth-century B.C. migrations to, 95–98; under Greek rule, 190; under the Persians, 143–45

Elat, M., 221

Elephantine, 145, 147

Elkab, 181

El-Yahky, F., 213

Enmarch, R., 216

Eph'al, I., 226

Epiphanius, 229

Esarhaddon, 119–20, 122

Ese, 92

Eskheby, 106

Euergetes III, 193

Euphrates River, 8

Eusebius, 229

Fairservice, W., 214

Fantar, M. H., 218

Faulkner, R. O., 216, 223

Favard-Meeks, C., 226

Fecht, G., 221

festivals/feast days: feast days of the Ram, 126; *sed*-festival/jubilee, 14

Fight for the Armor of Inaros, The, 123

Fischer, H. G., 214

folklore, 123, 136–37

forced labor, 41; decrees of immunity from, 43

Frame, G., 221

Frandsen, P. J., 217

Franke, D., 216, 217

Frankfurter, D., 229

Fraser, P. M., 227

Friedman, R. F., 213, 214, 218

Frontinus, 226

Galan, J. M., 217

Gamili, E., 212

Gardiner, A. H., 222

Gat, A., 212

Gaza, 117

Gebel Barkal stela, 123

Giveon, R., 224

Gledhill, J., 214

gods/goddesses: association of with animal and plant species (as "images" of), 89, 92; cults of parochial gods (nome deities) in Egypt, 128; prophetic power compared to oracular power of, 136. *See also* specific gods and goddesses

Goedicke, H., 217, 219

Goldwasser, O., 214

Gomaà, F., 219

Gophna, R., 212
Goyon, J. C., 223
Graefe, E., 221
Graham, G., 219
Grajetzki, W., 216
Grandet, P., 218
Grayson, A. K., 221
Great Black, 10
Great Green, 4
Great Syrian Sea. *See* Great Green
Greeks, 139, 141, 142, 182–83, 184–85, 190–91, 193, 199
Green, P., 227
Grenier, J.-C., 228
Griffith, F. Ll., 222, 228
Griffiths, J. G., 215
Griggs, C. W., 229
Grimal, N.-C., 211, 218, 221
Grunert, S., 215

Haider, P. W., 218
Hakoris, 154
Hansen, D. P., 211, 217, 225
Harpokration, 199
Harris, J. R., 226
Harsiese, 140
Hasel, M. G., 217
Hassan, Fikri, 213, 215
Hathor, 131
Ḥat-meḥyet ("She-Who-Is-Foremost-of-Fishes"), xvii, 14, 86, 89, 92, 99, 126
Hatshepsut, 217
Heerma von Voss, M., 216
Heinz, S. C., 217
Helck, W., 214, 216, 217, 218, 224
Heliopolis, 74, 99, 131
Hennessy, J., 212
Herakleopolis (ancient "Plantation-of-the-King's-Off-spring"), 59, 103, 112; siege of, 114–15
Herihor, 100
Hermopolis Parva (modern Baqlieh), 68, 74, 105, 131; as "the Seat where he [the Ram] settled on the First Occa-sion," 131
Herodotus, 133, 222, 224, 226
Hery, 85
Hezekiah, 118
Hinz, W., 225
Hittites, 75, 76, 95
Hoffmann, F., 221, 222
Hoffmann, I., 225

Holbl, G., 227
Holm-Rasmussen, T., 225
Hor-aha, 14, 19; as *Atjotji* ("the Seizer"), 19
Horemheb, 75, 76, 77
Hornakht II, 110, 111
Hornung, E., 211, 223
Horus ("Lord of Heaven"), 8, 13, 17; protection of by Nekhbit and Edjo, 14; punishment meted out by, 13; as the "Seizer," 14–15; unification of the "Two Lands," 13–15, 16
Horus-the-Child (Harpokrates), 131
House of Akhtoy (9th and 10th Dynasties), 59
"House of Amun," 103
"House of Ram," 23, 35, 124; burial grounds associated with, 166–68; decline of, 205–6; desecration and de-struction of, 207–8, 210, 229; during the 29th Dynasty, 148, 150–51, 153–55, 157, 161; during the Middle King-dom, 62; during the third century B.C., 196–97, 199; during the Time of the Residence, 36–40; fire damage in the last quarter of the 6th Dynasty, 46; and the "House of the Plough" (*pr-šn'*). 24, 25; and the "Man-sion of the Ewes," 166, 196, 208; and the "Mansion of the Rams," 157, 161, 188, 208; restoration of during the time of the empire pharaohs, 71, 78–80, 86; structure of the temple community, 128–31; various names for, 124. *See also* "Abiding Place" (*Djedet*); Ram of Mendes
Hunt, A. S., 228
Hutter, M., 221
Hyksos ("Foreign Rulers"), 65–66; defeat of, 67

Ibaba, 76, 85; statue inscription of, 76
Imhotpe, 40–41
Inaros, 144
"industrial" technology, 10
"Instruction for King Merikare," 50
Iphicrates, 181
Iran, 10
Ishtef-Tety, 28
Isis "the Great, the God's Mother," 131
Israel, 117
Ius-aas, 131

Jacob, C., 227
Jacquet-Gordon, H., 215
Janes, G., 222
Jansen-Winckeln, K., 219. 223–24
Janssen, J. J., 219
Jay, P., 212
Jecquier, G., 215

Johnson, A. C., 228
Johnson, A. W., 212
Johnson, J. H., 225, 226, 227
Johnson, M. E., 229
Jones, D., 215
Josephson, J., 226
Josephus, 205, 228

Kadesh, siege of, 76
Kaiser, W., 214
Kakosy, L., 223
Kambitsis, S., 228–29
Kanawati, N., 215
Karnak, 131
Katary, S., 219
Kees, H., 223
Kemp, B. J., 211
Keref-er-Ptah, 140
Kessler, D., 222
Khababash, 189
Khamwese, 74
Khasekhemwy ("The-Power-Has-Appeared"), 17, 214
Khemmis, 8
Khnum, 134, 136
Khufu, 40
Kienitz, F. K., 226
Killebrew, Ann, 218
Kitchen, K. A., 219, 221, 223
Klotz, D., 224
Koenen, L., 223
Kroeper, K., 212
Kruchten, J.-M., 219
Krywinski, A. S., 212
Krzyzaniak, L., 212
Kush/Kushites, 99, 112, 114–16, 117, 118, 120, 122, 138

Labu. See Libya/Libyans
Lacau, P., 217
Laʾda, C. A., 227
*Laḥaḫta ("Watery Place"), 1–2, 66
Lamerge-Karlovsky, C. C., 214
Laming MacAdam, M. F., 220
Land of the Flood, xviii, 8, 16, 60; as a middle ground in the exchange of goods, 4; resources of, 4; subdivision of into townships ("nomes"), 14; threats to from people of the south Nile, 12–15
Land of the *Shma*-plant," 10, 16; population growth and cultural expansion in, 10–11; subdivision of into townships ("nomes"), 14

Leahy, A., 218
Leclant, J., 214, 221
Lefebvre, G., 227
Lesko, L. H., 216
Levy, T. E., 212
Lewis, N., 227
Liberalis, 206
Libya/Libyans, 95–98, 99–100, 102–5, 112; expulsion of Libyans from Egypt (654 B.C.), 139; the family of the Libyan chiefs of Mendes, 219–20
Lichtheim, M., 216
"Life"/"River"/"Young Grain," 33–34, 35; hypostaseis of, 35; and the "Seat of the Celebrant" (*st-ir*), 33. See also ʾAnzata ("Shepherd"); Apis; Nepri; Ram (*bai*), the; Sokar
Lipinska, E., 224
Liverani, M., 217, 218
Lloyd, A. B., 211, 223, 224, 225, 226
Lotianu, 10
Lovell, N. C., 216, 228
Lucas, A., 226
Lüddeckens, Erich, 228
Lundh, P., 217

MacDonald, C. F., 217
Mackay, P., 211
Manassa, C., 218
Manetho, 19, 215
Manniche, L., 226
Margolith, O., 218
Mark, S., 213
Martin, G. T., 216, 217
Martin-Pardey, E., 215
Maspero, G., 219, 224
Masson, O., 224
McDowell, A. G., 219
Meeks, D., 226
Memphis, 42, 75, 99, 112, 115, 119. See also White Fort (the "Residence")
Mendes, 2, 8, 11, 17, 68; Asian influence on early architecture of, 6–7; Assyrian name of (Asshur-massu-urappish ["Asshur-Has-Expanded-His-Land"]), 120; building phases in evidence in excavations to date, 18–19, 21; as the center of satellite communities, 18; Christianity at, 207–8; in the Coffin Texts, 59; community structure and government through the "Big Man," 4–6; in the cycle of Petubastis tales, 221; decline of, 199, 201–2, 205, 206–7; during the 29th Dynasty, 148, 150–51; during the period of Libyan rule, 105–6, 108, 110; during the Saite revival, 139–40; during the third century B.C., 199; in

Mendes (*cont.*)

The Fight for the Armor of Inaros, 123; formalized public acts in, 7; as a garrison post for Ptolemaic troops, 228; in the Gebel Barkal stela, 123; harbors of, 150, 151, 172, 173, 176, 201–2; the "Hill of Bones" (*kom el-adhem*), 122, 151; history of compared to the overall history of Egypt, xviii–xix; the "House of Amulets," 172; the "House of the Dais," 131; the "House of the Ennead," 131; as an important source for evidence on ancient Egyptian history and society (longevity of occupation on the site), xvii–xix; lack of archaeological evidence for the Middle Kingdom period, 58; the "Libyan Palace," 186; as a middle ground in the exchange of goods, 4; "The Mound of the Souls," 128; natural resources of, 4; occupation of at the close of the Old Kingdom, 44; as part of Asian trade route, 4; perfume industry in, 173; prosperity of during the Time of the Residence, 36; in the Pyramid Texts/Coffin Texts, 34, 59; and the rebellion against Assyria, 122; and the rebellion against Persia, 146; reports on archaeological work done at the site of, 211; size and general configuration of, xvii–xviii; town council (*djadje*) of, 5; temenos wall construction in, 181; topography of during the early third century B.C., 195–96; as a township, 14; tutelary goddess of (Ḥat-meḥyet ["She-Who-Is-Foremost-of-Fishes"]), xvii, 14, 86, 89, 92, 99, 126; as a virtual type site for interests broader than those of Egyptology, xviii; wine industry in, 176. *See also* "House of Ram"

Merenptah, 78, 80, 97–98, 99

Meshwesh. *See* Libya/Libyans

Metjen, 215

mḥi ("to flood, drown"), 212

Michailidis, G., 223

Midant-Reynes, B., 213

military titles/epithets: *dux* ("leader"), 106; "Great Courtier in the Entire Land, High-Priest of Amun-re King of the Gods, Field-Marshal of Upper and Lower Egypt, Duke," 100

Mitanni, 68

Mittelmann, R., 218

Mokhtar, M. G., 223

Montet, P., 219, 222

Montuhotpe I (the Great), 60, 216

Morena Garcia, J. D., 215

Morenz, L. D., 213, 214

Moret, A., 223

Morris, E. F., 217

mortuary practices: domestic arrangements to the cemetery, 32; false door of the priest Nefer-shu-ba, 33; interment of the poor, 51, 57; interment of sacred animals, 89, 92, 128, 196; mastabas, 28–29; mortuary arrangements of the middle and lower classes at Mendes, 24; mortuary endowments, 41; the "mound" (*iȝt*), 128; Roman "burial society" (*collegium funeraticium*), 202; sarcophagi, 157, 161, 166; vaults, 51. *See also* "Abiding Place, the" (*Djedet*); Ram (*bai*), the, as the Lord of the Abiding Place (*Neb Djedet*)

Müller-Wollermann, R., 215

Murnane, W. J., 217

Murray, M. A., 212

Muslims, 208

Muthis, 148

Mysliwiec, K., 219, 223

Na'aman, N., 221

Nakht-hor-hebef. *See* Nektanebo II

names: displayed in pictographs, 17; displayed in script, 17; names favored by the Ramessides, 77; significance of, 136; theophoric names, 205, 207

naos (*kȝry*). *See* shrine (*iwnn*)

Naville, Edouard, 106, 124, 153, 206, 211, 224, 225

Nebuchadrezzar, 141, 142

Necho I, 122, 138, 186

Necho II, 140–41

Neferites I, 146–47, 179; tomb of, 89, 92, 168, 177–78, 186, 188

Neferites II, 147

Nefer-khau, 68

Nefer-shu-ba ("The Ram Is Fair of Shade"), 28

Nehemaway, 85

Nekaure, 215

Nekhbit, 14

Nekhen, 10

Nektanebo I, 148, 149, 150, 151, 155, 168, 179, 181–82, 225, 226; as the "defender of Egypt," 182; and "equalization payments," 181; temple-rebuilding program of, 181

Nektanebo II, 182, 183–85; character of, 183

Neo-Babylonian empire, 140–43

Nepri, 35

Nes-Hor, 141, 157, 161

Nile Delta. *See* Land of the Flood

Nile River, xviii, 10; Mendesian branch of, 2, 4, 24, 105, 151, 173, 228; summer flooding of, 4; third-millennium low floods of, 42–43; as a transit corridor, 11

Nile Valley. *See* Land of the *Shma*-plant

Nitocris, 138

Noort, E., 218

numerology: the number four (totality), 134; the number three (plurality), 134, 227

Nut, 128

Ny-onkh-ba, 40

Ny-su-ba-neb-djed ("He-Who-Belongs-to-the-Ram-Lord-of-the-Abiding-Place") (Greek "Smendes"), 100, 102, 105, 106, 108, 110, 111, 140, 144, 182, 183; tomb of, 167, 176–77

'nz (West Semitic "to wander"), 214

Oats, J., 213

Obsomer, C., 216

Ochus. See Artaxerxes III

O'Connor, D., 211, 217

Oman, L., 215

Ombos ("Gold-Town"), 10

Onasch, H.-U., 221

Onkh-Hor, 115, 118

oral tradition, 15

Oren, E. D., 212, 217, 218, 221

Osiris, 33, 35, 77, 131; the "classical" Osiris Myth, 213; and the deceased in Mendes, 36; and life, 41; as "Lord of the Tomb" in Mendes, 131; as manifest in the Ram, 35; mythic dismemberment of the body of, 131; as "pure in the Abiding Place," 35; relics of at Mendes, 131

Osorkon I, 104

Osorkon II, 105

Paramesses. See Ramesses I

Paser, 86

Pawlish, Larry, 211–12

Payom, 122, 199

Pe. See Buto

Peace of Antalcidas (386 B.C.), 147, 179

Peftjaudibast, 112

Pepy I, 42

Pepy II, 42–43, 45, 215; royal decree of exemption, 43

Pepy-yema, 28

Perdu, O., 224

Per-hebyet, 184

Pernigotti, S., 224

Persia/Persians, 142–43, 144–48, 179, 181–86, 188–90, 226, 227

Pestman, P. W., 228

Petosiris, 189

Petrie, W.M.F., 215

Pharnabazos, 181

Phileas, 207

Philip (III) Arrhidaeos, 190–91

Philolaus, 199

Piankhy, 100, 112, 114–16, 119

Piankoff, A., 223

"Pillar-City," 29

Pindar, 133

Pindidi. See Mendes

piracy, 95

Pliny, 173, 176, 226

Plutarch, 183, 223, 226, 227, 228

Polyaenus, 224, 226

Polycrates, 201

Polz, D., 217

Pomponius Mela, 228

Porten, B. H., 225

Posener, G., 215

pottery: "basket-handle" jars, 173; beer-jugs, 92–94; "East Greek" pottery, 173; Meidum bowls, 28; "Philistine" pottery, 92–94; "Phoenician crisp torpedo jars," 173; rope designs on, 4

Pressl, D. A., 224

Primordial Ocean (Nun), four hypostaseis of ([absolute] Darkness [Kkw], Infinity [Ḥḥw], Fluidity [Nw], and Directionlessness [Tnmw]), 134

processionals: "Coming-Forth," 7; "Rowing-on-the-River," 7

prophecy, 136–37

Psammuthis, 147–48

Psamtek, 146

Psamtek I, 138–39, 141

Psamtek II, 141

Psamtek III, 143

Psousennes II, 104

Ptah-Sokar, 77

Ptolemaeus, 207

Ptolemy I (Soter), 190, 191, 193

Ptolemy II (Philadelphos), 157, 193, 194–96; deference toward native tradition, 194–95

Ptolemy IV, 199

Ptolemy of Mendes, 199, 226, 228

Pyramid Texts, 59

pyramids: and the increased concentration of bovids (oxen and cows) at construction sites, 26, 28; "step-pyramids," 41

Quack, J., 216

Quaegebeur, J., 227, 229

Quirke, S., 211, 216

Ram (*bai*), the: as encompassing the four basic elements (water, light, air, earth), 35; epithets of, 134; as Lord of the Abiding Place, 29, 32, 35; and names incorporating the "ram," 40; as the "Soul of Air" (*Šw*), 35; as the "Soul of Earth" (*Gb*), 35; as the "Soul of Re," 35. *See also* Ram of Mendes

Ram of Mendes, 133–37; as archetypal Sire, 133–34; as the "Complete One" (*Itm*), 135; his person and power as unrestricted in the universe, 134; prophetic talent of, 136–37; as *quadrifrons* ("four faces on one neck"/four avatars: Light/Flame [Re], Air [Shu], Earth [Geb], and Flood [Osiris]), 40, 134–36, 157, 223; sexual proclivity of, 133

"Ramesside Age," 76

Ramesses I, 76

Ramesses II, 77–78, 80, 103; temple-building program of, 77–78

Ramesses III, 94, 98, 99, 218

Ramesses VI, 92

Ramesses XI, 100, 102

Ray, J. D., 225, 226, 227

Re, 35, 131

Red Sea. *See* Great Black

Redford, A. F., 225

Redford, D. B., 211, 213, 216, 217, 219, 220, 221, 222, 223, 224, 225, 227, 228

Redford, S., 211, 222

Reich, R., 221

religious titles/epithets: "Bishop of the Priests of the Ram," 129; "Chamberlain-Separator-of-the-Two-Gods," 131; "Chief Lector-Priest," 28; "Commander-of-the-Host," 128; "Divine Worshiper of Amun," 112; "ethnarch," 227; "Festival-Director of the Ram, Lord of *Djedet,* and Lector-Priest of Edjo," 77; "He-Whose-Decay-Is-Hidden," 128; "High-Priest of the Ram, Lord of the Abiding Place," 106; "One-with-the-Belly," 131; "Opener of the Doors of the God in His Temple," 130; "Overseer of the Priests of the Ram," 28, 106; "Priest of the Ram," 28; "Priest of the Ram of *Anepat*," 40; "Priestess of Hathor," 28; "Privy to the Mysteries," 28; "Prophet of the Ram and *Ḥ3t-mḥyt* and the Great Ennead which is in the Abiding Place," 131; "Prophet of the Ram of Re in the Horizon of Re," 131; Prophets (lit., Servants of God), 129; "Scribe of the God's-Book of the Ram . . . [in] 'The Shearing,'" 126; "Servant of Intimacy," 131; "she that makes hale his soul," 131; "Shorn-One in the Fish-Township," 130; "Son-Whom-He-Loves," 129; "Stewart of the Divine Income of Sobek of *Djedet,*" 61

Reymond, E.A.E., 227

rḫ ("to know"), 213

Ritner, R. K., 221

Robins, G., 221

Romans, 202, 206–7

Romer, M., 219, 224

Rothman, M. S., 213

Roux, G., 221

royal mythology, 8, 10, 14

Ryholt, K.S.B., 217, 220–21, 222

Sais/Saites: and the rebellion against Assyria, 122; and the rebellion against Persia, 146, 179; and township bureaucracy, 139

Sakhmet, the "Powerful One," 74, 131

Samuel, A. E., 227

saraḫu (Akkadian: "To be splendid, glorious, uplifted"), 213

Sargon II, 117

Sauneron, S., 223

Schade-Busch, M., 217

Schenkel, W., 216

schilby-fish, 14, 86, 89; as a decorative theme on stelae, 89; as "the Foremost of the Inundation," 4; misrepresentation of as a dolphin, xvii

Schneider, H. D., 222

Schofield, L., 218

Schumacker, I. W., 224

scripts, 16–17; commemorative tableaux/art, 15–17; Egyptian hieroglyphic, 17; origins of, 15, 16; phonetic value of "signs," 17; as precursor to a real alphabet, 16–17

SḎ(D) ("side, mountain"), 214

Sea Peoples, 94, 98

Sebennytos, xix, 176, 179

Seeher, J., 214

Seidelmayr, S., 215

Seka, 19

Sennacherib, 118, 118–19

Senwosret I, 62

Serapion, 207

Sesostris, 67

Seth, 17

Seth-nakhte, 98

Set-net-Pepy, 28

Sety I, 77, 78

Sety II, 98

Shabaka, 116, 117

Shebitku, 117, 118, 221

s(h)erakhu, 213

Sheshonq I, 104, 105

Sheshonq III, 106

Shinnie, P. L., 221

ships, 11; depictions of the Big Man in heraldic devices on ships, 12–13; markings of divine ownership, 11

shma-plant, 213

shrine (*iwnn*), 124, 130; as a "barque-block" (*tntзt*), 124; as "the Great Seat," 124; *mammisi* ("birth-house"), 126, 151; northern "type" of,14; *pr-nw* shrine, 161

Siheil, 134

Silverman, D. P., 211, 216

Smith, H. S., 224

Smither, P. C., 223

Snofru, 40

Sobek, 6, 61

Sokar, 35

Sourouzian, H., 218

Spalinger, A. J., 221–22, 224

Spencer, A. J., 214

Spencer, J., 211

Speyer, W., 228

Spiegelberg, W., 219

Squittier, K. A., 228

sr ("to proclaim [in advance]," "to announce" what is coming in the future, "to foretell, prophesy"), 136

sr ("sheep"), 136

Stanley, J. D., 215–16

Stern, M., 226

Sternberg-Hotabi, H., 225

Sturm, J., 217

Sumeria, 10

Syria, 10

Tз-mḥw ("the drowned land"), 212

Tachos, 106, 118, 120, 182

Taharqa, 118–19, 122, 138

Tamos, 146

Tanis ("Storm-Town" [*D'nt*]), 100, 104, 111, 112, 131; and the rebellion against Assyria, 122; as a Thebes *redivivus,* 100

Tanwetamani, 138

Tassie, G., 215

Tatian, 228

taxation, 41, 105; decrees of immunity from, 43

Tefnakhte, 112, 114–16

Tehneh, 112

Tel er-Rub'a. *See* Mendes

Tell Ibrahim Awad, 18

temples: conformity of temple activities to the model of the functioning of a rich man's house, 130; and guest cults, 124, 131; and the *lesonis*-priest, 130; music in 130–31; the Processional Temple, 124; and "prophets," 129–30; and priestesses, 130–31; and "rest-house" palaces, 106; and *w'eb* priests ("the pure ones/purifiers"), 130. *See also* shrine (*iwnn*)

Temple of the Ram. *See* "House of Ram"

Tennes, 184, 185

Tety, 42

Thebes (ancient "Township of the Scepter"), 59, 99, 103, 105, 111–12, 112, 114, 122, 131, 145, 181

Theopompus, 227

Thmuis, 176, 199, 201, 206, 207–8, 226, 229

Thompson, D. J., 224

Thoth, 131, 196

Thrasyllus, 199

Thucydides, 228

Thutmose III, 68; hymn to, 68–69; statue of, 71; temple-rebuilding program of, 68, 71, 80

Tiglath-pileser III, 117

Titus, 205

Tja-ba-neb-djed-memau, 140

Tja-hap-emmaw, 182

Tjehenu, 8

Torok, L., 221

trade, 8, 10, 94, 148, 173; trade goods, 10, 173; trade routes, 10, 96

Traunecker, C., 225

Trigger, B. G., 211

Tutankhaten, 75

Udjahoresne, 144

'Ummah ("Clan-Town"), 4, 17

Underworld Books, 168

Un-djeb-en-djede, 102

Valley of the Kings, 168

van den Brink, E.C.M., 212

Van Haarlem, W., 214

Vandier, J., 217, 222

Van't Dack, E., 228

Vernus, P., 223

Verreth, H., 222, 228

Vespasian, 205

"visible language," 15. *See also* scripts

Vittmann, G., 222, 224

Von Beckerath, J., 221

Von der Way, T., 213, 214

Von Kaenel, F., 223

Vos, R. L., 222

Wachsmann, S., 218

Waddell, W. G., 215

Wallinga, H. T., 224

Warburton, D., 217

Ward, W. A., 216, 217

Welsby, D. A., 221

Wenke, R. J., 214

Wessetsky, W., 224

White Fort (the "Residence"), 13–15, 18, 40, 41; collapse of, 50–51; influence of over the Nile Valley and Nile Delta, 13–15

Whyte, I., 216

Wilcken, U., 227

Wild, H., 224

Wilkinson, T., 214

Willems, H., 216

Wilson, J. A., 216

Wilson, Karen L., 172, 211

Winnicki, K., 227

Wright, M., 212

Xerxes, 144

Xois, 99, 112

Yardeni, A., 225, 226

Yewepet, 104

Yoyotte, J., 219, 220, 221, 224, 226, 228

Zenon, 228

Zivie, A., 219, 222, 223

Zivie-Coche, C., 222